International Political Economy Series

Series Editor: Timothy M. Shaw, Visiting Professor, University of Massachusetts Boston, USA, and Emeritus Professor, University of London, UK.

The global political economy is in flux as a series of cumulative crises impacts its organization and governance. The IPE series has tracked its development in both analysis and structure over the last three decades. It has always had a concentration on the global South. Now the South increasingly challenges the North as the centre of development, also reflected in a growing number of submissions and publications on indebted Eurozone economies in Southern Europe.

An indispensable resource for scholars and researchers, the series examines a variety of capitalisms and connections by focusing on emerging economies, companies and sectors, debates and policies. It informs diverse policy communities as the established trans-Atlantic North declines and 'the rest', especially the BRICS, rise.

Titles include:

Tony Heron
PATHWAYS FROM PREFERENTIAL TRADE
The Politics of Trade Adjustment in Africa, the Caribbean and Pacific

Martin Geiger, Antoine Pécoud (editors)
DISCIPLINING THE TRANSNATIONAL MOBILITY OF PEOPLE

Leila Simona Talani
THE ARAB SPRING IN THE GLOBAL POLITICAL ECONOMY

Xiaoming Huang (editor)
MODERN ECONOMIC DEVELOPMENT IN JAPAN AND CHINA
Developmentalism, Capitalism and the World Economic System

Gopinath Pillai (editor)
THE POLITICAL ECONOMY OF SOUTH ASIAN DIASPORA
Patterns of Socio-Economic Influence

Rachel K. Brickner (editor)
MIGRATION, GLOBALIZATION AND THE STATE

Yang Jiang
CHINA'S POLICYMAKING FOR REGIONAL ECONOMIC COOPERATION

Jewellord Singh and France Bourgouin (editors)
RESOURCE GOVERNANCE AND DEVELOPMENTAL STATES IN THE GLOBAL SOUTH
Critical International Political Economy Perspectives

Bonnie K. Campbell (editor)
MODES OF GOVERNANCE AND REVENUE FLOWS IN AFRICAN MINING

Yildiz Atasoy (editor)
GLOBAL ECONOMIC CRISIS AND THE POLITICS OF DIVERSITY

Eirikur Bergmann
ICELAND AND THE INTERNATIONAL FINANCIAL CRISIS
Boom, Bust and Recovery

Felipe Amin Filomeno
MONSANTO AND INTELLECTUAL PROPERTY IN SOUTH AMERICA

Gabriel Siles-Brügge
CONSTRUCTING EUROPEAN UNION TRADE POLICY
A Global Idea of Europe

Greig Charnock, Thomas Purcell and Ramon Ribera-Fumaz
THE LIMITS TO CAPITAL IN SPAIN
Crisis and Revolt in the European South

Monique Taylor
THE CHINESE STATE, OIL AND ENERGY SECURITY

Toni Haastrup, and Yong-Soo Eun (editors)
REGIONALISING GLOBAL CRISES
The Financial Crisis and New Frontiers in Regional Governance

Bartholomew Paudyn
CREDIT RATINGS AND SOVEREIGN DEBT
The Political Economy of Creditworthiness through Risk and Uncertainty

Andreas Nölke (editor)
MULTINATIONAL CORPORATIONS FROM EMERGING MARKETS
State Capitalism 3.0

Lourdes Casanova and Julian Kassum
THE POLITICAL ECONOMY OF AN EMERGING GLOBAL POWER
In Search of the Brazil Dream

Bhumitra Chakma
SOUTH ASIA IN TRANSITION
Democracy, Political Economy and Security

Benedicte Bull, Fulvio Castellacci and Yuri Kasahara
BUSINESS GROUPS AND TRANSNATIONAL CAPITALISM IN CENTRAL AMERICA
Economic and Political Strategies

Karen E. Young
THE POLITICAL ECONOMY OF ENERGY, FINANCE AND SECURITY IN THE
UNITED ARAB EMIRATES
Between the Majilis and the Market

International Political Economy Series
Series Standing Order ISBN 978- 0–333–71708–0 hardcover
Series Standing Order ISBN 978- 0–333–71110–1 paperback

You can receive future titles in this series as they are published by placing a standing order. Please contact your bookseller or, in case of difficulty, write to us at the address below with your name and address, the title of the series and one of the ISBNs quoted above.

Customer Services Department, Macmillan Distribution Ltd Houndmills, Basingstoke, Hampshire RG21 6XS, England

Latin America's Emerging Middle Classes

Economic Perspectives

Edited by

Jeff Dayton-Johnson
Associate Professor, Monterey Institute of International Studies, USA

Editorial matter, production and preface © Jeff Dayton-Johnson 2015.
Chapters © Contributors 2015.

All rights reserved. No reproduction, copy or transmission of this publication may be made without written permission.

No portion of this publication may be reproduced, copied or transmitted save with written permission or in accordance with the provisions of the Copyright, Designs and Patents Act 1988, or under the terms of any licence permitting limited copying issued by the Copyright Licensing Agency, Saffron House, 6-10 Kirby Street, London EC1N 8TS.

Any person who does any unauthorized act in relation to this publication may be liable to criminal prosecution and civil claims for damages.

The author(s) has/have asserted his/her/their right(s) to be identified as the author(s) of this work in accordance with the Copyright, Designs and Patents Act 1988.

First published 2015 by
PALGRAVE MACMILLAN

Palgrave Macmillan in the UK is an imprint of Macmillan Publishers Limited, registered in England, company number 785998, of Houndsmills, Basingstoke, Hampshire, RG21 6XS

Palgrave Macmillan in the US is a division of St Martin's Press LLC,
175 Fifth Avenue, New York, NY 10010.

Palgrave is the global academic imprint of the above companies and has companies and representatives throughout the world.

Palgrave® and Macmillan® are registered trademarks in the United States, the United Kingdom, Europe and other countries

ISBN: 978–1–137–32078–0

This book is printed on paper suitable for recycling and made from fully managed and sustained forest sources. Logging, pulping and manufacturing processes are expected to conform to the environmental regulations of the country of origin.

A catalogue record for this book is available from the British Library.

A catalog record for this book is available from the Library of Congress.

Contents

List of Tables and Figures		ix
Preface		xiii
Notes on Contributors		xvii
List of Acronyms and Abbreviations		xxiii
1	Making Sense of Latin America's Middle Classes *J. Dayton-Johnson*	1
2	Inequality, Mobility and Middle Classes in Latin America *J. P. Azevedo, L. F. López-Calva, N. Lustig and E. Ortiz-Juárez*	32
3	Latin America's Global Middle Class: A Preference for Growth over Equality *M. Cárdenas, H. Kharas and C. Henao*	51
4	Brazil's New Middle Classes: The Bright Side of the Poor *M. Neri*	70
5	Who Is the Latin American Middle Class? Relative-Income and Multidimensional Approaches *F. Castellani, G. Parent and J. Zenteno Gonzales*	101
6	Covering the Uncovered: Labor Informality, Pensions and the Emerging Middle Class in Latin America *C. Daude, J. R. de Laiglesia and Á. Melguizo*	130
7	Business Sector Responses to the Rise of the Middle Class *L. Casanova and H. B. B. Renck*	150
8	Feeling Middle Class and Being Middle Class: What Do Subjective Perceptions Tell Us? *E. Lora and J. Fajardo-González*	173
9	Political Attitudes of the Middle Class: The Case of Fiscal Policy *C. Daude, H. Gutiérrez and Á. Melguizo*	186
Index		205

List of Tables and Figures

Tables

1.1	Different Estimates of the Size of the Latin American Middle Class (% of population)	17
3.1	Change in the Share of the Middle Class between 2005 and 2030 (in percentage points)	55
3.2	Trends in Income Distribution: Gini Coefficient	56
3.3	Peruvian Middle-Class Values and Attitudes (regression results)	62
4.1	How Much Income Inequality Is Explained by Economic Classes?	76
4.2	Economic Classes Defined by Total Household Income (R$)	78
4.3	Individual Characteristics, Education and Work by Economic Classes	88
4.4	Public Services Quality and Individual Perceptions by Economic Classes	89
4.5	Marginal Contribution to Income Inequality	94
4.6	Individual Characteristics, Education and Work by Economic Classes	96
5.1	Size of the Middle Class in Latin America in or around 2011 (% of households)	105
5.2	Size of the Middle Class According to Relative and Absolute Measures in Selected Latin American Countries, in or around 2000 and 2011 (% of households)	107
5.3	Perceptions of Public Services, Colombia, 2003 and 2010 (% of households)	111
5.4	Determinants of Middle-Class Status: Multinomial Probit Estimations around 2010	114
5.5	Multidimensional Poverty Rates for Different Numbers of Deprivations in Colombia (%)	118
5.6	Deprivations of Multidimensionally Poor and Non-poor Families in Colombia (% of households)	119
5.7	Colombian Middle Class and Their Deprivations (% of households)	122
8.1	Income Distribution and Self-Assessment of Social Position (percentage of individuals)	175

8.2	Matching Coefficients for Two Objective Definitions of Middle Class	176
8.3	Correlation and Matching Coefficients by Country (objective definition)	177

Figures

2.1	Annual Percentage Change in the Gini Coefficient, by Country; c. 2001–11	34
2.2	Contribution of Proximate Determinants to the Decline in Inequality (%); Latin America, c. 2000–10	35
2.3	Contribution of the Decline in Inequality to Changes in Poverty (%); c. 2001–10	36
2.4	Percentage of Households Living on $2–10, $2–13 and $10–50 per Person per Day in Mexico; 1992–2012	38
2.5	Income and the Probability of Being Poor; Chile, Mexico and Peru	40
2.6	Percentage of Population in Economic Groups; Latin America, c. 2000–12	42
2.7	Percentage of Middle-Class Population 2012, and Its Change over the 2000s in Percentage Points	43
2.8	Correlation between Changes in the Size of the Middle Class and Changes in Inequality and Income; c. 2000–11	44
2.9	Contribution of the Decline in Inequality to Changes in the Size of the Middle Class (%); c. 2003–10	45
3.1	Peruvian Individual Top Priorities	64
4.1	World Income Distribution, BRICs and the US	72
4.2	Gini Coefficients, Brazil and the World (cross-country)	73
4.3	Changes in Shares of National Income, Brazil (bottom 50 per cent, mid 40 per cent and top 10 per cent)	75
4.4	The Population Pyramid and Economic Classes 2003–14, Brazil	79
4.5	Class Composition 1992 to 2014	80
4.6	Evolution of Class ABC Shares, Brazilian States	81
4.7	Cumulative Income Growth Rates 2011 to 2013, by Vintile	84
4.8	Chances of Going Up and Down across the Median – Odds Ratio (2002 = 1)	85
5.1	Evolution of the Size of the Middle Class, Selected Latin American Countries, 2000–11 (% of households)	106
5.2	Middle Class and Type of Employment, Selected Latin American Countries, 2011	109
5.3	Middle Class and Activity Sector, 2011	110
5.4	Dimensions and Variables of Multidimensional Poverty Index (MPI)	118

5.5	Multidimensional Poverty Index and Income Classes in Colombia (% of households)	120
5.6	Deprivations and Middle Class in Colombia (% of middle-class households deprived)	121
6.1	Non-agricultural Middle-Income Workers in Colombia, Chile, Mexico and Peru by Occupation (Percentage of workers – 14 to 64 years old)	136
6.2	Workers Contributing to the Pension System by Level of Income in Colombia, Chile, Mexico and Peru (Percentage of the total workers – 14 to 64 years old)	139
9.1	Demand for Redistribution by Self-Reported Middle-Class Respondents in Selected Latin American countries, China and the US (%)	191
9.2	'Corruption among Government Officials Is Common or Very Common' in Latin America (% of respondents, by income decile, 2010)	196

Preface

This book began as a conversation. More prosaically, it began as a policy research project at the OECD Development Centre, where some years ago I served as the head of the Americas Desk, the unit that publishes the annual *Latin American Economic Outlook*. The conversation started among the Desk staff: while we did not all agree on how to address the issue, we were all stimulated by the prospect of fresh thinking about the problem of what it meant to be middle class in the developing world. We devoted our 2011 *Outlook* to the Latin American middle sectors (OECD, 2010). The report was presented by OECD Secretary-General Angel Gurría, alongside then-president of the Dominican Republic Leonel Fernández (who invoked the sociologist C. Wright Mills in his impromptu analysis of the Dominican middle class) at the Ibero-American Summit in Mar del Plata, Argentina. The theme and our analysis of it struck a chord with heads of state, policymakers and policy analysts alike.

The conversation spread to other multilateral and intergovernmental organizations, to representatives of Latin American governments, to academics. People disagreed with our definition of the middle class. They took issue with our characterization of the middle class in the region. They engaged with our policy recommendations. It turned out that we were part of a wave of policy research projects on the middle class in Latin America: notably, major studies from other international organizations would coincide with our OECD report: to wit, the United Nations Economic Commission for Latin America and the Caribbean (Franco et al., 2010) and the World Bank (Ferreira et al., 2013). We all sought to build upon a burgeoning multidisciplinary research literature and to respond to demands posed by policymakers. All of a sudden, it seemed, there was a variety of different perspectives on the middle class in Latin America and in the developing world more generally.

This book tries to embrace some of that debate and discussion by inviting several of the principal participants in this latest wave of economically oriented policy research to contribute. By construction, therefore, the different chapters do not always agree with each other. I hope to have captured some of the inherent interest in these still-unresolved debates about how to measure and how to interpret the changes in Latin America's emerging middle classes.

Despite the heterogeneity in conclusions and approaches among the contributors to this volume, all share a similar two-fold methodological framework. First, all of us are primarily motivated by the concerns of development economics and particularly issues of poverty and income inequality, their measurement and trends. Second, all are exponents of a new style of political-economy analysis. The contributors to this book thus straddle the boundary between economic analysis and other disciplinary approaches. It's probably not coincidental that they also straddle the lines between academia, policy analysis and politics in a professional sense. Between the time this conversation started and the publication of this book, several of the authors crossed from universities or think tanks to government ministries to international organizations and back. At press time, for example, there are two cabinet ministers in the table of contents who were in research jobs when we started the book.[1] Marcelo Neri's chapter on Brazil's middle class, in which he triangulates among various data sources, none of them ideal, to track the growth of the middle class in real time, is a telling example of the value of this kind of analysis, at once rigorous and pragmatic.

I am grateful to all of those colleagues and friends who have been a part of this multi-year conversation on what is meant by Latin America's middle classes, and I am particularly thankful to those who were my colleagues back at the OECD when we started this project and to the eighteen experts who contributed chapters to this book. In that regard, I am doubly in debt to those colleagues in both groups, OECD colleagues who contributed to this volume: Francesca Castellani, Christian Daude, Juan Ramón de Laiglesia, Hamlet Gutiérrez, Ángel Melguizo and Gwenn Parent. My thinking on these and so many other aspects of Latin American reality has been indelibly marked by them. Thanks, too, are due to other former OECD colleagues who supported and informed this research, including Carlos Álvarez, Mario Pezzini and Javier Santiso.

For their help in the writing and preparation of this book, I am also grateful to Fernando de Paolis, Rafael Hernández, Robert McCleery, Richard Salvucci, Jessica Yoo, several students and workshop participants who helped me understand this material better and the staff at the William Tell Coleman Library at the Monterey Institute of International Studies. Special thanks are due to Tim Shaw, editor of the International Political

---

[1] In this way, these authors embody several of the characteristics of Latin American political economy highlighted in a recent collection I edited with Javier Santiso, a book which included academic contributions from former and current heads of state and cabinet ministers (Santiso and Dayton-Johnson, 2012).

Economy series, and to Christina Brian and Ambra Finotello of Palgrave Macmillan. The project received the financial support of a faculty development award from the Monterey Institute. I'm grateful for the patience shown by all of those, at work and at home, who were pretty sure I should be doing something other than working on this book. Finally, I want to express my gratitude and appreciation to Jennifer and Nell, to whom I owe a lot more than gratitude and appreciation.

My fondest hope is that the stimulating contributions contained herein will inform a broader and more inclusive conversation about economic development, inequality and social justice in Latin America and the Caribbean.

Jeff Dayton-Johnson

References

Ferreira, F. H. G., J. Messina, J. Rigolini, L. F. López-Calva, M. A. Lugo and R. Vakis (2013) *Economic Mobility and the Rise of the Latin American Middle Class* (Washington, DC: The World Bank).

Franco, R., M. Hopenhayn and A. León, eds. (2010) *Las clases medias en América Latina* (Mexico City: Siglo XXI Editores and CEPAL).

OECD [Organisation for Economic Co-operation and Development] (2010) *Latin American Economic Outlook 2011: How Middle-Class Is Latin America?* (Paris: OECD Publishing).

Santiso, J. and J. Dayton-Johnson, eds. (2012) *The Oxford Handbook of Latin American Political Economy* (Oxford and New York: Oxford University Press).

Notes on Contributors

João Pedro Azevedo is a senior economist at the World Bank Poverty Global Practice, focusing on Central Asia and Turkey and leading the Europe and Central Asia Statistical Team. Before joining the Bank, Azevedo served as the superintendent of monitoring and evaluation at the Secretary of Finance for the State of Rio de Janeiro in Brazil, as well as a research fellow at the Institute of Applied Economic Research in the Brazilian Ministry of Planning. He is a former chairman of the Latin American Network on Inequality and Poverty and holds a PhD in economics.

Mauricio Cárdenas is the minister of finance and public credit in Colombia (since September 2012). He has also served as minister of mines and energy, minister of economic development, minister of transport and director of the National Planning Department. Cárdenas has also been the director of the Latin American Initiative of the Brookings Institution and executive director of Fedesarrollo, a Colombian think tank. Cárdenas has published widely on issues related to economic development. His private-sector experience includes serving as general manager of Empresa de Energía de Bogotá and as president of Titularizadora Colombiana. Cárdenas has published widely on issues related to economic development. He holds a Ph.D. in economics from the University of California at Berkeley.

Lourdes Casanova, a senior lecturer and academic director of the Emerging Markets Institute at the Johnson School of Business at Cornell University (US) and formerly at INSEAD, specializes in international business with a focus on emerging-market multinationals. She is the author or coauthor of *The Political Economy of an Emerging Global Power: In Search of the Brazil Dream* (Palgrave Macmillan, 2014), *Global Latinas: Latin America's Emerging Multinationals* (Palgrave Macmillan, 2009) and *Innovalatino, Fostering Innovation in Latin America* (Ariel, 2011). Casanova is a member of Latin America Global Agenda Council and the Competitiveness in Latin America taskforce of the World Economic Forum and Advisory Committee of European Union/Brazil.

Francesca Castellani has served as advisor to the manager of the Andean countries of the Inter-American Development Bank (IDB) in Washington, DC, since February 2014. Previously, she was lead economist at the IDB Country Office in Bogotá. She joined the IDB in 2003, working in Washington, DC, on macroeconomic analysis and research. Castellani also worked at the OECD, the World Bank and the United Nations Commission on Trade and Development in Geneva. Castellani earned an economics degree from Bocconi University in Milan and a master's and a doctorate in economics from the University of Geneva, Switzerland.

Christian Daude is a senior economist at the OECD Economics Directorate, where he currently heads the Colombia Desk, leading the team in charge of Colombia's economic survey, macroeconomic forecasts and structural surveillance. He has also been the head of the Americas Desk for three years, responsible for producing the OECD's flagship publication on Latin America, as well as several country studies. Before joining the OECD in 2008, he worked as a research economist at the Inter-American Development Bank and the European Central Bank. Daude holds a Ph.D. and M.A. in economics from the University of Maryland at College Park.

Jeff Dayton-Johnson is an associate professor of Development Practice and Policy and interim dean of the Graduate School of International Policy and Management at the Monterey Institute of International Studies in Monterey (US). He was previously a senior economist at the OECD Development Centre, where he led the *Latin American Economic Outlook* team, and a professor of economics at Dalhousie University in Canada. His research interests include Latin American economic development, inequality, international migration, fiscal policy and the policymaking process. Dayton-Johnson is co-editor (with Javier Santiso) of the *Oxford Handbook of Latin American Political Economy* (2012).

Juan Ramón de Laiglesia is an economist in the Conditions of Work and Equality department of the International Labour Office. He previously worked at the OECD Development Centre, where he contributed to several reports on socioeconomic issues in Latin America and the developing world. He has written on a diverse set of topics related to the impact of institutions on the welfare of the poor and those in developing countries, including labor informality, poverty measurement, land tenure economics, polygamy and their links to investment and saving behavior. De Laiglesia is an engineer of the École Polytechnique and holds a PhD and an MSc in economics from the London School of Economics.

Johanna Fajardo González is a Ph.D. student in applied economics at the University of Minnesota (US). She received her B.A. in economics from Universidad Nacional de Colombia in 2005 and her M.Sc. in economics from University College London in 2009. Her research focuses on microeconomic issues in developing countries, including household behavior, education and health. Prior to commencing her doctoral studies, Fajardo spent two years as a research assistant at the Inter-American Development Bank.

Hamlet Gutiérrez is an economist with the General Directorate of Internal Revenue of the government of the Dominican Republic, where he advises the director-general on tax policy. He previously worked at the Ministry of Economy, Planning and Development of the Dominican government and the OECD Development Centre. His main areas of research include fiscal policy, public policies for development and infrastructure in Latin America. Hamlet holds a bachelor's degree in economics from the Instituto Tecnológico de Santo Domingo, a master's degree in applied economics from the Johns Hopkins University and is certified in forecasting practice by the International Institute of Forecasters.

Camila Henao Arbeláez is currently pursuing her doctoral studies at the University of Illinois at Urbana-Champaign (US). While at the International Monetary Fund, she conducted macro-financial research on Brazil, Venezuela and Central America. She also worked for the Brookings Institution, where she conducted research on Latin America's middle class. Furthermore, she has been a consultant for the Inter-American Development Bank. Henao holds a B.S. from Universidad de Los Andes (Colombia).

Homi Kharas is a senior fellow at the Brookings Institution (US). Formerly a chief economist in the World Bank, Kharas currently studies policies and trends influencing developing countries, including aid to poor countries, the emergence of a middle class, the food crisis and global governance and the G20. He served as the lead author of the High Level Panel report on the post-2015 development agenda presented to the UN secretary-general. His most recent coauthored books are *Getting to Scale*

(2013); and *After the Spring: Economic Transitions in the Arab World* (2012). He holds a PhD in economics from Harvard University.

Luis Felipe López-Calva is lead economist in the Poverty, Equity and Gender Unit for Latin America and the Caribbean at the World Bank. He has served as director of the Mexican national Human Development Report for the United Nations Development Programme, as well as professor of economics at Universidad de Las Américas-Puebla (Mexico) and El Colegio de México. López-Calva is a member of Mexican government commissions on macroeconomics, health, the measurement of poverty and social development. His research addresses child labor, poverty and inequality, institutional economics and development. López-Calva studied economics at the Universidad de Las Américas-Puebla, Boston University and Cornell University (from which he holds a Ph.D.).

Eduardo Lora is a senior fellow at the Center for International Development at Harvard University. Formerly chief economist at the Inter-American Development Bank, he has authored or edited dozens of books on Latin American development issues, the latest of which are *More than Revenue: Taxation as a Development Tool* (2012) and *Entrepreneurship in Latin America* (2013). He holds a master's of science in economics from the London School of Economics, which awarded him the title of Distinguished Alumnus.

Nora Lustig is Samuel Z. Stone Professor of Latin American Economics at Tulane University and a non-resident fellow at the Center for Global Development and the Inter-American Dialogue. She is currently the director of the Commitment to Equity project (CEQ), editor of the *Journal of Economic Inequality*'s forum and vice-chair of the Board of Directors of the Global Development Network (GDN). She is a founding member and past president of the Latin American and Caribbean Economic Association (LACEA), was a co-director of the World Bank's *World Development Report 2000/1: Attacking Poverty* and is a member of the Stiglitz et al. Commission on Measuring Economic Performance and Social Progress. Lustig received her doctorate in economics from the University of California, Berkeley.

Ángel Melguizo is head of the Americas Desk at the OECD Development Centre, coordinating the annual *Latin American Economic Outlook*, the OECD's flagship publication on the region. He worked as lead specialist in the Labor Markets Unit at the Inter-American Development Bank, where he coordinated work on pensions policy. Previously, he was a senior adviser at the Economic Bureau of the Spanish prime minister and a principal economist at the BBVA Financial Group, specializing in research on pension reform in Latin America, fiscal policy and long-term economic growth. He holds a Ph.D. in public economics and a B.A. in economics from Complutense University of Madrid.

Marcelo Neri is the minister of strategic affairs in the Brazilian Cabinet. He founded the Center for Social Policies (CPS) at Getúlio Vargas Foundation (FGV) and teaches in the Graduate School of Economics (EPGE) at FGV. He was secretary general of the Council of Economic and Social Development (CDES) and president of the Institute of Applied Economic Research (Ipea). Neri works actively in the formulation and evaluation of public policies: he created a system of state minimum wages and conditional cash transfer programs. He has edited books on microcredit, social security, diversity, rural poverty, Bolsa Família, consumption, perceptions and the middle class. His areas of research include well-being and microeconometrics. Neri holds a Ph.D. in economics from Princeton University.

Eduardo Ortiz-Juárez is an economist at the UNDP's Regional Bureau for Latin America and the Caribbean (New York); non-resident associate research fellow at the Center for Inter-American Policy and Research, Tulane University (New Orleans); and consultant at the Poverty and Gender Unit of PREM-LAC, the World Bank (Washington, DC). Prior to that, he was deputy director of economic and social analysis at the Mexican Ministry of Social Development. His fields of interest relate to poverty, inequality, middle classes, social policy and development with particular emphasis on Latin America. He has coauthored several papers, book chapters and articles in peer-reviewed journals.

Henrique Renck is a senior intelligence analyst at eCornell. He holds bachelor's and master's degrees in economics from Universidade Federal do Rio Grande do Sul, Brazil, as well as a graduate degree in business administration from Cornell University. Renck's previous professional experience includes private equity and development banking in Brazil, and his research interests range from applied economics to law and economics and institutional economics.

Jannet Zenteno Gonzales is the acting head of the Social Indicators and Statistics Unit of the National Institute of Statistics of Bolivia. She has also worked for the National Planning Department of the Colombian government. Zenteno worked as a research fellow at the Inter-American Deveopment Bank and as a research assistant in the Center of Economic Development Studies (CEDE) at the Universidad de los Andes in Colombia. Zenteno studied at the Universidad Técnica de Oruro (Bolivia) and earned a master's degree in environmental economics and natural resources at the Universidad de los Andes.

List of Acronyms and Abbreviations

ADECOMP	Azevedo/Sanfelice/Nguyen decomposition (Stata module)
ATM	Automated teller machine
BEPS	Servicio Social Complementario de Beneficios Económicos Periódicos (Complementary Social Service of Periodic Economic Benefits, Colombia)
BPC	Benefício de Prestação Continuada (Continuing Cash Benefit, Brazil)
Bradesco	Banco Brasileiro de Descontos (Brazilian Discount Bank)
BRF	Brasil Foods
CAF	Corporación Andina de Fomento (Andean Development Corporation)
CASEN	Encuesta de Caracterización Socioeconómica Nacional (National Socio-economic Characterization Survey, Chile)
CBD	Companhia Brasileira de Distribuição (Brazilian Distribution Company)
CCTs	Conditional cash transfers
CEDLAS	Centro de Estudios Distributivos Laborales y Sociales (Center for Distributive, Labor and Social Studies, Universidad Nacional de La Plata, Argentina)
Cemex	Cementos Mexicanos S.A. (Mexican Cement, Inc.)
Cencosud	Centros Comerciales Sudamericanos S.A. (South American Shopping Centers, Inc.)
CEPAL	Comisión Económica para América Latina y el Caribe de las Naciones Unidas (United Nations Economic Commission for Latin America and the Caribbean)
CIAT	Centro Interamericano de Administraciones Tributarias (Inter-American Center of Tax Administrations)
Codelco	Corporación Nacional del Cobre de Chile (National Copper Corporation of Chile)
CPS/ FGV	Centro de Políticas Sociais/Fundação Getúlio Vargas (Center for Social Policies, Getulio Vargas Foundation, Brazil)
DNP	Departamento Nacional de Planeación (National Planning Department, Colombia)
DRDECOMP	Datt/Ravallion decomposition (Stata module)
ECLAC	United Nations Economic Commission for Latin America and the Caribbean

EGR	Esteban, Gradin and Ray measure of polarization
ENAHO	Encuesta Nacional de Hogares (National Household Survey, Peru)
ENIGH	Encuesta Nacional de Ingresos y Gastos de los Hogares (National Household Income and Expenditure Survey, Mexico)
EQ-5D	European Quality of Life-5 Dimensions Index
FEMSA	Fomento Económico Mexicano, S.A.B. de C.V. (Mexican Economic Development, Inc.)
GDP	Gross Domestic Product
GEIH	Gran Encuesta Integrada de Hogares (Large Integrated Household Survey, Colombia)
IBGE	Instituto Brasileiro de Geografia e Estatística (Brazilian Institute of Geography and Statistics)
ICLS	International Conference of Labour Statisticians
ICP	International Comparison Program
IDB	Inter-American Development Bank
IIA	Independence of irrelevant alternatives
ILO	International Labour Organization
IMF	International Monetary Fund
INSS	Instituto Nacional do Seguro Social (National Social Security Institute, Brazil)
IPEA	Instituto de Pesquisa Econômica Aplicada (Institute of Applied Economic Research, Brazil)
LAC	Latin America and the Caribbean
LAPOP	Latin American Public Opinion Project
MPI	Multidimensional Poverty Index
MPS	Ministério da Previdência Social (Ministry of Social Pensions, Brazil)
NAFTA	North American Free Trade Agreement
OECD	Organisation for Economic Co-operation and Development
OEM	Original equipment manufacturers
PCA	Principal components analysis
PDVSA	Petróleos de Venezuela S.A. (Petroleum of Venezuela, Inc.)
Pemex	Petróleos Mexicanos (Mexican Petroleum)
Petrobras	Petróleo Brasileiro S.A. (Brazilian Petroleum, Inc.)
PISA	Programme for International Student Assessment
PME	Pesquisa Mensal de Emprego (Monthly Employment Survey, Brazil)
PNAD	Pesquisa Nacional por Amostra de Domicílios (National Household Survey, Brazil)

POF	Pesquisa de Orçamentos Familiares (Household Budget Survey, Brazil)
POUM	Prospect of upward mobility hypothesis
PPP	Purchasing power parity
PRI	Partido Revolucionario Institucional (Institutional Revolutionary Party, Mexico)
PT	Partido dos Trabalhadores (Labor Party, Brazil)
SEDLAC	Socio-Economic Database for Latin America and the Caribbean (Universidad Nacional de La Plata/World Bank)
SIPS	Sistema de Indicadores de Percepção Social (System of Indicators of Social Perceptions, Brazil)
SISBEN	Sistema de Identificación de Potenciales Beneficiarios de Programas Sociales (Identification System for Potential Social Program Beneficiaries, Colombia)
SNA	System of National Accounts
UNDP	United Nations Development Programme
WVS	World Values Survey
ZTE	Zhongxing Telecommunication Equipment Corporation

1
Making Sense of Latin America's Middle Classes
Jeff Dayton-Johnson

What does it mean to be middle class in Latin America? How is the Latin American middle class changing? What are the implications of these changes for Latin American development? The contributions to this volume, taken together, attempt to answer these questions and to make sense of the emerging middle classes in Latin America. This initial chapter motivates recent interest in the Latin American middle class by situating the topic in three narratives about the region's development experience in recent years, having to do with development success (in comparison to past decades, including the so-called 'Lost Decade' that stretched to almost twenty years in some countries), self-sustaining economic growth and a reduction of dependence on the US and European markets and the social critique formulated by the Brazilian demonstrations of 2013–14; each of these stories has an important middle-class dimension. The chapter then provides an overview for understanding the numerous ways the middle class has been defined and measured in recent years, arguing that the various definitions serve an array of explanatory purposes. The final section surveys the answers provided by the contributors to this volume to the research questions raised here.

What emerges from the collective work of the authors of this book is a middle class that is internally heterogeneous in terms of its socioeconomic characteristics as well as its political views and attitudes. There are vulnerable households whose circumstances are not too different from those of the poor in their countries; there is also a growing share of households whose consumption behavior is beginning to resemble that of their rich-country counterparts. Middle-class Latin Americans espouse political views consistent with a more activist, development-oriented State, while at the same time expressing reservations about the effectiveness of the State to solve social problems. This amalgamated emerging middle class is nevertheless vulnerable in the aggregate and stands to benefit from public policies that would promote its social and economic well-being and a more inclusive model of development.

What three recent narratives about Latin America tell us about the middle class

Three vignettes illustrate the growing importance of, and the reasons for our interest in, Latin America's middle classes. Each is, to a certain extent, a caricature that partially obscures a more complicated reality; we will return to the evidence supporting each of these narratives later in this chapter.

Narrative #1: The 'Latin American Decade'

At an international forum in Paris in January 2011, Colombian president Juan Manuel Santos made the case that the world was at the dawn of a 'Latin American Decade'.[1] Abundant natural resources, reformed and stable financial sectors and coherent fiscal and monetary policymaking added up, in Santos's reckoning, to a positive prognosis for the region in a global context of lingering recession in the US and Europe. Santos foresaw vigorous inflows of portfolio and investment capital and bolstered trade relationships that would maintain historically high growth rates and transform Latin American societies in beneficial ways. In this same vein, others have noted approvingly the spread of a new post-ideological pragmatism in policymaking, including the flourishing of aggressive new social policies.

The 'Latin American Decade' narrative envisages economic performance better than other countries and parts of the world, rich and poor alike. Moreover, the story is one of a definitive break with the region's past, evidenced by inflection points in a broad range of social, economic and political indicators. While less than a half decade later, fewer are ready to endorse the Colombian president's optimism, the burgeoning middle classes of many Latin American societies can be adduced as an additional element in this upbeat analysis of the region's economic performance.

Indeed, in a very direct way, growth of the middle class can be seen as a more or less automatic byproduct of one of the most remarkable achievements leading up to – and continuing beyond – Santos's Paris speech: the dramatic reduction in the incidence of poverty and inequality in Latin America. According to statistics calculated by the UN Economic Commission for Latin America and the Caribbean, the poverty rate declined from a high of 48.4 per cent of the population in 1990 to 27.9 per cent in 2013; that is a drop from 204 million at the earlier date to 164 million at the latter date (CEPAL, 2013, p. 51). Different countries have witnessed different rates of poverty reduction: in some, like Chile and Uruguay, the decline occurred earlier than in its neighbors; in others, like El Salvador and Guatemala, rates of poverty remain well above the regional average. In all its complexity, the decline in Latin American poverty is relevant to the discussion in this book because for many observers, Latin Americans who manage to emerge from poverty are automatically members of the middle class. Not all definitions of the middle class would embrace all of these households, as we shall see, but about a fifth of Latin America's population that was poor at the height of the region's 'Lost Decade' of growth (which lasted more than a decade) is not poor today. (Chapter 2 in this volume, by Azevedo et al., analyzes the relationship between economic growth, poverty reduction and middle-class growth.)

In this 'Latin American Decade' reading, the very appearance – let alone the growth and dynamism – of a middle class in Latin American countries is another indicator of positive economic performance, of success, in a region marked by decades, if not centuries, of underdevelopment.

Narrative #2: Decoupling from the Center

In 2008, when the US and Europe were plunged into economic recession, economic growth rates in Latin America were astonishingly resilient – in many cases, remaining well above growth rates registered in OECD countries.[2] This resilience followed on the heels of a near-decade of booming growth in the years preceding the financial crisis, during which many observers boldly declared that Latin America – and many other developing countries, indeed – had 'decoupled' from their dependence upon the hegemonic economies of the US and Europe. If true, this claim would mark a historic break with the patterns analyzed by Argentinian economist Raúl Prebisch's 'center-periphery' framework and the vast dependency school of Latin American development studies. Specifically, the champions of decoupling averred, economic downturns in the US no longer led to downturns in Latin American economies (or, as the maxim once had it, 'When the US sneezes, Latin America catches the flu').[3]

Decoupling from the center, in a slightly broader interpretation of the narrative, means relying more on the periphery to fuel development.

A major part of the decoupling story is that Latin American countries no longer depended as centrally upon US or European demand for their exports: they had expanded their portfolio of trade partners to include rapidly growing emerging economies in Asia, particularly China (indeed, China displaced the US as the principal trade partner of several South American countries during the first decade of the millennium). A secondary motif in the decoupling account is the role of domestic demand. Latin American businesses could depend not only on China for demand, but on the more robust spending power of people in the middle of the income distributions in their own countries. In this narrative, the middle class emerges, by virtue of its consumption spending, as a potential motor for economic growth. Chapter 3 in this volume, by Cárdenas et al., considers the purchasing power of the middle class as a motor for growth and compares it to the emerging Chinese and Indian middle classes. Chapter 7, meanwhile, addresses the strategic response of Latin American businesses to this new class of consumer.

Narrative #3: Bus Fares, Football and Demonstrations
On 2 June 2013, the fare for riding a bus or the subway in São Paulo was raised from R$3 to R$3.2, a move that was met with immediate protest. Four days later, 2,000 protesters voiced their disapproval along the Avenida Paulista; by 17 June, the protest had swollen to 65,000 in São Paulo, blocking major arteries, while in Brasília, protesters occupied the National Congress. On 19 June, the fare increase was reversed (and fares in Rio de Janeiro were reduced as well), but it was too late to stem the growth of the movement the initial price rise had engendered. Approximately one million Brazilians – 300,000 in Rio alone – marched on 20 June in various cities of the country.[4] Before long, protesters linked their demands with condemnation of sizeable public spending to host the 2014 World Cup and the 2016 Summer Olympics; the opening of the World Cup in June 2014 was met with renewed demonstrations.

Observers in Brazil, and later internationally, immediately remarked upon the 'middle-class' character of the protesters. The content of their demands, moreover, could be characterized as a kind of middle-class politics. Their argument sees fiscal policy as a reflection of the social contract linking citizens and the government. Citizens transfer resources to government – like bus fares – in exchange for which governments provide goods and services – like bus service – of reasonable quantity and quality. The Brazilian protests were a way of refusing to pay more for a service of dubious quality. And the protesters quickly made the link to other publicly provided services, including health care and education, and to the issue of corruption in government. It was, in short, a furious defense of democratic consolidation – holding the elected government accountable for its promises – in Brazil, a country, like many of its neighbors, that emerged from military dictatorship only a few decades ago. (Chapter 4 in this volume, by Marcelo Neri, addresses the growth and characteristics of the Brazilian middle class.)

That the middle class might be a constituency for progressive, if not revolutionary, political platforms is not new: The political scientist John Johnson argued as early as the late 1950s that emerging Latin American 'middle sectors' of urban wage workers in commerce and industry were political defenders of State-led development efforts, public education, social welfare programs and democracy itself. Johnson credited middle-class elector support for the political success of a long series of political leaders, ranging from José Batlle y Ordoñez in Uruguay, Hipólito Irigoyen in Argentina at the start of the twentieth century, through the Partido Revolucionario Institucional (PRI) presidents that followed the 'stabilizing development' model in Mexico and Juscelino Kubitschek in Brazil in the mid-century.[5] Many recent electoral processes in Latin America have likewise courted the middle-class vote: those resulting in the election of Sebastián Piñera in Chile in 2010 and Luis Guillermo Solís in Costa Rica in 2014, to name just two.

In this formulation, the emerging middle classes, represented by the Brazilian protesters, send a strong signal to their elected leaders that they will hold them accountable to respect and protect their fledgling democracies.[6] Alternatively, it could be that the middle class protests and lobbies for things of clear value to them, even at the expense of social welfare programs and the poor. Examples include drives to maintain or increase large subsidies for gasoline and higher education, items that feature far more prominently in the consumption baskets of the middle class than the poor, and the expansion of formal sector pensions and other parts of the 'social safety net' that frequently does not extend to the poor, or often even the 'vulnerable'. Chapter 9 in this volume, by Daude et al., considers these possibilities.

These three vignettes – a new decade of Latin American economic effervescence, a shuffling off of economic dependence on the US and Europe and the rise of a new form of street protests – each shine a light on different aspects of the importance of the emerging middle class in Latin America. Taken together, these perspectives raise a number of questions:

1 How is the emergence of the middle class related to recent successes in social and economic development in the region?
2 What is the relationship between poverty reduction and middle-class growth in Latin America?
3 In a related vein, how is the growth of the middle class related to the recent decline in inequality in many countries in Latin America and to changes in the income distribution more generally?
4 Can the Latin American middle class serve as a motor for economic growth? How?
5 Are the middle classes defenders of democratic consolidation in Latin America? And what kind of public policies do middle-class Latin Americans support?

Just who is the Latin American middle class?

Each of these questions has been systematically analyzed in a growing body of research – much of which is represented by the other chapters in this volume. The first step in approaching any of these questions, however, is defining the middle class. Who is the middle class – in Brazil, in the Dominican Republic, in China; in developing economies, in rich countries; today, fifty years from now or in the nineteenth century? Most readers will have had some image in their mind as they read the chapter up to this point. Perhaps that image is of Martín Santomé, the hapless office worker in Uruguayan author Mario Benedetti's classic *La tregua* (1960), who wanly tells us on the first page of the novel that he will be eligible to retire in six months and twenty-eight days.[7] More likely, the reader's image is informed by stereotypical notions of middle-class life that developed in rich countries or perhaps by accounts of the middle class in developing countries that have popped up with regularity in the business press in recent years.[8]

Economic Approaches to Defining the Middle Class

The approach adopted in this volume is unapologetically economic in nature: that is, the middle class is defined in terms of economic characteristics such as household income or consumption or occupational status. Indeed, Benedetti's protagonist exhibits characteristics that align with some researchers' definitions: a formal-sector professional job in the city, a solid level of schooling, the prospect of a pension, all of which would make Santomé's material well-being substantially better than most Uruguayans' in the late 1950s. By establishing concrete criteria, households in a given Latin American country can be assigned to the middle class (or not) for the purposes of measurement and in order to track changes in the middle class (including, notably, its size) over time. Note that this research objective – definition for the purpose of measurement – is also economic in nature, or at least aligned with a quantitative approach to social science.

This quantitative economic approach is different from, and complementary to, others. For example, historians have frequently addressed the challenge of the middle class, not in terms of counting middle-class people, but by answering the question of how people in different settings define themselves or others as middle class. In this conception, the historical study of the middle class in Latin America or anywhere else is the systematic analysis of changes in middle-class status and identity: How do the boundaries change, and why do they change?[9] For the purposes of most of the research included in this book, the lesson of this rich historical literature is twofold: 1) any boundaries we use here to delimit the middle class are necessarily context-specific and not likely to be useful everywhere and always, and 2) a valuable complement to the quantitative-economic approach would look carefully at how those limiting boundaries came to be used in a manner far more critical than the descriptive perspective employed in this section.

Let us turn then to the various income-based boundaries that have been proposed and used to research the extent of the middle class in developing countries. Many of the income limits are expressed in terms of US dollars per day – for example, people with incomes higher than $2 a day are 'middle class' for some of these authors. Some methodological considerations – which will be commonplace to readers who are economists – should be clarified, particularly for readers in Latin American countries who may find the per capita income numbers reported in the chapters in this volume to be at odds with the earnings that they observe around them every day.

First, these figures are generally based on household surveys now widely available in most developing economies for many years (Chapter 2 in this volume, by Azevedo et al., for example, uses analysis of successive household survey data sets from Chile, Mexico and Peru). Though the degree of harmonization and rigor in these surveys has progressed markedly in recent years, the precision of the income estimates they provide is not always perfect, especially for agricultural households or those headed by own-account workers. Moreover, some surveys focus on household consumption rather than income, slightly complicating the comparison of data from disparate sources. As for wealth, at least as important as income or consumption spending to any measure of economic inequality, the available data are spotty, especially for the wealthiest households, who tend to be underrepresented in household surveys.

At least two adjustments are then made to survey-based household income data. Total household income is converted to per capita income by dividing the total by the number of household members; typically children are given a lower weight than adults in this calculation, so that a household with two adults and four children might be treated as containing four 'adult equivalents'. Finally, per capita income expressed in local currency units – Honduran lempiras, Argentinian pesos – is converted to US dollars, adjusting for international differences in purchasing power parity (PPP). The PPP adjustment corrects for differences in the prices of so-called 'non-traded goods' (like haircuts, cement and personal services) between rich and poor countries – these prices tend to be lower in poor countries than in rich ones. The PPP adjustment as such raise per capita income figures in developing countries relative to simply using the market exchange rate to compute dollar figures.[10] These, then, are the figures used to demarcate the middle class from other groups in society in what follows.

Absolute-Income Definitions of the Middle Class in Developing Countries

One group of authors has chosen absolute measures of income to delimit the middle class. That is, they define lower and upper per capita income levels to comprise the middle class, which are applied to all countries under analysis, regardless of average or median income levels in those countries. A pair of influential studies in this regard begin with the criterion that middle-class people should not be poor: thus, they set the lower threshold at income of $2 per person per day, a widely used poverty-line income level. Abhijit Banerjee and Esther Duflo (2008) look at households with per capita daily consumption expenditures between $2 and $10, using household survey data from thirteen countries (including Guatemala, Mexico, Nicaragua and Panama from Latin America). Among the commonalities Banerjee and Duflo identify among middle-class households thus defined: their heads tend to have steady work and they have fewer and healthier children than poorer households. Ravallion (2009) stretches the upper income bound of the Banerjee-Duflo definition to $13 a day, on the grounds that this corresponds to the median of poverty lines in rich countries. Thus, Ravallion's developing-country middle class contains those households that would be poor by rich-country standards but are not poor in the context of their own country.

Ravallion then extends it to the developing world as a whole and finds a net increase of 1.2 billion people in this middle class between 1990 and 2002, four-fifths of which occurred in developing Asia. Moreover, most of the new members of the developing world's middle class are quite close to the lower $2-a-day cutoff, and Ravallion therefore emphasizes the vulnerability of this group to falling (back) into poverty.

An alternative middle-class definition applies to all countries, rich and poor alike. Homi Kharas (2010) accordingly sets the lower and upper bounds at $10 and $100 income per person per day to delimit a middle class that can be found in every country. (This research is extended in Chapter 3 of this volume, by Cárdenas et al.) These daily income levels correspond to large segments of the population in rich countries today and could quite plausibly serve as a measure of the middle class in high-income economies. In contrast, the share of households in developing countries with incomes this high is generally small, but for large-population countries like China, India or Brazil, this minority nevertheless includes a lot of people in absolute numbers. Kharas forecasts the growth of this global middle class and estimates that by 2020, roughly one-half of the group will be in Asia, versus one-quarter today. These new middle-class Asian households will be found largely in China and India (indeed, Kharas forecasts that India's middle class will outstrip China's in size). Latin America's share of Kharas's global middle class (excluding Mexico, which is included in North America), meanwhile, will decline from 10 per cent today to 6 per cent in 2030.

The World Bank's major report on the Latin American middle class (Ferreira et al., 2013) included different income cutoffs better tailored to the economic characteristics of the region and arguably less ad hoc in nature. (Chapter 2 in this volume, by Azevedo et al., is partly based on the World Bank research and provides an account of how the income cutoffs were developed.) The World Bank's middle class falls between per capita incomes of $10 a day and $50 a day (Ferreira et al., 2013, fig. 5.2; these cutoff points were advocated in an earlier paper by Milanovic and Yitzhaki, 2002). The lower bar is raised deliberately to exclude the vulnerable – those with a greater than 10 per cent chance of falling into poverty based on an econometric model of income levels over time estimated with repeated household surveys in Chile, Mexico and Peru.

These absolute-income definitions of the middle class, whether $2 to $10, $2 to $13, $10 to $50 or $10 to $100, facilitate comparisons across countries and over time in a reasonably transparent way. Nevertheless, it is difficult to develop an absolute-income definition that is both applicable to all countries, rich and poor alike, and more often than not includes people in the middle of the income distribution. Kharas's global middle class is universally applicable, for example, but in most developing countries the definition draws in a tiny minority of households at the upper end – sometimes the extreme upper end – of the income distribution.

Ravallion's developing-country middle class, meanwhile, does a better job of embracing people in the middle of the income distribution in lower-income countries, but there would be, by construction, zero middle-class households according to this definition in rich countries. Indeed, as Chapter 2 by Azevedo et al. in this volume demonstrates, Ravallion's middle-class limits are low even for a middle-income country like Mexico; by this definition, they show, Mexico's middle class paradoxically swells during economic downturns – but only because more households *drop* into this relatively low income bracket. For developing countries much poorer than Mexico, these measures can likewise miss the middle from the other direction: Banerjee and Duflo find, for example, that rural households that spend $2 a day on consumption in India and Pakistan have consumption levels higher than more than 80 per cent of their neighbors.

This criticism is not meant to invalidate the usefulness of absolute-income definitions. Indeed, these measures are particularly well-suited to discussions of middle-class consumption spending as a motor of growth: given that consumption spending typically accounts for the lion's share of national income, increased spending capacity among the middle class will fuel growth of national income. If, in contrast, the mechanism linking the middle class to higher growth rates operates through the effect of lower inequality on growth, then relative-income measures like those described in the following section are more useful.

Relative-Income Definitions of the Middle Class in Developing Countries

For these reasons, other authors have opted for relative-income definitions of the middle class. Thus, the OECD (2010) study of the Latin American middle class considers households with per capita income between 50 per cent and 150 per cent of median per capita income.[11] (This research is extended in Chapter 5 by Castellani et al. and Chapters 6 and 9 by Daude et al. in this volume.) The lower cutoff is a frequently used relative poverty line in rich countries, so that the motivation for this measure is the relative-income analog to the Banerjee, Duflo and Ravallion measures: households with per capita income above 50 per cent of the median lie above an internationally comparable poverty line, albeit one that varies from country to country. The middle class (and indeed, the poor and the rich) as a share of total population will vary from country to country depending upon the shape of the income distribution.

An alternative relative-income measure is used by William Easterly (2001) in an influential econometric study. This measure relies upon the notion of income quintiles: imagine that all of the households in an economy are lined up from lowest to highest income and then divided into equal-sized fifths (or quintiles). Easterly defines the middle class as those households in the second, third and fourth quintiles. In this conception, the middle class will always constitute exactly 60 per cent of the total population, but Easterly analyzes the share of national income earned by this middle 60 per cent (averaged over the years 1990 to 1996). For the 103 countries in his data set, the average income share earned by the middle class is 47 per cent; the measure ranges from a low of 30 per cent to a high of 58 per cent. Easterly analyzes the relationship between the middle-class share of national income and economic growth (also accounting for other important variables, ethnic fractionalization among them). He finds that a higher middle-class income share is associated with higher income levels and growth rates, as well as better social and physical infrastructure, better policymaking and lower levels of conflict (among other beneficial outcomes).[12]

These relative-income measures – whether the OECD's '50–150' definition or the use of quintiles or deciles of the income distribution – succeed in a way that the absolute-income measures do not: they can be meaningfully applied to all countries, and they always include people in the middle of the income distribution. Thus, for example, OECD (2010, fig 1.1) compares the size of this middle class in several Latin American countries with that of Italy around 2006. The smallest middle classes in the Latin American countries included in the comparison were Bolivia (37 per cent of the population) and Colombia (39 per cent); the largest were Mexico (53 per cent) and Uruguay (56 per cent). None, however, were as large as Italy's, at 66 per cent. Of course, the income level that separates those below the middle class from the middle class itself in these relative-income measures differs from one country to the next.

The relative-income measures, additionally, tell us something about inequality in a given economy. The Latin America–Italy comparison demonstrates that, in an important way, income inequality is greater in Latin America than it is in Italy. Moreover, income inequality is more acute in Bolivia and Colombia than it is in Mexico or Uruguay, in the specific sense that proportionally more Mexicans and Uruguayans than Bolivians and Colombians find themselves between 50 and 150 per cent of median income in their country. Indeed, these comparisons of the size of the '50 to 150' middle class match up with comparisons of the Gini index, a widely used synthetic measure of income inequality (which ranges from zero for perfect equality to one hundred for perfect inequality), for these five countries around 2006. According to the World Bank's World Development Indicators, the Gini indices were as follows: Colombia, 59; Bolivia, 56; Mexico, 48; Uruguay, 47; Italy, 36.

In this way, relative-income measures allow us to link discussion of the middle class to the issue of income inequality, long relevant in Latin America, but also to recently observed declines in inequality.[13] The middle class can grow because economic growth raises many poor households above the poverty line, or it can grow because the level of income inequality declines, and more households find themselves in the middle of the income distribution. Chapter 2 in this volume, by Azevedo et al., disaggregates the growth of the middle class into these two components. They find that about a little more than a fifth of the growth in the middle class is due to inequality reduction, while four-fifths is due to economic growth and poverty reduction. (Azevedo et al. use an absolute-income measure of the middle class: the $4 to $50 delimitation.) This is similar to the forecasting exercise reported by Kharas et al. in Chapter 3, which suggests that economic growth has far greater potential to drive middle-class growth than does redistributive public finance. (One issue not addressed by most contributors to this volume is the difference in 'middle class' in rural and urban contexts. Many countries now have separate rural and urban PPP measures and poverty lines, so that in principle there could in turn be two relative income definitions of 'middle class', even for the same country and year.)

Income-Based Measures and the Poverty Line

Many of the income-based measures of the middle class use the poverty line as their lower limit, whether it's the absolute international poverty line of $2 a day (as in the Banerjee-Duflo and Ravallion definitions), or the relative poverty line equal to 50 per cent of median per capita income (as in the OECD definition). As a result, much of the debate regarding how the middle class should be defined perfectly mirror debates about how poverty should be defined, and vice versa. Thus there are disagreements regarding the appropriate international absolute poverty line; some researchers opt for $1-, $2- and $4-a-day lines, and each of those choices has immediate consequences for the size of the middle class.

Adam Smith, in *The Wealth of Nations*, famously argued that poverty is a relative concept, in that the 'necessaries' consistent with being a 'creditable person' vary across countries and over time:

> By necessaries I understand, not only the commodities which are indispensably necessary for the support of life, but whatever the custom of the country renders it indecent for creditable people, even of the lowest order, to be without. A linen shirt, for example, is, strictly speaking, not a necessary of life. . . . But in the present times, through the greater part of Europe, a creditable day-labourer would be ashamed to appear in public without a linen shirt . . . Custom, in the same manner, has rendered leather shoes a necessary of life in England. The poorest creditable person of either sex would be ashamed to appear in public without them. . . . Under necessaries, therefore, I comprehend, not only those things which nature, but those things which the established rules of decency have rendered necessary to the lowest rank of people.[14]

Smith's view leads to the use of a relative poverty line for measuring and analyzing the extent of poverty in a given economy. This view likewise establishes a relative, time- and place-specific boundary between shame and creditability, between poverty and what we would now call middle-class life.

Confusion can emerge because these relative poverty lines generally differ from national poverty lines set by national statistical offices. The OECD (2010, fig. 1.10) report on the middle sectors compares the 50 per cent of median income poverty line with national poverty lines for eight Latin American countries. To put it simply, how many people does the OECD report consider middle class that are considered poor by their own governments? The results are mixed. In Chile and Costa Rica, and to a lesser degree Argentina and Brazil, the poverty line is not far from 50 per cent of median income, so there is little to no overlap between this conception of the middle class and local definitions of the poor. At the other extreme, in Mexico, Peru and the Dominican Republic, virtually all of those considered 'moderately poor' (though not 'extremely poor') fall within the OECD report's definition of the middle class.

But are all the non-poor automatically middle class? Not everyone would say so. The World Bank report on the middle class (Ferreira et al., 2013) explicitly seeks to eliminate from the group the 'vulnerable' so important to Ravallion's conception of the developing world's middle class. The World Bank team does so essentially by moving the lower income boundary from $2 to $10 a day.

Less controversial, and generally less remarked upon, is the suitability of the upper income boundaries of the middle class. This is primarily because our interest in economic mobility is fundamentally focused on crossing the lower threshold. Per capita incomes of $50 or $100 a day are quite high by international standards: the World Bank team, which sets the upper bar at $50 a day, notes that this corresponds to the ninety-eighth percentile of the income distribution in many Latin American countries.

Nevertheless, some of the discussion of the middle class in the media appears, unwittingly perhaps, to be concerned with Latin American households near or beyond these upper-income limits. For example, a Mexico City public relations professional told journalist David Lida (2008, p. 30) that he was bullish about the middle class:

> 'I don't believe what the papers say,' he said recently. 'There are a lot of new middle-class people in Mexico City.' It surfaced that his conception of middle class meant those who earn close to two hundred thousand dollars a year, drive a Mercedes or an Audi, have mortgaged a lavish apartment, sport a Cartier or Rolex watch, and wear designer clothing. 'That kind of money doesn't buy you everything,' he said ruefully. 'I live in a small apartment and drive a six-year-old car, but I travel to New York or Paris once a month.' He scoffed at a Mexican fashion designer whose shirts retail at three hundred fifty dollars. 'I buy my clothes on sale in San Diego,' he said. 'I pay one hundred dollars for shirts. The most I've ever spent on a shirt is two hundred fifty dollars, and that was Comme des Garçons.'

Meanwhile, in Lima, real-estate professionals note that 'middle-class demand' is pushing up apartment prices in neighborhoods like Surquillo and Breña. The price of a 60 m² apartment in the desirable Barranco district averages about $100,000 at current exchange rates (and between $50,000 and $70,000 in less expensive districts neighboring Miraflores). Contrast this with Peru's per capita income, converted using current exchange rates like the apartment prices quoted, which is only $6,000.[15] If indeed the middle class corresponds to people in the middle of the income distribution (and, as we have seen, not all specialists would define it that way), then clearly many observers are mistaken about where the dividing line between the middle class and the rich is to be found. Chapter 8 in this volume, by Lora and Fajardo, compares Latin Americans' self-reported position in the income distribution with their actual position; they find that the confusion of Lida's Mexico City PR man and Lima real-estate professionals is widespread.

Occupational Status

Income is not the only economic variable one might use to craft a definition of the middle class. Indeed, Adam Smith's relative boundary between poverty and creditability was not explicitly stated in terms of income, but rather in terms of ownership of goods, such as a linen shirt and shoes (although it could be translated into the income necessary to purchase the required goods). In Smith's conception, income is primarily useful as a means to acquire symbols of status.

Perhaps the most important economic marker of middle-class status, aside from income itself, is one's job. A certain stereotypical conception of middle-class work holds that such workers have stable, well-paid (if humdrum) office jobs, like Martín Santomé in *La tregua*. Do working people in the developing world's middle class have good or bad occupations? Different studies (and different definitions of the middle class) yield different answers to this question. Banerjee and Duflo (2008) found that steady work was among the commonalities of their $2 to $10 middle class in thirteen developing countries. Chapter 6 in this volume, by Daude et al., in contrast, finds that a substantial share of middle-income workers (using the OECD's 50–150 relative measure of the middle class) have informal-sector jobs and are therefore less secure than their formal-sector counterparts.

In the extreme, two people might have the same income, but one might be considered middle class and the other not based on their occupational characteristics. Parker's (1998) fascinating history of the rise of the middle class in Lima in the first half of the twentieth century shows that income differences were small between white-collar office workers and blue-collar workers. It was precisely on the basis that their superior status required higher expenditures on clothing and housing that the former mobilized to demand better wages (which they achieved) and social benefits.

The important study of the Latin American middle class carried out by the UN Economic Commission for Latin America and the Caribbean (ECLAC), reported in Franco et al. (2010, 2011), explicitly combines income and occupational characteristics into its two-dimensional definition of the middle class. In brief, they define the middle class as all people in the middle-income stratum plus people in the low-income stratum but with middle-level occupational characteristics. The middle-income stratum is bounded below by four times the urban poverty-line income and above by the ninety-fifth income percentile. In both bounds, the ECLAC income measure is close in spirit to the World Bank's (Ferreira et al., 2013) lower limit on the middle class, which seeks to exclude the vulnerable non-poor and include all but the highest-income households. The ECLAC's innovation is to include lower-income workers with 'good' jobs: that is, non-manual occupations, whether as public- or private-sector employees or as own-account workers. The share of these low-income but middle-level job holders varies from 12 per cent of the population in Costa Rica and Panama in 2006 to as much as 27 per cent of the population in Brazil (León, 2010, table 14).

Comparing Different Measures of the Latin American Middle Class

The relatively young research literature on the contemporary Latin American middle class already contains a handful of measures of the phenomenon under study. Many of these different definitions are represented among the various chapters of this volume. This multiplicity can create confusion.

Consider the very basic measure of the *size* of the middle class (table 1.1). The disparities among estimates of the size of the middle class in six Latin American countries are large: Argentina's middle class ranges from 6 per cent of the population, according to the Banerjee and Duflo $2 to $10 definition, to 74 per cent of the population, according to the ECLAC income-plus-occupation definition. The gaps are similarly large for other countries. Many of these divergences are by design, of course. The Kharas $10 to $100 definition by construction includes no one in the Banerjee and Duflo $2 to $10 definition. Some measures move together, in the sense that they are high in the same countries and low in the same countries. For example, by the ECLAC, OECD and World Bank definitions, Argentina, Chile and Mexico have larger middle classes, while Colombia and Peru have smaller middle classes. The Banerjee-Duflo and Ravallion definitions overlap substantially at relatively low per capita incomes, and both identify the same largest (Colombia) and smallest (Argentina) middle classes.

Despite the potential for confusion, these different measures have been developed to answer different questions. Accordingly, it is to the research questions raised earlier in this chapter that we now return.

Table 1.1 Different Estimates of the Size of the Latin American Middle Class (% of population).

Definition	(1) 4 times Urban Poverty Line – 90th percentile (ECLAC)	(2) $10–100/day (Kharas)	(3) '50–150' (OECD)	(4) $2–10/day (Banerjee & Duflo)	(5) $2–13/day (Ravallion)	(6) $10–50 (World Bank)
Year	2006	2005	2010	2010	2010	2010
Argentina	74	53	55	6	10	66
Brazil	53	34	43	28	38	56
Chile	70	46	52	18	30	66
Colombia	39	25	47	36	49	51
Mexico	48	60	53	27	41	64
Peru	32	31	51	21	39	65

Note: Definitions of these different measures are provided in the text. Years are not consistent for all countries; consult original sources for more details.

Sources: 1) Leon et al., table 14; 2) Chapter 3, this volume, table 3.1; 3–6) Chapter 5, this volume; table 5.2.

Revisiting Narratives about the Latin American Middle Class: What the studies in this volume tell us

In this final section, we revisit the research questions raised at the end of the opening section of this chapter in light of the methodological discussion regarding the measurement of the middle class and attempt to synthesize some of the key findings of the research collected in this volume. Under each question, I will pay particular attention to the different answers that would be provided depending upon whether an absolute- or relative-income measure of the middle class is used.

The Middle Class and the Latin American Decade

How is the emergence of the middle class related to recent successes in social and economic development in the region? Marcelo Neri neatly links the rise of Brazil's 'Classe C' with the boom years of the 'pequena grande década' (2003–2008, for most countries in the region).[16] Neri describes the Brazilian income distribution as 'Belindia': those income classes (A and B) with incomes below the middle C class have incomes, on average, similar to those of India; those classes (D and E) with higher incomes have average income levels on par with those of Belgium (hence 'Belindia'). For Neri, then, the new middle classes of emerging economies like Brazil stand between current definitions of poverty and prosperity; their increased standard of living is a clear sign of progress and most definitely a component of the larger set of improvements that led Juan Manuel Santos to decree a 'Latin American Decade'. In a sense, the normative evaluation of the emergence of Latin America's middle classes embodies all of the research questions raised earlier in this chapter, the remainder of which are considered below.

The Middle Classes, Poverty and Inequality

What is the relationship between poverty reduction and middle-class growth in Latin America? The question is most readily answered with absolute-income definitions of the middle class. The previous section documented disagreement about whether not being poor is necessary or sufficient (or neither, or both) for being in the middle class. Whatever one's view about these measurement debates, the incidence of poverty in the region has fallen dramatically in the last two decades, and at least some of those Latin Americans who have emerged from poverty are now members of the middle class. But the contribution of poverty reduction to the growth of the middle class depends critically on the middle-class measure chosen.

Ravallion's (2008) middle-class measure, recall, lies between the relatively extreme international poverty-line income of $2 per person per day and the rich-world poverty-line income level of $13 per person per day. Growth of Ravallion's middle class should be particularly sensitive to reduction in the most extreme poverty. Chapter 5 in this volume, by Castellani et al. (table 5.2), nevertheless shows that this group, relatively far to the left in the income distribution, has been shrinking in size over Latin America's 'little great decade', sometimes precipitously: in Argentina from 48 per cent to 10 per cent of the population; in Peru, from 61 per cent to 39 per cent.

In Latin America's recent experience, poverty reduction translates into middle-class growth more readily when poverty lines higher than $2 a day are used to define poverty. The World Bank $10-a-day cutoff deliberately seeks to eliminate the vulnerable – who are consubstantial with the developing world's middle class for Ravallion. Using this higher base income, the middle class grew during the first decade of the millennium for all eight of the countries in table 5.2 of Chapter 5, sometimes quite substantially: Bolivia's middle class thus defined rose from 31 per cent to 55 per cent of the population.

How is the growth of the middle class related to changes in the income distribution more generally? This question is more appropriately answered using relative-income measures, which capture changes in the shape of the income distribution. The OECD measure of the middle class as households with per capita incomes between 50 and 150 per cent of the median swells as income becomes more equitably distributed and shrinks as it becomes more polarized.

As noted, income inequality has fallen over the last decade in a majority of Latin American countries for which data are available. López-Calva and Lustig (2010a) emphasize two primary drivers of this decline. The first is a decline in the 'wage premium' earned by more-educated workers: supply of more-educated workers has outstripped demand for them, leading to a smaller gap between incomes of more-educated and less-educated workers. Second, innovative social programs, including conditional cash transfer programs like Bolsa Família in Brazil and Progresa/Oportunidades in Mexico have raised incomes among the poorest households. Both factors relate directly to the fortunes of the middle class.

Arguably, these changes are better reflected in the relative-income measure of the OECD middle class used in Chapter 5 than in the absolute-income measures of Chapters 2 or 3. The largest percentage-point increases in the middle class among the eight countries in the first decade of the 2000s in table 5.2 were witnessed in Bolivia (twelve percentage points) and Argentina (nine points). Percentage-point increases in the World Bank absolute-income measure were larger overall, and the biggest gainers were not the same as with the OECD measure: Peru and Bolivia (twenty-four percentage points each), followed by Brazil (sixteen points). The simple correlation between improvements in the OECD and World Bank measures of the middle class in table 5.2 is 0.67: strong but not ironclad. Two different things are being measured by these two measures over time. The World Bank absolute-income measure detects how many households are being lifted above a fixed benchmark ($10 of income per person per day, in this case). The OECD relative-income measure, meanwhile, measures how many people are gathered within a band of incomes centered on the median income level. The first is therefore more sensitive to overall economic growth, the second to changes in inequality. The gross pattern represented by a comparison of these two measures is that rising incomes have mattered more for middle-class growth than declining inequality. This finding is confirmed by the exhaustive disaggregation reported in Chapter 2 by Azevedo et al., which finds that roughly a fifth of the growth in the World Bank's middle-class measure is due to declining income inequality (and the rest is due to economic growth).

The Middle Class as a Motor for Growth

Can the Latin American middle class serve as a motor for economic growth? Affirmative responses to this question lie behind much of the enthusiasm for the middle class in the business media, focused on this group's buying behavior. In this connection, an index of the global middle class proposed by Dadush and Ali (2012) is based on car ownership. Absolute-income measures of the middle class scaled to rich-country consumption levels, like that used by Cárdenas et al. in Chapter 3, are arguably best suited to analyzing this potential, at least in a macroeconomic sense.

In the first instance, this macro perspective on the middle class is concerned with the extent to which this group can be a driver for global, and not only domestic, growth. In this case, it is not the proportion of the population with daily incomes between $10 and $100 that matters; it is the absolute number of such consumers and their associated purchasing power. World Bank economist Branko Milanovic, using data presented in Lakner and Milanovic (2013), tweeted a figure with the largest middle classes, using the Kharas definition from Chapter 3.[17] The urban Chinese middle class is numerically largest, with 450 million people; the US middle class is a distant second, at just under 250 million. Brazil places fourth, with about 90 million middle-class members. Indeed, both Brazil and Mexico (approximately 60 million) have numerically larger middle classes than India (around 10 million). Thus, Latin America's two most populous nations have large middle classes and therefore larger potential motors for consumption-fueled growth. Nevertheless, Kharas's (2010) projections forecast a future in which they will be dwarfed in size and spending power by the emerging middle classes of developing Asia.

Even if the capacity of Latin America's middle classes to fuel global growth is limited, however, the growing share of the population with daily incomes over $10 could serve as a lucrative market for new economic activities. From this meso perspective, even the economies of small countries like Costa Rica and Uruguay, with middle classes under the Kharas definition in excess of half the population, stand to benefit.

At the micro level, the rise of this new class of consumer provides opportunities for businesses to profit from innovative new strategies. Chapter 7 in this volume, by Casanova and Renck, explores the range of strategies deployed by firms like Grupo Monge (a Costa Rican retailer of electronic consumer durable goods) or Natura (a Brazilian cosmetics company). A feature common to several of Casanova and Renck's company stories is the expansion from one Latin American country to another. Chapter 7, furthermore, shows that the effect of middle-class growth on company strategies can be indirect, as in the increased demand for buses from public-transport companies, much of it met by Brazilian Marcopolo.[18]

The potential for the middle class to drive growth is hampered by its vulnerability. Measures of the middle class that include households vulnerable to falling (back) into poverty paint a picture of a group of consumers ill-equipped to sustain meaningful growth of consumption. Absolute-income measures of the middle class bounded below by the $10 per person per day income line exclude the vulnerable by design; Ravallion's developing-world middle-class measure focuses solely on the vulnerable. Relative-income measures like the OECD '50–150' definition look at the households in the middle of the income distribution, allowing us to ask: how many of them are vulnerable? In this vein, Chapter 6 in this volume, by Daude et al., finds that a majority of middle-class workers thus measured in Chile, Colombia, Mexico and Peru have informal-sector jobs, and fewer than half are covered by any sort of social-protection or social-insurance scheme. Chapter 5, meanwhile, uses the multidimensional poverty index developed by the Colombian National Planning Department – which measures non-income aspects of poverty, including poor education, health and housing conditions. Castellani et al. ask, how many middle-class Colombians (in terms of their income) are at the same time 'multidimensionally poor'? This ambiguous group has fallen as a share of the middle-class population but remains considerable: 58 per cent of middle-class Colombians (always using the '50–150' definition) were multidimensionally poor in 1997, while 27 per cent were in 2010.

Other mechanisms linking middle classes and economic growth have to do with inequality, better captured by relative-income measures. Easterly's (2001) econometric study, which showed that countries in which the middle class earned a larger share of national income also had higher economic growth rates, uses a relative-income measure. In this way, his paper is part of a larger research literature that shows that inequality is bad for growth.[19] In this analysis, a larger middle class is good for growth not because it embodies a mass of purchasing power to drive aggregate demand, but because it signifies lower inequality. The arguments linking high inequality and low growth come in at least three varieties. According to the first, where high inequality is matched with poorly functioning capital markets, investment will suffer because many potential entrepreneurs with good ideas but no collateral are unable to get loans to start up businesses. In the second variety, high-inequality countries are more prone to violence and instability that diverts resources from economic growth. Easterly's paper is, in fact, part of this school of thought. In the third, voters in highly unequal countries are more likely to vote for fiscal redistribution – that is, high taxes on the rich to fund government transfers to the non-rich – that discourages investment and thereby depresses growth. Doubt has lately been cast upon this third mechanism, in the light of a research paper that emerged from, of all places, the International Monetary Fund (Ostry et al., 2014). The IMF study found that more unequal countries do tend to redistribute more income, but that it does not depress growth.

The Middle Classes, Politics and Policy

Regardless of the measured effects of fiscal redistribution on growth, this brings us to the final research question raised regarding the middle class: What kind of policy platforms do they favor? In particular, do they favor higher taxes and higher government spending? The question is not merely of theoretical interest, as most Latin American countries, as we have seen, have growing middle classes and high (though declining) levels of inequality, and they also have comparatively low levels of tax revenues and government spending, relative to the size of their economies.[20] If middle classes support a more activist State – a hypothesis going back to Johnson in the late 1950s – why have they failed to elect governments that reflect this view?

By the logic of the median voter theory, Latin America arguably should have governments that profess the political platforms favored by the middle class, at least the middle class defined on the basis of relative income. These are the voters in the middle of the spectrum, after all. Chapter 9 in this volume, by Daude et al., considers different reasons why Latin American electoral processes might not satisfy assumptions of the median-voter theory. Chapter 9, furthermore, provides valuable insights into the policy preferences of middle-class Latin Americans and the degree to which they match the demands voiced by Brazilian demonstrators on the eve of the 2014 World Cup.

The football demonstrator view, in a nutshell, is that fiscal policy is a snapshot of the health of the social contract linking citizens and their government. Daude et al. analyze several opinion surveys and find support for this 'football demonstrator' thinking as well as reasons for guarded optimism: in short, there may be a constituency for higher taxes (and the tax reform that would be required), but it would require improvements in the quantity and quality of publicly provided goods and services, such as health care, education and public transport. That is, there is a potential virtuous circle that could be exploited by sufficiently adroit political leaders. Cárdenas et al., in Chapter 3, analyze apparently contradictory survey evidence from Peru, which shows high levels of distrust of government and support for fairly laissez-faire politics. It could be, however, that these results are consistent with those of Chapter 9, only that Peru suffers from a vicious circle of poor perceptions of public services and concomitant low willingness to pay more in taxes.

Chapters 9 and 6 in this volume, by Daude et al., highlight public policies that could better the lot of middle-class Latin Americans – particularly, but not exclusively, the vulnerable lower fringe of the group. Chief among these is a set of social-protection policies (notably including pensions) that, by design, attempt to reduce vulnerabilities of working people against the vagaries of poor health, injury, unemployment, natural disasters and old age. This policy package is conceptually distinct from the broader social-contract mechanism mentioned above: these social-protection measures derive from an objective consideration of the circumstances of a segment of the population marked by high rates of informal employment and incomes not far above the poverty line. Moreover, these policy proposals are based on a survey of innovative policy experiments in social protection, some more promising than others, in Latin America and beyond.

Not all observers regard the middle class as a progressive or potentially progressive political force. Critics of Johnson's (1957, 1958) view, tinged as it was with then-prevalent notions of modernization theory, note that Johnson's middle sectors aligned themselves with the economic elites and military dictatorships in Latin America. This mistrust of the middle class endures today, in the era of democratic consolidation. For example, Marilena Chauí, a Brazilian academic close to the leftist governing Partido dos Trabalhadores, was heard telling a group of sympathizers, 'The middle class is a political abomination, because it is fascist; an ethical abomination, because it is violent; a cognitive abomination, because it is ignorant' (Nunes, 2013). This was duly reported by a scandalized Brazilian mainstream press, habitually hostile to the party of Lula and Dilma Rousseff.

Stepping back from the critical issue of fiscal policy or even the political preferences of the middle class, a more basic question has to do with the size of the middle class as a voting bloc. The size of the middle class varies considerably according to the definition employed (table 1.1); nevertheless, all but the most leftward-shifted definitions (that is, the Banerjee/Duflo and Ravallion measures) generate groups that are sizable fractions – often a majority – of the population. Even the smaller middle-class measures, like Ravallion's vulnerable, could play a powerful role in a coalition of various constituencies: arguably, the vulnerable, thus defined, have provided critical electoral support to the variety of left-leaning governments in the region (including the Brazilian PT). And recent electoral processes, such as Chile in 2009 and Costa Rica in 2013, have witnessed presidential candidates explicitly targeting the middle class as a constituency. A careful analysis of how these and other candidates defined the middle class, whose votes they sought, would make a useful complement to the economic and political-economy analysis that predominates in this book.

A final question regarding the capacity of the middle class to be a progressive voting bloc has to do with whether the group – whichever of the definitions is used to describe it – is conscious of itself as a group or class. The survey data analyzed by Lora and Fajardo in Chapter 8 suggest that the answer is no. Survey respondents were asked to locate themselves on one of ten 'rungs' on the ladder of income in their country; Lora and Fajardo combine this information with respondents' actual income levels and the income distribution of the countries in question. They find that two-thirds of Latin Americans believe they are sitting on rungs three through five, where by construction there is only room for 30 per cent of the population. This finding could explain the political appeal of targeting the middle class for votes, as the self-identified middle class far outnumbers any objective measure of the number of people in the middle of the income distribution. We arrive full circle back to our discussion of historians' approaches to the middle class: Who considers themselves middle class (identity) and who is considered middle class (status)? In the consideration of voting behavior, these approaches may matter as much as objective measures of the middle class. Lora and Fajardo, however, demonstrate the utility of a quantitative approach to these subjective indicators of the middle class.

Many Measures, Many Questions

At this relatively early stage in the economic analysis of the Latin American emerging middle classes, one is left with the sensation of a dizzying multiplicity of definitions of the middle class. Researchers spend a lot of time and effort justifying their choice of definition. This book, which gathers eight excellent studies by some of the most prominent experts in the area, reflects that proliferation of measures and the methodological debates that accompany it. New students of the Latin American middle class might feel disappointed by the absence of a consensus regarding which measure is the right one. They need not. I have tried to establish in this introductory chapter that researchers have proposed many different measures precisely because they are trying to answer many different questions. And indeed, answering any single question with two different measures of the middle class frequently shines light on different aspects of that question (for example, the relationship between poverty reduction and the growth of the middle class). The explosion of research questions, in turn, is a sign of the importance and relevance of middle-class emergence in Latin America (and elsewhere in the developing world) to a broad range of actors: academics with an interest in social and economic development, to be sure, but also policymakers, politicians, policy advocates, social movements, businesses and more. By focusing attention on the research questions first, and their relation to varying interpretations of current Latin American reality, I hope to have placed the methodological debates in their proper context.

A middle class that is an amalgam of the various measures reviewed here emerges as a working concept to synthesize these various concerns. This superset of middle classes includes a sizeable share of vulnerable Latin American households more similar to the poor than to the elite; it also includes a growing share of households whose consumption behavior is beginning to resemble in absolute terms that of the lower rungs of the middle class of rich countries. This socioeconomic heterogeneity is mirrored by some of the dispersion in political views and attitudes that people in this amalgamated class express in opinion polls. Is the upper end of the middle class sufficiently robust to drive economic growth, even as the vulnerable fringe clearly cannot? Is the nascent social-contract thinking expressed by many members of the middle class sufficiently coalesced to influence voting behavior and electoral outcomes? Can this political platform be translated into public policies that promote the well-being of the vulnerable middle-class members (not to mention those still below the poverty line) even as they promote more inclusive economic growth? These are the second-round questions raised by the contributions to this volume.

Notes

1 Santos was addressing the International Economic Forum on Latin America and the Caribbean, organized by the OECD, the IADB and the French Ministry of Finance on 24 January 2011 (Santos, 2011). Conservative columnist

Andres Oppenheimer (2011) would be among the first to debunk the notion of a Latin American Decade, barely begun. On the advent of pragmatic, post-ideological policymaking in the region, an important component of Santos's analysis and a recurrent theme in the analyses in this volume, see Santiso (2005). Tommasi and Scartascini (2012) review the literature on the quality of policymaking in the region.

2 Growth rates in Latin America and OECD countries in the immediate aftermath of the financial crisis are analyzed comparatively in the Macroeconomic Overview chapter of OECD (2010). The average growth rate in the OECD area is reported there as -4.6 per cent in 2009, versus -3.6 per cent in Latin America. Both figures mask important heterogeneity, but the most important lesson is that the downturn in the rich countries was not amplified when its impact struck Latin America, as might have been the case in crises past.

3 The decoupling hypothesis is critically assessed in the Latin American context by Levy Yeyati and Cohan (2011, 2012).

4 I have followed the version of events reported in the 6 July 2013 issue of *Folha de São Paulo*, accompanying an editorial by Marcelo Coelho, who notes that for the first time, the protests revealed opposition to the left-wing Partido de Trabalho (PT) government that could not be credibly written off as 'right-wing coup plotters' (Coelho, 2013). Daude et al. (2013) link the Brazilian demonstrations to political debates surrounding fiscal policy; see Daude and Melguizo (2012) and Elizondo and Santiso (2012) for in-depth explorations of the political economy of taxation and fiscal policy, respectively, in Latin America.

5 See Johnson (1957, 1958). Johnson's critics would concede that his middle sectors played a progressive role in the struggle against the oligarchies in the early twentieth century, but they would also point out that these same sectors later aligned themselves with the elites in their countries and supported the military dictatorships that swept through the region; see Hoselitz (1962), Pike (1963) and Parker (2013).

6 Post-neoliberal politics in the developing world and beyond are addressed by Kyung-Sup et al. (2012) and Overbeek and van Apeldoorn (2012).

7 Benedetti's short story 'The Budget', a compact criticism of the idiocy of government office life, is reprinted in Parker and Walker (2013).

8 See, for example, the Special Report on 'The New Middle Classes in Emerging Markets' in the 12 February 2009 issue of *The Economist*, or 'Middle Class in Emerging Markets Means Growth: Cutting Research', in *Bloomberg Business Week* dated 18 October 2012. There are scores more articles that could be added.

9 Excellent sources for the long sweep of national histories of middle-class life include Adamovsky (2009) for Argentina, Barr-Melej (2001) for Chile, Owensby (1999) for Brazil and Parker (1998) for Peru, as well as many of the chapters in Parker and Walker (2013). Outside of Latin America, useful and very critical summaries of historical research on middle-class identity and status are provided in López and Weinstein, eds. (2012). The editors argue persuasively in their introduction against the use of rich-country models of the middle class for understanding the phenomenon elsewhere. See also the chapters in that collection by Simon Gunn (on England), Marina Moskowitz

(on the US) and Carol E. Harrison (on France) for comprehensive critical perspectives on changing understandings of the middle classes in canonical rich-country cases.

10 Deaton (1997) provides a now somewhat dated, but nevertheless still comprehensive, guide to the use of household surveys in developing countries. The purchasing power parity adjustment is summarized usefully in Ray (1998, ch. 2). The latest PPP adjustments, dating from 2011, are presented in ICP (2014).

11 Note that the OECD study uses the median income – the per capita income earned by the household precisely in the middle of the income distribution, with an equal number of households above and below it – rather than the mean income. In economies with highly unequal income distributions, like virtually all Latin American countries or the US, extraordinarily high incomes at the upper end raise the mean income level above the median; the latter is more representative than the former of potential command over resources for people genuinely in the middle. The '50–150' definition had been used in a study of the declining size of the middle class in the US by Davis and Huston (1992).

12 Piketty's (2013, pp. 536–7) celebrated study of capital and inequality uses a measure similar to Easterly's when he interprets the rise of a 'classe moyenne patrimonial' in rich countries in the second half of the twentieth century. Piketty defines this middle class based on income from capital – that is, income earned from ownership of real estate or financial assets, mostly, for the middle class. He traces the rise in the relative importance of this income for households in the fiftieth to ninetieth percentile of the total population of a country. Thus Piketty's middle class is always equal to 40 per cent of the population, and though it is 'in the middle', it is skewed to the right. Even in rich countries, ownership of capital among the poorer half of the population is extremely limited. Piketty's 50–40–10 breakout of the income distribution is also similar to the Brazilian 'Belindia' definition of the middle class proposed by Neri in Chapter 4 of this volume.

13 The recent decline in inequality in Latin America is thoroughly analyzed by López-Calva and Lustig, eds. (2010ab). The vast literature on the region's inequality is situated in its historical context by Coatsworth (2008) and Thorpe (2012).

14 Smith (1776, Book 5, ch. 2, part 2, article 4). On relative poverty lines in developing countries, refer to Garroway and de Laiglesia (2012).

15 The middle-class demand for apartments was reported by Escalante Rojas (2014) in the Lima daily *El Comercio*; the figure for gross national income per capita is taken from the World Bank's *World Development Indicators*.

16 See Neri (2011) and Chapter 4, this volume. Casanova and Kassam (2014) provide a more general treatment of the rise of Brazil as an emerging economy, while Cohn (2012) explores employment and the role of the state in Brazil's current development strategy.

17 I hope that this figure appears in a more conventional publication soon. In the meantime, the tweet's URL is https://twitter.com/BrankoMilan/status/480882446909452288/photo/1.

18 For a more general treatment of the rise of multinational firms based in emerging economies, see Nölke (2014).

19 Bénabou (1996) provides a major contribution to the first wave of quantitative research into this question, as well as an authoritative review of the research up to that point. Many of the empirical contributions to this literature took the form of cross-country econometric studies – like Easterly's (2001), in fact – that have fallen slightly out of favor, particularly since Forbes (2000) called into question the robustness of the results to the use of more appropriate statistical models. The hypotheses have nevertheless retained significant appeal and have been tested in more appropriate settings, including looking at single countries over time.

20 Daude and Melguizo (2012), OECD (2008) and OECD-ECLAC-CIAT (2014) summarize the comparative data on tax-to-GDP ratios in Latin American countries and elsewhere. Governments in OECD countries typically collect taxes on the order of 35 to 40 per cent of GDP, while Latin American countries (with some notable exceptions, like Argentina and Brazil) collect taxes that amount to less than 20 per cent of GDP. These ratios are low relative to other developing countries as well. Lower government revenues are reflected in lower government spending and the consequent inability to address important development deficits.

References

Adamovsky, E. (2009) *Historia de la clase media argentina: Apogeo y decadencia de una ilusión, 1919–2003* (Buenos Aires: Planeta).

Banerjee, A. and E. Duflo (2008) 'What Is Middle-Class About the Middle Classes Around the World?' *Journal of Economic Perspectives*, vol. 2., no. 2 (Spring), 3–28.

Barr-Melej, P. (2001) *Reforming Chile: Cultural Politics, Nationalism and the Rise of the Middle Class* (Chapel Hill, NC, and London: University of North Carolina Press).

Benabou, R. (1996) 'Inequality and Growth', *NBER Macroeconomics Annual*, vol. 11, 11–92.

Casanova, L. and J. Kassum (2014) *The Political Economy of an Emerging Global Power: In Search of the Brazil Dream*, International Political Economy Series (Basingstoke and New York: Palgrave Macmillan).

CEPAL [Comisión Económica para América Latina y el Caribe] (2013) *Panorama social de América Latina* (Santiago: United Nations Economic Commission for Latin America and the Caribbean).

Coatsworth, J. H. (2008) 'Inequality, Institutions and Economic Growth in Latin America', *Journal of Latin American Studies*, vol. 40, 545–569.

Coelho, M. (2013) 'Manifestações expõem o fato de que o poder não muda', *Folha de São Paulo*, 6 July, http://www1.folha.uol.com.br/cotidiano/2013/07/1307302-opiniao-manifestacoes-expoem-o-fato-de-que-o-poder-nao-muda.shtml, date accessed 1 July 2014.

Cohn, S. (2012) *Employment and Development under Globalization: State and Economy in Brazil*, International Political Economy Series (Basingstoke and New York: Palgrave Macmillan).

Dadush, U. and S. Ali (2012) 'In Search of the Global Middle Class: A New Index', *The Carnegie Papers: International Economics* (Washington, DC: Carnegie Endowment for International Peace).

Daude, C., J. Dayton-Johnson and A. Melguizo (2013) 'Legitimidad fiscal y protestas en la calle: sobre Brasil y América Latina', *VOX.Lacea*, http://www.vox.lacea.org/?q=cambios_politica_fiscal_brasil, date accessed 1 July 2014.

Daude, C. and A. Melguizo (2012) 'Taxation and Democracy in Latin America', in J. Santiso and J. Dayton-Johnson, eds., *The Oxford Handbook of Latin American Political Economy* (Oxford: Oxford University Press), 532–556.

Davis, J. and J. H. Huston (1992) 'The Shrinking Middle-Income Class: A Multivariate Analysis', *Eastern Economic Journal*, vol. 18, no. 3, 277–285.

Dayton-Johnson, J., J. Londoño and S. Nieto Parra (2011) 'The Process of Reform in Latin America: A Review Essay', OECD Development Centre Working Paper No. 304 (Paris: OECD Publishing).

Deaton, A. (1997) *The Analysis of Household Surveys: A Microeconometric Approach to Development Policy* (Baltimore, MD: Johns Hopkins University Press).

Easterly, W. (2001) 'The Middle Class Consensus and Economic Development', *Journal of Economic Growth*, vol. 6, 317–335.

Elizondo, C. and J. Santiso (2012) 'Killing Me Softly: Local Termites and Fiscal Violence in Brazil and Mexico', in J. Santiso and J. Dayton-Johnson, eds., *The Oxford Handbook of Latin American Political Economy* (Oxford: Oxford University Press), 457–502.

Escalante Rojas, J. (2014) 'La demanda de la clase media sostendrá el negocio inmobilario durante el 2014', *El Comercio*, (24 January), A2.

Ferreira, F. H. G., J. Messina, J. Rigolini, L. F. López-Calva, M. A. Lugo and R. Vakis (2013) *Economic Mobility and the Rise of the Latin American Middle Class* (Washington, DC: The World Bank).

Forbes, K. (2000) 'A Reassessment of the Relationship Between Inequality and Growth', *American Economic Review*, vol. 90, no. 4, 869–887.

Franco, R., M. Hopenhayn and A. León, eds. (2010) *Las clases medias en América Latina* (Mexico City: Siglo XXI Editores and CEPAL).

Franco, R., M. Hopenhayn and A. León (2011) 'The growing and changing middle class in Latin America: An update', *CEPAL Review*, no. 103, 7–25.

Garroway, C. and J. R. de Laiglesia (2012) 'On the Relevance of Relative Poverty Lines for Developing Countries', OECD Development Centre Working Paper 314 (Paris: OECD Publishing).

Hoselitz, B. F. (1962) 'El desarrollo económico en América Latina' *Desarrollo Económico*, no. 2 (October), 49–65.

ICP [International Comparison Program] (2014) *Purchasing Power Parities and Real Expenditures of World Economies: Summary of Results and Findings of the 2011 International Comparison Program* (Washington, DC: The World Bank).

Johnson, J. J. (1957) 'Middle groups in national politics in Latin America', *Hispanic American Historical Review*, vol. 37, no. 3, 313–29. Excerpted in Parker and Walker (2013), 25–34.

Johnson, J. J. (1958) *Political Change in Latin America: The Emergence of the Middle Sectors* (Stanford, CA: Stanford University Press).

Kyung-Sup, C., B. Fine and L. Weiss, eds. (2012) *Developmental Politics in Transition: The Neoliberal Era and Beyond*, International Political Economy Series (Basingstoke and New York: Palgrave Macmillan).

Lakner, C. and B. Milanovic (2013) 'Global Income Distribution from the Fall of the Berlin Wall to the Great Recession', Policy Research Working Paper 6719 (Washington, DC: The World Bank).

León, A., E. Espíndola and C. Sémbler (2010) 'Clases medias en América Latina: Una visión de sus cambios en las dos últimas décadas', in Franco et al., eds. (2010), 43–116.

Levy Yeyati, E. and L. Cohan (2011) *Latin America Economic Perspectives: Innocent Bystanders in a Brave New World* (Washington, DC: The Brookings Institution).

Levy Yeyati, E. and L. Cohan (2012) 'What have I done to deserve this? Global winds and Latin American growth', *VoxEU*, http://www.voxeu.org/article/uncoupling-decoupling-latin-america-s-experience, date accessed 1 July 2014.

Lida, D. (2008) *First Stop in the New World: Mexico City, Capital of the 21st Century* (New York: Riverhead/Penguin).

López, A. R. and B. Weinstein, eds. (2012) *The Making of the Middle Class: Toward a Transnational History* (Durham, NC, and London: Duke University Press).

López-Calva, L. F. and N. Lustig (2010a) *Declining Inequality in Latin America: A Decade of Progress?* (Washington, DC: Brookings Institution Press and United Nations Development Programme).

López-Calva, L. F. and N. Lustig (2010b) 'Declining Latin American Inequality: Market Forces or State Action?', *VoxEU*, http://www.voxeu.org/article/declining-latin-american-inequality-market-forces-or-state-action, date accessed 1 July 2014.

Milanovic, B. and S. Yitzhaki (2002) 'Decomposing World Income Distribution: Does the World Have a Middle Class?', *Review of Income and Wealth*, vol. 48, no. 2, 155–178.

Neri, M. C. (2011) *A nova classe média: O lado brilhante da base da pirâmide* (São Paulo: Editora Saraiva).

Nölke, A., ed. (2014) *Multinational Corporations from Emerging Markets: State Capitalism 3.0*, International Political Economy Series (Basingstoke and New York: Palgrave Macmillan).

Nunes, A. (2013) 'O video revela por que Marilena Chauí, a musa do PT, odeia a classe média', *Veja*, (17 May), http://veja.abril.com.br/blog/augusto-nunes/direto-ao-ponto/o-video-revela-por-que-marilena-chaui-a-musa-do-pt-odeia-a-classe-media/, date accessed 1 July 2014.

OECD [Organisation for Economic Co-operation and Development] (2008) *Latin American Economic Outlook 2009* (Paris: OECD Publishing).

OECD [Organisation for Economic Co-operation and Development] (2009) *Latin American Economic Outlook 2010* (Paris: OECD Publishing).

OECD [Organisation for Economic Co-operation and Development] (2010) *Latin American Economic Outlook 2011: How Middle-Class Is Latin America?* (Paris: OECD Publishing).

OECD-ECLAC-CIAT (2014) *Revenue Statistics in Latin America* (Paris: OECD Publishing).

Oppenheimer, A. (2011) 'A "Latin American Decade" or Wishful Thinking?' *Miami Herald*, (5 February).

Ostry, J. D., A. Berg and C. G. Tsangarides (2014) 'Redistribution, Inequality, and Growth', IMF Staff Discussion Note SDN/14/02 (Washington, DC: International Monetary Fund).

Overbeek, H. and B. van Apeldoorn, eds. (2012) *Neoliberalism in Crisis*, International Political Economy Series (Basingstoke and New York: Palgrave Macmillan).

Owensby, B. P. (1999) *Intimate Ironies: Modernity and the Making of Middle-Class Lives in Brazil* (Stanford, CA: Stanford University Press).

Parker, D. S. (1998) *The Idea of the Middle Class: White-Collar Workers and Peruvian Society, 1900–1950* (University Park, PA: Pennsylvania State University Press).
Parker, D. S. (2013) 'Introduction: The Making and Endless Remaking of the Middle Class' in Parker and Walker, eds. (2013), 1–22.
Parker, D. S. and L. E. Walker, eds. (2013) *Latin America's Middle Class: Unsettled Debates and New Histories* (Lanham, MD: Lexington Books).
Pike, F. B. (1963) 'Aspects of Class Relations in Chile, 1850–1960', *Hispanic American Historical Review*, vol. 43, no. 4, 445–54. Excerpted in Parker and Walker (2013), 35–44.
Piketty, T. (2013) *Le Capital au XXIe siècle* (Paris: Éditions du Seuil). Also published in 2014 as *Capital in the Twenty-First Century* (Cambridge, MA: Harvard University Press).
Prebisch, R. (1981) *Capitalismo periférico: Crisis y transformación* (Mexico: Fondo de Cultura Económica).
Ravallion, M. (2009) 'The Developing World's Bulging (but Vulnerable) Middle Class', *World Development*, vol. 38, no. 4, 445–54.
Ray, D. (1998) *Development Economics* (Princeton, NJ: Princeton University Press).
Santiso, J. (2005) *Amérique latine. Révolutionnaire, libérale et pragmatique* (Paris: Éditions Autrement). Also published in 2006 as *Latin America's Political Economy of the Possible: Beyond Good Revolutionaries and Free-Marketeers* (Cambridge, MA: MIT Press).
Santos, J. M. (2011) 'Intervención del Presidente Santos en el Foro Económico Internacional América Latina y el Caribe', Presidencia de la República de Colombia, http://wsp.presidencia.gov.co/Prensa/2011/Enero/Paginas/20110124_03.aspx, date accessed 23 June 2014.
Smith, A. (1776) *An Inquiry into the Nature and Causes of the Wealth of Nations*, E. Cannan, ed. (New York: Modern Library).
Thorp, R. (2012) 'A Historical Perspective on the Political Economy of Inequality in Latin America', in J. Santiso and J. Dayton-Johnson, eds., *The Oxford Handbook of Latin American Political Economy* (Oxford: Oxford University Press), 149–167.
Tommasi, M. and C. Scartaschini (2012) 'How (Not) to Produce Effective Policies? Institutions and Policymaking in Latin America', in J. Santiso and J. Dayton-Johnson, eds., *The Oxford Handbook of Latin American Political Economy* (Oxford: Oxford University Press), 263–284.

2
Inequality, Mobility and Middle Classes in Latin America

João Pedro Azevedo, Luis F. López-Calva, Nora Lustig and Eduardo Ortiz-Juárez

Introduction

What is the link between middle class and income inequality? This chapter will assess the relationship between changes in income distribution and the growth of the middle class. Interest in the latter has peaked worldwide, as the rise of the global middle class is increasingly recognized as a key megatrend (*Global Trends 2030*, 2013). Zooming in on the concrete case of Latin America and the Caribbean, we know that, as economic activity has grown and poverty levels have fallen alongside economic growth, the middle class is on the rise. We also know that income inequality has fallen in the region. Within this context, following a discussion on the middle class and inequality and presenting some recent trends, this chapter asks how much of the expansion of the middle class in Latin America is explained by economic growth, and how much by the decline in income inequality.[1]

The chapter is organized as follows. First, we outline trends in income inequality and its determinants, showing the reduction of inequality in Latin America. Following, we present the definitions on which further measurements are based – what exactly do we mean by middle class? This section draws from the definition proposed by López-Calva and Ortiz-Juárez (2014), further applied empirically by Ferreira et al. (2013) to Latin American countries. The concept is based on an absolute threshold that defines the middle class by exploiting the link between income and vulnerability to poverty. It sets economic security as the condition that defines the middle class – that is, those households who face a low probability of falling into poverty. This section ends with a review of regional trends, applying this definition to look at how the middle class has been expanding in Latin American countries. Finally, using an extension of the decomposition method proposed by Datt and Ravallion (1992) to allow for multiple thresholds and address the issue of path-dependency (Azevedo et al., 2012a), we look to disentangle the effect of both the decline in inequality and of income growth on the growth of the middle class. We find that, in addition to economic growth, the reduction in income inequality experienced in the region indeed contributes to explain part of the expansion of the middle class in Latin America. The final section offers some concluding remarks.

Income Inequality: Trends and Determinants

Income inequality has declined in Latin America over the last decade, as evidenced in the substantial amount of research published in recent years.[2] The Gini coefficient, a measure of inequality ranging from zero (perfect equality) to one (perfect inequality), fell from a weighted average of 0.550 in the early 2000s to 0.496 circa 2011, motivated by the decline that took place in sixteen of seventeen countries (fig. 2.1). The rates of decline range from over an annual average of −2 per cent in Nicaragua and Bolivia to −0.28 per cent in Venezuela. The changes were statistically significant in all countries where inequality receded, as well as in Honduras – where inequality rose at an annual rate of 0.61 per cent. The only exception to the statistical test is Costa Rica, where the available data indicates that inequality remained practically unchanged.

The question that follows naturally is, what factors lay behind the decline of income inequality in Latin America? A recent survey by Lustig et al. (2013) points to two main explanations: first, the decline in non-labor income inequality, particularly motivated by the effect of direct transfers and to a lesser extent to the effect of pensions; and second, the reduction of labor income inequality. Two different decomposition methods confirm these accounts (fig. 2.2). On one hand, Azevedo et al. (2013a) apply a non-parametric decomposition on the change of inequality of different income sources and demographic indicators, observing that the most important determinant of the decline in inequality is a relatively strong growth in earnings for workers at the bottom of the income distribution (on average, 54 per cent of the reduction in the Gini coefficient can be attributed to changes in labor income). In terms of non-labor income, their results suggest that changes in government transfers contributed to 21 per cent of the observed regional decline in

34 *Latin America's Emerging Middle Classes*

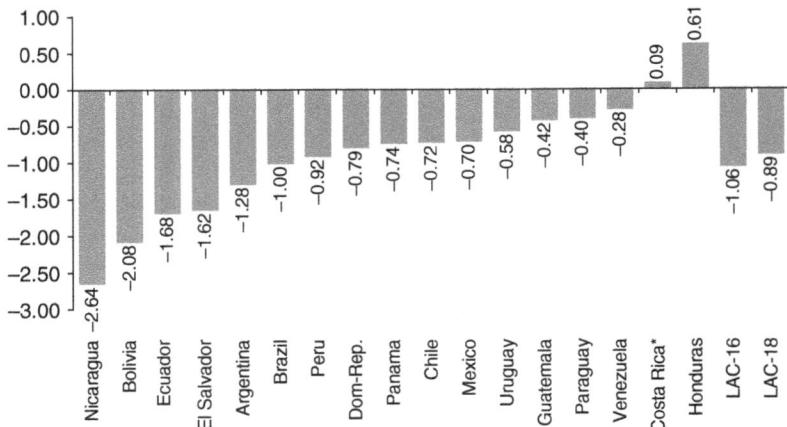

Figure 2.1 Annual Percentage Change in the Gini Coefficient, by Country; c. 2001–11.

Source: Authors' calculations, based on data from SEDLAC (CEDLAS and the World Bank), August 2013./ᵃ The average change in the Gini coefficient for each country is calculated as the percentage change between the end year and the initial year, divided by the number of years. The average for LAC-16 is the simple average of the changes in sixteen countries in which inequality fell; the average for LAC-18 is the average of the changes in all eighteen countries. The following time periods were used to estimate the percentage changes: Argentina (2000–13), Bolivia (2001–12), Brazil (2001–12), Chile (2000–11), Costa Rica (2001–09), Dominican Republic (2000–11), Ecuador (2003–12), El Salvador (2004–12), Guatemala (2000–11), Honduras (2001–11), Mexico (2000–12), Nicaragua (2001–09), Panama (2001–12), Paraguay (2001–11), Peru (2000–12), Uruguay (2000–12) and Venezuela (2000–06). The change in Colombia should be interpreted with caution due to problems of data comparability across years. Data for the early 2000s and the late 2000s in El Salvador and Venezuela, respectively, are currently under revision by CEDLAS. Using the bootstrap method, with a 95 per cent significance level, the changes were not found to be statistically significant in Costa Rica, which is represented by a gray-filled bar.

inequality, while changes in pensions contributed 9 per cent. On the other hand, the results from a parametric decomposition provided by CEDLAS on the level of inequality, following the Lerman and Yitzaki (1985) methodology, confirms the previous evidence: during the 2000s, changes in labor income accounted for 62 per cent, on average, while transfers and pensions accounted, respectively, for 17 and 2 per cent.

More robust and progressive government transfers across Latin American countries (such as Bolsa Família in Brazil and Progresa/Oportunidades in Mexico) explain the reduction in *non-labor* income inequality. What is behind the reduction in the *labor* component of overall income inequality? The aforementioned survey by Lustig et al. suggests that returns to education drove the decline in labor income inequality. That is, during

Reasons for the decline in inequality

- not considering economic crises as detonators or important factors. (Baran and Sweezy?)

Labor and non-labor
↓ ↓
education transfers
↓ (CCT)
supply pensions
demand
quality | what about
_____| business and
self-employment, financial
income and rental value?

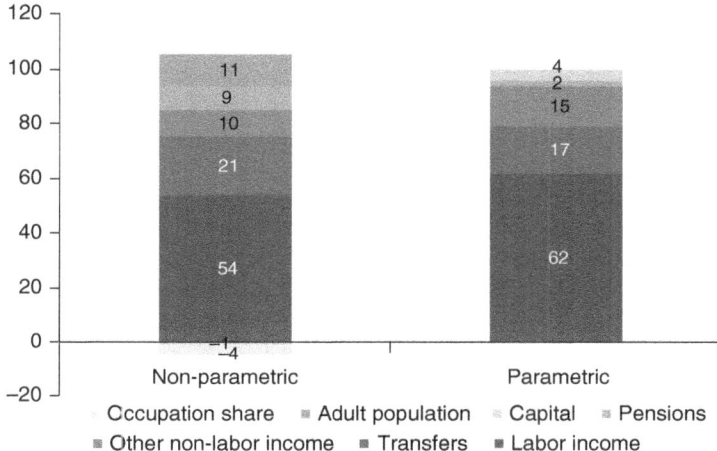

Figure 2.2 Contribution of Proximate Determinants to the Decline in Inequality (%); Latin America, c. 2000–10./a

Source: Non-parametric decomposition results from Azevedo et al. (2013a) using ADECOMP (Azevedo et al., 2012b) and parametric results provided by CEDLAS, based on data from SEDLAC (CEDLAS and the World Bank)./a The negative (positive) sign indicates an unequalizing (equalizing) effect of each determinant. The results shown refer to averages for fourteen countries in the case of the non-parametric decomposition (Argentina, Brazil, Chile, Colombia, Costa Rica, Dominican Republic, Ecuador, El Salvador, Honduras, Mexico, Panama, Paraguay, Peru and Uruguay) and twelve countries in the case of the parametric decomposition (Argentina, Bolivia, Brazil, Dominican Republic, Ecuador, El Salvador, Mexico, Nicaragua, Peru, Paraguay, Uruguay and Venezuela). The latter decomposition does not estimate the contribution of the demographic determinants as it focused on labor and non-labor income sources only.

the 2000s, the wage premium earned by those with primary, secondary and tertiary education (vis-à-vis those with no formal education or an incomplete basic education) decreased in the majority of the sixteen countries where overall inequality declined.

Why did returns to education decline? While no clear consensus exists, there are three potential explanations: a reduction in the relative demand for skilled workers; an increase in the relative supply of skilled workers; and a deterioration in the quality of education.[3] In the first case, the demand-side explanation, the evidence suggests that Latin America's commodity boom in the 2000s induced a reallocation of labor from non-commodity tradable sectors, like high-tech manufacturing, to sectors less intensive in skilled labor, such as services. This trend could reduce returns to education and thus wage inequality.[4] In terms of the supply side, the evidence reflects that returns to education declined due to an increase in the relative supply of workers with complete secondary and tertiary education, which, in turn, resulted from the substantial increases in school enrollment at all levels over the last two decades. The expansion of education, which eased supply-side constraints, was associated with higher public spending on basic education and an increase of coverage in rural areas. At the same time, the conditional cash transfers (CCTs) schemes implemented in the late 1990s reduced demand-side constraints by compensating poor households for the opportunity costs of keeping their children in school.[5] The third explanation links declining returns to a degradation of education levels, mainly in tertiary education. This could have taken place due to a combination of an expansion of low-quality tertiary education and/or because those entering tertiary education programs increasingly include individuals with lower abilities.[6]

Whether the decline in income inequality was predominantly the result of supply-side effects, a decline in the demand for workers with higher skills or even a deterioration in educational quality – among

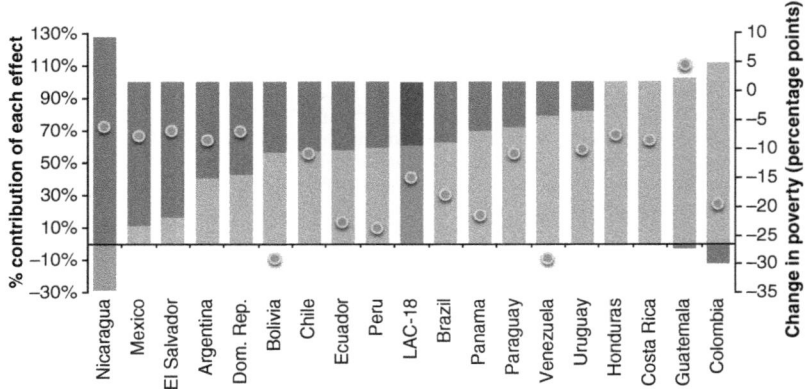

■ Growth effect   ■ Redistribution effect   ● Change in poverty ($4 a day) in percentage points

Figure 2.3 Contribution of the Decline in Inequality to Changes in Poverty (%); c. 2001–10.[/a]

Source: Estimates provided by CEDLAS, based on data from SEDLAC (CEDLAS and the World Bank)./a The contribution of the decline in inequality toward reducing poverty was calculated using the Maasoumi-Mahmoudi decomposition method (Maasoumi and Mahmoudi, 2013). The following time periods were used: Argentina (1998–11), Bolivia (2000–11), Brazil (2003–11), Chile (2000–09), Colombia (2003–10), Costa Rica (2002–09), Dominican Republic (2003–11), Ecuador (2003–11), El Salvador (1998–2010), Guatemala (2000–11), Honduras (2003–11), Mexico (2000–10), Nicaragua (2001–09), Panama (2001–11), Paraguay (2004–10), Peru (1997–2010), Uruguay (2004–11) and Venezuela (2004–11). The average for LAC-18 refers to the simple average of the effect in all eighteen countries.

other potential causes – has not been unequivocally established. The fact remains that inequality unambiguously – and significantly – declined over the last decade. An indication of its quantitative significance is the contribution of declining inequality upon poverty reduction. Between 2000 and 2011 (circa), the incidence of poverty, defined as the proportion of households with per capita earnings of less than $4 (in purchasing power parity, PPP, dollars) per day, fell from 41.7 to 26.3 per cent, the equivalent of about 55.5 million fewer people in poverty. Of course, poverty could decline because of economic growth, even in the absence of changes in the income distribution. The Maasoumi-Mahmoudi (2013) decomposition of the determinants of poverty reduction reveals that, on a regional average, 39 per cent of the reduction in poverty was due to the decline in inequality. The magnitude was significant in Nicaragua, Mexico, El Salvador, Argentina and the Dominican Republic, where the decline in inequality accounted for more than 50 per cent of the reduction in poverty (fig. 2.3).[7]

What does the decline of inequality mean for middle classes in Latin America?

The fact that inequality declined and that it contributed significantly to the reduction of poverty, as illustrated above, suggests two possibilities. First, that the reduction of poverty levels could have reshaped the composition of the population, as individuals transited from poverty to a relatively better income level. Secondly, the expansion of the group above the poverty threshold – namely the middle stratum or the middle class (depending on how we define and measure it) – may be correlated with the reduction in income inequality; in other words, the observed decline in inequality could have had a positive impact on mobility.

The analysis of these possibilities requires as a first step the clear establishment of the criteria by which the middle class is to be measured in order to examine its expansion. What exactly do we mean by 'middle class'? Following this discussion, we apply decomposition methods to quantify the relative contributions of growth and redistribution to changes in the size of the middle class.

The middle class has traditionally been defined in terms of income or consumption patterns in the economic realm, or as occupational status in the sociological practice (refer to the overview provided in Chapter 1 of this volume). Regardless of the approach used, the definition of thresholds for the measurement of the middle class is dependent on a particular period and place and on specific research and policy purposes.

For instance, in the economic tradition, measurement has mainly focused on *relative* definitions, most of which quantify the middle class as those individuals with an income or consumption around the median of the distribution,[8] or as those individuals whose income lies between fixed positions (i.e., at given percentiles) in the distribution.[9] These relative measures, however, impose important constraints upon cross-country comparisons of the evolution and composition of the middle class. The most evident limitation, naturally, is that this group may differ from place to place as income distributions vary between countries. That is, using relative measures, the income that qualifies a given Honduran as middle class, for example, might consign a Uruguayan with the same income to the ranks of the poor.

Under these circumstances, an *absolute* approach is more advantageous, as it characterizes the middle class as those households with an income or consumption in a specific and comparable range. While most absolute measures enable comparison across countries, the drawback is that they may end up as descriptive statistics of income groups, sometimes even giving counterintuitive results. For instance, Ravallion (2010) and Banerjee and Duflo (2008) define the middle class as those individuals living on $2–13 and $2–10 per person per day, respectively. Applying these thresholds to cross-sectional data for Mexico, we observe that the

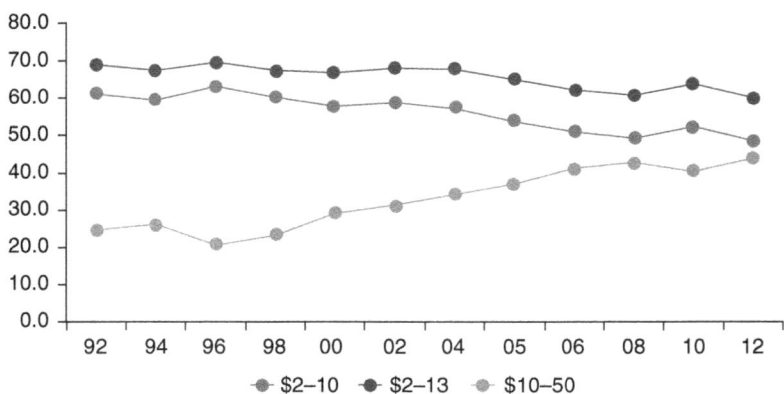

Figure 2.4 Percentage of Households Living on $2–10, $2–13 and $10–50 per Person per Day in Mexico; 1992–2012./a

Source: Author's calculations, based on data from the Mexican National Household Income and Expenditure Survey (ENIGH) between 1992–2012./a The monetary intervals of $2–10, $2–13 and $10–50 correspond, respectively, to the middle-class definitions by Banerjee and Duflo (2008), Ravallion (2010) and López-Calva and Ortiz-Juárez (2014).

middle class would have *decreased* over 1992–2012 – a counterintuitive result given the (moderate) rate of economic growth over the period – and conversely it would have *increased* in times of economic downturns, moving in parallel with poverty levels (fig. 2.4). Indeed, by these thresholds, the size of the middle class would have increased in Mexico during the crisis of 1995 when the incidence of poverty rose significantly. The same pattern occurred during the recent crisis of 2008–09: while the Mexican economy fell by almost −7 per cent and the incidence of poverty rose, by those definitions the size of the middle class would have increased as well.

Why do the thresholds proposed by Ravallion (2010) and Banerjee and Duflo (2008) lead to counterintuitive results? The patterns shown are based on the lower threshold to measure the middle class proposed under both definitions: $2 a day, which is half the international threshold of $4 a day for poverty measurement in Latin America. Thus, people who were previously above the established threshold but who fell back into being *near-poor* with the crisis, would be seen as moving into the middle class (increasing the size of this group).[10] In contrast, under the middle-class characterization proposed by López-Calva and Ortiz-Juárez (2014) – defined as those living on $10–50 a day – the middle class in the region is growing overall (and dipping in times of economic downturns, as expected, see fig. 2.4). The difference between approaches highlights the need of a robust conceptual framework to support the definition of thresholds.

How to Measure the Middle Class

Based on a vulnerability to poverty approach, López-Calva and Ortiz-Juárez (2014) propose a middle-class measure that seeks to provide conceptual clarity on what it means to be in the middle, capturing the economic component of class. The measure is also consistent with the notion of *directional mobility*, and, given its applicability to different contexts, it can provide useful insights from a public policy perspective.

In line with Amartya Sen's (1983) capabilities approach, the authors develop a framework in which the middle class is absolute in terms of the *functionings* that define it but relative in terms of the *means* through which those functionings can be achieved. Arguing that vulnerability to poverty is the functioning that defines the middle class, the lower threshold is established at an absolute level using a regression-based approach on panel data to determine the amount of income associated with the probability of falling into poverty (income is used as the relative measure of vulnerability to poverty).

The three-stage methodology requires two or more household data sets from the same population at different points in time in order to make inferences about people's upward or downward mobility in the income distribution. Accordingly, our methodology is applied to longitudinal data for Chile (2001–06), Mexico (2002–05) and Peru (2002-06). In the first stage, transition matrices are computed using the poverty line of $4 a day to classify households into four categories: 1) non-poor, 2) always poor, 3) falling into poverty and 4) newly poor. In the second stage, a logistic regression model is estimated to analyze the factors correlated with the probability of falling into poverty. In this model, the dependent variable takes a value of '1' if households remain in poverty in the second period and '0' otherwise. The set of explanatory variables includes demographic, occupational, educational and risk-related indicators. In the third stage, the explanatory variables of the logistic model are used to estimate a linear regression model, where the dependent variable is the household per capita income in the first period. The authors then obtain the average of the independent variables for an array of estimated probabilities of falling into poverty and, in combination with the coefficients estimated from the linear regression, use these averages to predict the income associated to each probability.

López-Calva and Ortiz-Juárez (2014) propose that the middle class should, ideally, consist of those households facing a low risk of falling into poverty over time. In this sense, they put forward the use of a

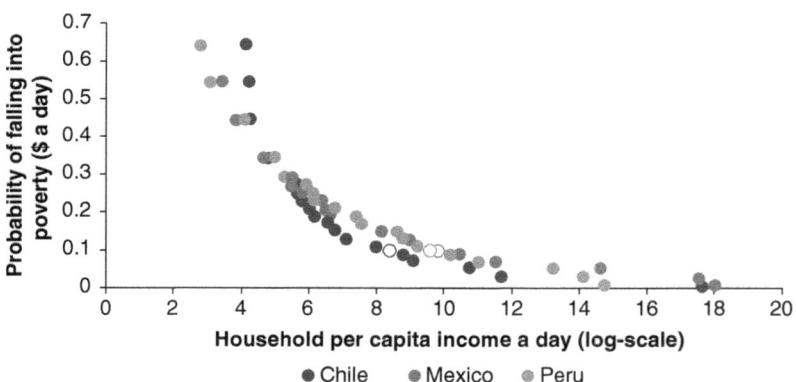

Figure 2.5 Income and the Probability of Being Poor; Chile, Mexico and Peru.[/a]

Source: López-Calva and Ortiz-Juárez (2014).[/a] Household per capita income a day in purchasing power parity dollars. White dots represent the per capita income value associated to a 10 per cent probability of falling into poverty in each country.

10 per cent probability of falling into poverty as a dividing line between economic security and vulnerability and define the predicted income associated to that probability as the lower threshold for the middle class. At higher levels of predicted (log) income, the probability of falling into poverty declines sharply (fig. 2.5).

What about the upper threshold? The authors establish it at $50 a day, an income figure that lies between the 97th and 98th percentile of the income distribution in all three countries, which suggests that crossing this threshold would have a very low impact on the size of the middle class. This is consistent with results obtained by Ferreira et al. (2013), who find that, for the Latin American-wide income distribution, the threshold of $50 lies in the 98th percentile. The sensitivity analysis for both thresholds shows that moving the top threshold up or down the income distribution indeed has a less relevant impact on the percentage of households in the middle class and even less on its change (versus moving the lower one) (López-Calva and Ortiz-Juárez, 2014).

Given that the lower threshold of a 10 per cent probability of falling into poverty coincides closely with income of $10 a day in all three countries (fig. 2.5), the middle class is defined as those *households living with a per capita income of $10–50 a day*. It is worth highlighting that the lower threshold is derived from a concept of economic security, which may be made operational for specific contexts; in other words, a 10 per cent probability of falling into poverty can be used anywhere as a general standard that divides economic security and vulnerability (even though the monetary value associated to it could be different from $10 a day, depending on the context).

An additional feature of this methodology is the emergence of an additional group of individuals, which is not part of the 'poor' population, as their income lies above the poverty line of $4, while at the same time, their probability of falling into poverty is higher than 10 per cent – or in other words, they have an income below the threshold of $10 a day. López-Calva and Ortiz-Juárez refer to this group as the *vulnerable*; their existence highlights the need for comprehensive social security schemes that prevent the near-poor population from falling back into poverty in the face of adverse shocks.

Regional Trends

Ferreira et al. (2013) apply the absolute definition proposed by López-Calva and Ortiz-Juárez (2014) to eighteen cross-sectional surveys in Latin America, confirming that the middle class is indeed on the rise in the region. The middle class as a percentage of the population has increased significantly, from 21.9 per cent in 2000 on a regional weighted average, to 34.3 per cent in 2012 (fig. 2.6). This expansive pattern appears almost as a reflection of the reduction in regional poverty, which, as mentioned, declined from 41.7 to 25.3 per cent over the same period. However, not all of the population leaving poverty reached middle-class status. A proportion of people transited from poverty to vulnerability, with a consequent increase in the proportion of vulnerable population: from 34.4 per cent in the early 2000s to 37.8 per cent in the late 2000s. Nonetheless, it is clear that the composition of Latin American society has changed. Indeed, since 2009, the size of the middle class exceeds the share of population in poverty.

As Ferreira et al. (2013) illustrate, the middle class has been on the rise since the early 1900s. Yet, it is mainly over the last decade that its growth has been both sustained and widespread, ranging from nineteen percentage points of the population in Peru to almost one percentage point in Uruguay, with only the Dominican Republic, Guatemala and El Salvador experiencing a slight decrease in the proportion of the middle class (fig. 2.7).

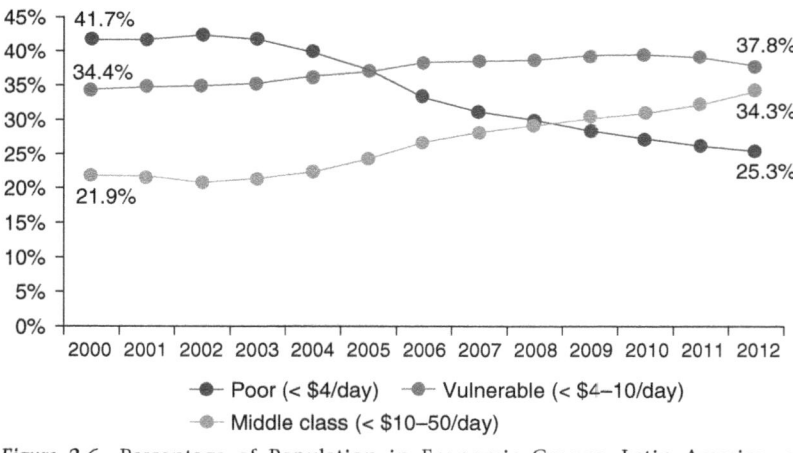

Figure 2.6 Percentage of Population in Economic Groups; Latin America, c. 2000–12.[a]

Source: Authors' calculations with country estimates provided by CEDLAS, based on data from SEDLAC (CEDLAS and the World Bank).[a] Weighted average of the percentage of population in each social group in the following countries: Argentina, Bolivia, Brazil, Chile, Colombia, Costa Rica, Dominican Republic, Ecuador, El Salvador, Guatemala, Honduras, Mexico, Nicaragua, Panama, Paraguay, Peru, Uruguay and Venezuela.

Try these graphs

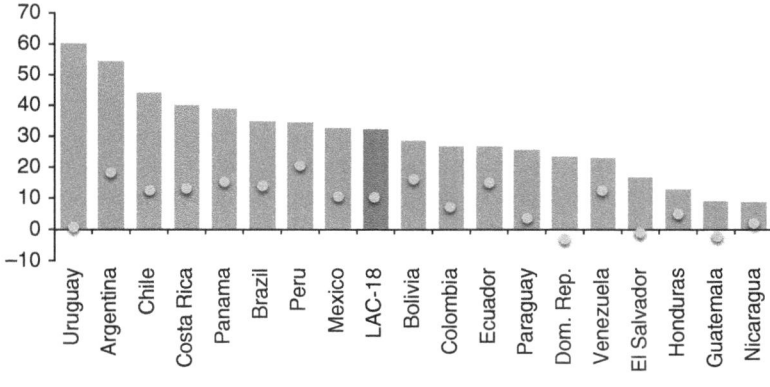

- % of middle class population
- Change in the size of the middle class, in percentage points

Figure 2.7 Percentage of Middle-Class Population 2012, and Its Change over the 2000s in Percentage Points.
Source: Authors' calculations with country estimates provided by CEDLAS, based on data from SEDLAC (CEDLAS and the World Bank).

The expansive trends of the middle class in the region are relevant in light of the reasons outlined by a broad literature that argues that the size and composition of the middle class is critical for strengthening and stabilizing the democratic system and its institutions, for better economic performance and for social cohesion, among others.[11] Nevertheless, significant heterogeneity persists in the region between countries in terms of the size of their middle classes. For instance, the difference between Southern Cone countries like Uruguay, Argentina or Chile, and Central American countries like El Salvador, Honduras, Guatemala and Nicaragua, exceeds forty percentage points (fig. 2.7).

Growth, Inequality and Directional Mobility

Let us take stock. The previous section demonstrated that the decline in income inequality influenced the reduction in poverty incidence in Latin America over the last decade by a regional average of 39 per cent. Is it possible to say the same about its influence on the expansion of the middle class? What is the relationship, if any, between changes in the distribution of income and the expansion of the middle class?

Correlations between changes in the size of the middle class and those in inequality and per capita income over the last decade give the expected results (fig. 2.8). The negative correlation in the first comparison (reaching −13.6 per cent) indicates that the size of the middle class increased by a greater magnitude in those countries where inequality declined at a higher annual rate. Likewise, the positive correlation (30.9 per cent) of the second comparison suggests that the fastest-growing economies experienced a significant growth in the size of their middle class. In both cases, the correlation was statistically significant at the 95 per cent significance level.

With no change in the shape of the income distribution, and absolute lower and upper income thresholds ($10 and $50 per person per day, in

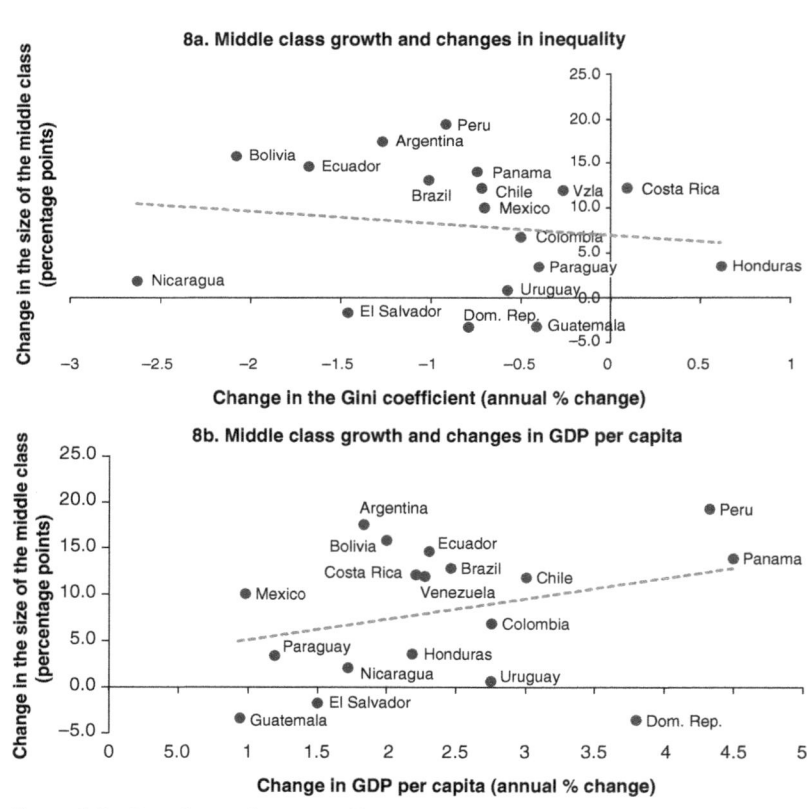

Figure 2.8 Correlation between Changes in the Size of the Middle Class and Changes in Inequality and Income; c. 2000–11.

Source: Authors' calculations, based on data from the World Development Indicators (World Bank) for GDP per capita and on data used in figs 2.1 and 2.7 for changes in inequality and size of the middle class, respectively.

this case) defining the middle class, steady growth of income per capita will automatically increase the size of the middle class in a developing country. But if the income distribution, whatever its mean or median, becomes less unequal, less polarized, that too will swell the ranks of the middle class. To disentangle the effect of both the decline in inequality and of income growth on the growth of the middle class, we follow the decomposition method illustrated in fig. 2.3. In this way we are able to decompose changes in the share of population belonging to the middle class into those changes which can be attributed to growth in average income per capita and to those related to the shape of the income distribution (i.e., inequality).

The decomposition reveals that, on a regional average, 21 per cent of the changes in the size of the middle class were due to the decline in inequality. The effect is particularly large in Mexico, Bolivia, Nicaragua and the Dominican Republic, where the decline in inequality accounted for more than 50 per cent of the changes in the size of the middle class (fig. 2.9). In Honduras, Costa Rica and El Salvador, the two effects work in different directions: income distribution grew more unequal, counteracting

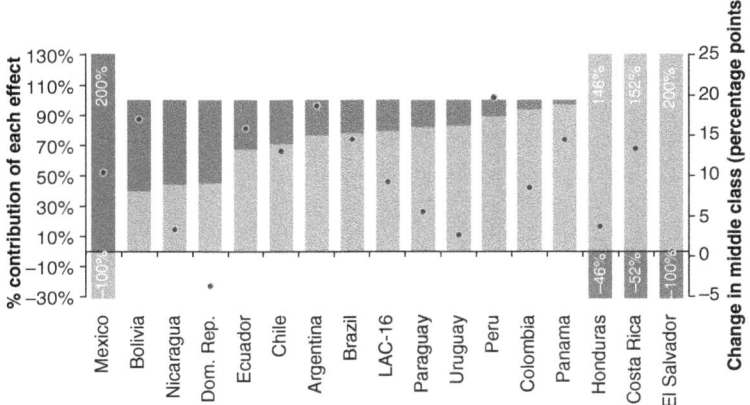

Figure 2.9 Contribution of the Decline in Inequality to Changes in the Size of the Middle Class (%); c. 2003–10.[/a]

Source: World Bank estimates using DRDECOMP (Azevedo et al., 2012a), based on data from SEDLAC (CEDLAS and the World Bank).[/a] The contribution of the decline in inequality toward changes in the size of the middle class is calculated using the Datt-Ravallion decomposition method (Datt and Ravallion, 1992). The following time periods were used: Argentina (2004–11), Bolivia (2002–08), Brazil (2004–11), Chile (2003–09), Colombia (2003–11), Costa Rica (2003–09), Dominican Republic (2003–11), Ecuador (2003–11), El Salvador (2003–10), Honduras (2003–11), Mexico (2004–10), Nicaragua (2005–09), Panama (2007–11), Paraguay (2003–11), Peru (2004–11) and Uruguay (2003–11). The average for LAC-16 refers to the simple average of the effect in all sixteen countries.

the positive effect of economic growth on the size of the middle class. For Mexico, meanwhile, it was poor growth that undermined the effects of a more equal income distribution. These findings indicate that even though economic growth explains the largest proportion of the change in the middle class, redistribution has played a significant role as well. Moreover, this result entails that a process focused solely on growth (or on one that increases inequality along the growth path) will have a weaker capacity to strengthen the middle class. Indeed, redistribution, overall, seems to play an important role in directional mobility.

Concluding Remarks

A substantial body of evidence indicates that income inequality has decreased in Latin America over the last decade. As illustrated in previous research, the main factors behind this trend refer to the decline in non-labor income inequality – explained by the effect of direct transfers and pensions on one hand, and on the other, to a reduction in labor income inequality resulting from declining returns to education. The unambiguous decline in income inequality in the first decade of the 2000s has contributed to the reduction of poverty incidence in the region. Decomposing the effects of economic growth and distribution on poverty reveals that close to 40 per cent of the reduction in poverty in Latin America is due to the decline in inequality.

What has been the effect of declining inequality on the middle class? To answer this question, we first present a discussion of what is meant by 'middle class'. The chapter follows López-Calva and Ortiz-Juárez (2014), who propose an absolute income-based threshold, setting economic security as the condition that defines the middle class (using a regression-based approach, they establish the lower threshold by determining the amount of income associated with the probability of falling into poverty). The basis of the concept thus explores the link between income and vulnerability to poverty. On the basis of this definition, the chapter then reviews recent research on middle-class trends in the region, confirming that the Latin American middle class is on the rise – although significant heterogeneity persists between countries and a large part of the population remains vulnerable.

Recognizing that income inequality has declined in Latin America and that the middle class has grown, the chapter then turns to the relationship between income distribution and the size of the middle class over the last decade. The significant results show a negative correlation between the middle class and income inequality (the middle class grew more where inequality declined more) and a positive correlation between the middle class and per capita income (economic activity and the middle class grow together). Decomposing the effects, we find that 21 per cent of the changes in the size of the middle class, on a regional average, were explained by the decline in inequality between 2003 and 2010. Mexico, Bolivia, Nicaragua and the Dominican Republic are the countries where the effect was larger. Income inequality, in addition to economic growth, plays an important part in the changes in the middle class. Policies that pay attention to the distribution of income (vis-à-vis focusing only on growth) have the capacity of contributing to strengthen the middle class.

Notes

1 While the Dominican Republic is included in many of the estimations, for simplicity's sake, we will refer to Latin America (instead of Latin America and the Caribbean) from here on.
2 See for example, Azevedo et al. (2013a); Azevedo et al. (2013b); Cornia (2013); Cruces et al. (2011); Gasparini et al. (2011); Gasparini and Lustig (2011); Lopez-Calva and Lustig (2010); and Lustig et al. (2013).
3 A fourth hypothesis refers to the increase in minimum wages and unionization rates that benefitted low-wage workers more than high-wage ones.
4 See, for example, Gasparini et al. (2011), De la Torre et al. (2012) and Azevedo et al. (2013b).
5 See, for example, López-Calva and Lustig (2010), Barros et al. (2010), Esquivel et al. (2010) and Campos et al. (2012).
6 See, for instance, Filmer and Schady (2013), who suggest that the increase in students in school as a consequence of CCTs has reduced quality of education, as there is no available evidence of higher scores or wages, and Reyes et al. (2013), who argue that the quality of certain types of tertiary education has decreased the skill premium in Chile.
7 The Maasoumi-Mahmoudi approach quantifies the relative contributions of economic growth and redistribution to changes in poverty. It is equivalent to an average of the Datt-Ravallion (1992) decomposition for different periods. While the latter decomposes changes in poverty into growth, redistribution and residual components, the Maasoumi-Mahmoudi approach eliminates the residual term.
8 See, for example, Birdsall et al. (2000) who suggest that the middle stratum comprises those individuals with an income of around 25 percent of the median or Davis and Huston (1992), who propose an income of around 50 per cent of the median as a threshold. In this vein, OECD (2010) defined the Latin American middle class as households with per capita incomes between 50 and 150 per cent of the median.
9 For instance, see Alesina and Perotti (1996), who suggest that the middle class lies between the 40th and the 80th percentile; Barro (1999) and Easterly (2001), who favor the space between the 20th and the 80th percentile;

Partridge (1997), between the 40th and the 60th percentile; and Solimano (2008), who proposes that the middle class lies between the 20th and the 90th percentile.
10 López-Calva and Ortiz-Juárez (2014) show similar results for Peru, where the incidence of poverty increased as a result of the adverse episodes experienced during 1998–99, and where, counterintuitively, the middle class would have also increased under the definitions proposed by Ravallion and Banerjee and Duflo.
11 See, for instance, Easterly (2001), Lipset (1959), Murphy et al. (1989), Doepke and Zilibotti (2008), Birdsall et al. (2000) and Barro (1999). Refer also to the discussion in Chapter 1 of this volume.

References

Alesina A. and R. Perotti (1996) 'Income Distribution, Political Instability and Investment', *European Economic Review*, vol. 40, no. 6, 1203–1228.

Azevedo, J. P., A. Castaneda and V. Sanfelice (2012a) 'DRDECOMP: Stata module to estimate Shapley value of growth and distribution components of changes in poverty indicators', Statistical Software Components S457563 (Boston, MA: Department of Economics, Boston College).

Azevedo, J. P., M. C. Nguyen and V. Sanfelice (2012b) 'ADECOMP: Stata module to estimate Shapley decomposition by components of a welfare measure', Statistical Software Components S457562 (Boston, MA: Department of Economics, Boston College).

Azevedo, J. P., G. Inchauste and V. Sanfelice (2013a) 'Decomposing the recent inequality decline in Latin America', Policy Research Working Paper Series 6715 (Washington, DC: The World Bank).

Azevedo, J. P., M. E. Dávalos, C. Díaz-Bonilla, B. Atuesta and R. A. Castañeda (2013b) 'Fifteen Years of Inequality in Latin America: How Have Labor Markets Helped?' Policy Research Working Paper 6384 (Washington, DC: The World Bank).

Banerjee, A. V. and E. Duflo (2008) 'What Is Middle Class about the Middle Classes around the World?' *Journal of Economics Perspectives*, vol. 22, no. 2, 3–28.

Barro, R. J. (1999) 'Determinants of Democracy', *Journal of Political Economy*, vol. 107, no. 6, 158–183.

Barros, R., M. de Carvalho, S. Franco and R. Mendonça (2010) 'Markets, the State and the Dynamics of Inequality in Brazil' in L. F. López-Calva and N. Lustig, eds., *Declining Inequality in Latin America: A Decade of Progress?* (Washington, DC: Brookings Institution and UNDP).

Birdsall, N., C. Graham and S. Pettinato (2000) 'Stuck in the tunnel: is globalization muddling the middle class?' Center on Social and Economic Dynamics Working Paper 14 (Washington, DC: Brookings Institution).

Campos, R., G. Esquivel and N. Lustig (2012) 'The Rise and Fall of Income Inequality in Mexico, 1989–2010', UNU-WIDER Working Paper No. 2012/10 (Helsinki: United Nations University-World Institute for Development Economics Research).

Cornia, A. (2013) 'Inequality Trends and Their Determinants: Latin America over 1990–2010', in A. Cornia, ed., *Falling Inequality in Latin America: Policy Changes and Lessons* (Oxford: Oxford University Press).

Cruces, G., L. F. López-Calva and D. Battistón (2011) 'Down and Out or Up and In? Polarization-Based Measures of the Middle Class for Latin America', CEDLAS Working Papers No. 113 (La Plata, Argentina: Universidad Nacional de La Plata).

Datt, G. and M. Ravallion (1992) 'Growth and Redistribution Components of Changes in Poverty Measures: A Decomposition with Applications to Brazil and India in the 1980s', *Journal of D evelopment Economics*, vol. 38, 275–295.

De la Torre, A., J. Messina and S. Pienknagura (2012) 'The Labor Market Story Behind Latin America's Transformation', Semiannual Report, Regional Chief Economist Office, Latin America and the Caribbean (Washington, DC: The World Bank).

Doepke M. and F. Zilibotti (2008) 'Occupational Choice and the Spirit of Capitalism', *Quarterly Journal of Economics*, vol. 123, no. 2, 747–93.

Easterly, W. (2001) 'Middle Class Consensus and Economic Development', *Journal of Economic Growth*, vol. 6, no. 4, 317–336.

Esquivel, G., N. Lustig and J. Scott (2010) 'A Decade of Falling Inequality in Mexico: Market Forces or State Action?' in L. F. López-Calva and N. Lustig, eds., *Declining Inequality in Latin America: A Decade of Progress?* (Washington, DC: Brookings Institution and UNDP).

Filmer, D. and N. Schady (2009) 'School enrollment, selection and test scores', Policy Research Working Paper Series 4998 (Washington, DC: The World Bank).

Ferreira, F. H. G, J. Messina, J. Rigolini, L. F. López-Calva, M. A. Lugo and R. Vakis (2013) *Economic Mobility and the Rise of the Latin American Middle Class* (Washington, DC: The World Bank).

Gasparini, L. and N. Lustig (2011) 'The Rise and Fall of Income Inequality in Latin America', Working Paper 1110 (New Orleans, LA: Tulane University).

Gasparini, L., S. Galiani, G. Cruces and P. Acosta (2011) 'Educational Upgrading and Returns to Skills in Latin America. Evidence from a Supply-Demand Framework, 1990–2010' Policy Research Working Paper 5921 (Washington, DC: The World Bank).

Global Trends 2030 (2013) *Global Trends 2030 Alternative Worlds*, National Intelligence Council (NIC), http://gt2030.com/, date accessed 1 July 2014.

Lipset, S. M. (1959) 'Some Social Requisites of Democracy: Economic Development and Political Legitimacy', *American Political Science Review*, vol. 53, no. 1, 69–105.

Lerman, R. I. and S. Yitzhaki (1985) 'Income Inequality Effects by Income Source. A New Approach and Applications to the United States', *Review of Economics and Statistics*, vol. 67, 151–156.

López-Calva, L. F. and N. Lustig, eds., (2010) *Declining Inequality in Latin America. A Decade of Progress?* (Washington, DC: Brookings Institution and UNDP).

López-Calva, L. F. and E. Ortiz-Juárez (2014) 'A Vulnerability Approach to the Definition of the Middle Class', *Journal of Economic Inequality*, vol. 12, no. 1, 23–47.

Lustig, N., L. F. López-Calva and E. Ortiz-Juárez (2013) 'Deconstructing the Decline in Inequality in Latin America', Policy Research Working Paper 6552 (Washington, DC: The World Bank).

Murphy, K. M., A. Shleifer and R. W. Vishny (1989) 'Income Distribution, Market Size and Industrialization', *Quarterly Journal of Economics*, vol. 104, no. 3, 537–64.

Maasoumi, E. and V. Mahmoudi (2013) 'Robust Growth-equity Decomposition of Change in Poverty: The Case of Iran (2000–2009)', *Quarterly Review of Economics and Finance*, vol. 53, no. 3, 268–276.

OECD [Organisation for Economic Co-operation and Development] (2010) *Latin American Economic Outlook 2011: How Middle-Class Is Latin America?* (Paris: OECD Publications).

Partridge, M. D. (1997) 'Is Inequality Harmful For Growth? Comment', *American Economic Review*, vol. 87, no. 5, 1019–1032.

Ravallion, M. (2010) 'The Developing World's Bulging (but Vulnerable) Middle Class', *World Development*, vol. 38, no. 4, 445–454.

Reyes, L., J. Rodríguez and S. S. Urzúa (2013) 'Heterogeneous Economic Returns to Postsecondary Degrees: Evidence from Chile', NBER Working Paper No. 18817 (Cambridge, MA: National Bureau for Economic Research).

Solimano, A. (2008) 'The Middle Class and the Development Process'. *Macroeconomía del Desarrollo* 65 (Santiago: United Nations Economic Commission for Latin America and the Caribbean).

Middle class in Peru is opposed to democracy and to redistributive policies. They want economic growth.

Economic growth drives the size of the middle class more than redistribution.

52

Benefits of the me from production and consumption side. → No need to do it as families do it as individuals (equivalent income)

3
Latin America's Global Middle Class: A Preference for Growth over Equality

Mauricio Cárdenas, Homi Kharas and Camila Henao

The middle class plays an important role in explaining comparative development as a source of consumption demand, innovation and political support for the public provision of infrastructure, health and education. The middle class has sufficient discretionary income to satisfy an increasing desire for consumption that drives the demand for higher-quality goods (Schor, 1999). This means that the demand for consumer durables increases rapidly as household income passes a critical threshold, normally associated with middle-class status. From a production standpoint, meanwhile, the middle class is sometimes identified with entrepreneurship and the corresponding side effects on job creation, innovation and the strengthening of a country's productivity: this sequence of quality-improving innovations is argued to be the engine of economic growth (Aghion and Howitt, 1992). The middle class also plays an active role in domestic politics, in promoting democratic attitudes, favoring progressive political platforms and providing a strong constituency for public investment in human and infrastructure capital that is vital for long-term economic growth (OECD, 2010). But on occasion the middle class can be a regressive force, using their political clout to protect their own position by encouraging populist policies like subsidies for pensions, housing and universities that can generate macroeconomic instability and undermine democracy and economic growth alike.

In this chapter, we estimate the size of Latin America's middle class and forecast its likely expansion during the next two decades. In our simulations, we build scenarios that differ according to two crucial assumptions regarding economic growth and income distribution. We start by defining the middle class, adopting a definition that is based not on relative incomes but on an *absolute* level, which is useful for international comparisons. In the scenarios, we find that faster economic growth has a much larger impact on the size of the middle class compared to redistribution. To better understand the attitudes and values of the middle class, we look at two recent surveys from Peru and find that the middle class in that country is adamantly opposed to taxation and redistribution, and tends to favor less democratic governance, relative to the attitudes expressed by poorer survey respondents. This is a sharp contrast to attitudes in the developed world. More analysis is needed to see if the Peruvian findings are more broadly applicable to other developing countries in Latin America.[1] The policy implications of this exercise suggest that the acceleration of economic growth is a more politically viable strategy than redistribution through taxes and public spending to expand the middle class.

Definitions

There is no standard definition of the middle class: several alternatives are analyzed and interpreted in this volume, but here we use a definition based on absolute per capita household income levels. Alternative definitions include relative measures of social class that categorize individuals according to their placement in each country's income distribution (also called central tendency measures). Absolute measures, in contrast, establish a given range of income to classify individuals into classes. The former are unappealing for international comparisons as households in the middle can have dramatically different incomes from country to country. Absolute definitions require a choice as to which is the level of income (or expenditures) that truly identifies middle-class living standards, and this choice is somewhat arbitrary; for example, some studies define the middle class as individuals with an annual income over $3,900 in purchasing power parity (PPP) terms, or those with daily expenditures between $2 and $4 or $6 and $10. We define the middle class as individuals with daily expenditures between $10 and $100 per person in purchasing power parity (PPP) terms.[2]

One crucial issue is whether the measure of the middle class in developing countries should use the same yardstick as in developed economies. Some have differentiated between the *developing world's middle class* (those who are not considered poor by the standards of developing countries but are still poor by the standards of rich countries), *developing world's upper middle class* (those who are still poor by the standards of rich countries, but whose income is larger than the highest poverty line for developing economies) and the *Western middle class* (those whose income is at least as high as the US poverty line) (Ravallion, 2009). We use a concept of a 'global' middle class applicable to people regardless of their country of residence. The lower bound of $10/day is chosen with reference to the average poverty line in Portugal and Italy, the two advanced European countries with the lowest poverty lines. The upper bound is chosen as twice the median income of Luxemburg, the richest advanced country. Defined in this way, the global middle class excludes those who are considered poor in the poorest advanced countries and those who are considered rich in the richest advanced country.

We do not favor a wide definition of the middle class that would suit just developing countries, say between $2 and $13 (adjusted for PPP). We want to avoid proclaiming somebody who is almost abjectly poor by Western standards to be a global middle-class individual. And these individuals purchase consumer durables of higher quality and higher [...] characterize countries with [...] size of the middle class [...] Latin American members [...] als in the upper end of [...] es, not in the middle of [...] some very poor countries [...] ciated with a *reduction* [...] countries, redistribution [...] ls who are in the $10– [...] are under $10 per day. [...] Latin America has not [...] Latin American econo- [...] population) as recently [...] 1.8 per cent), Mexico [...] livia had the smallest [...] population, followed by [...] nt). The average size of [...] data for 2005).

> *[Handwritten margin note:] In very poor countries, redistribution means a reduction of the mc. → Mexico is upper-middle income country, why has redistribution affected the mc?*

Simulations: the effects of economic growth

How will Latin America's middle class evolve between 2005 and 2030 under various economic growth scenarios, holding the distribution of income constant? Growth in output per capita can be modeled as a function of technological progress, capital accumulation and labor force growth. We obtain estimates of the future evolution of these determinant variables as follows: The rate of capital accumulation is based on the average investment rate between 1998 and 2007 (with a 6 per cent depreciation rate). Labor force growth is taken from UN population projections of the working-age (fifteen to sixty-four years) share of the population. The rate of technological improvement in each country is assumed to depend on the global technology frontier (which shifts out with new advances in science, new products and new processes) as well as the rate at which individual countries catch up with that technological frontier. We assume that the speed of convergence is inversely proportional to the gap between the per capita income level of each country and that of the United States, considered the global leader in technology. Countries with very low income levels are therefore predicted to catch up faster, while countries with per capita incomes closer to that of the United States will experience less rapid technological improvements. The global technology frontier is assumed to increase at a rate of 1.3 per cent per year (the historical rate of total factor productivity growth in the US). This rate of technological improvement has been very stable and can therefore be taken as a good proxy for future potential technology growth.

The evolution of Latin America's middle class will depend critically on economic growth. If we assume the gap between the income per capita of the US and Latin America is closed at a speed of 1 per cent per year, growth will be much faster than under an alternative assumption that Latin America will not converge to the US level. This latter scenario is more consistent with Latin America's own track record (with the exception of Chile). We thus assume two possible growth scenarios: the business-as-usual scenario (based on factor accumulation – that is, growth in capital and the labor force – but no productivity convergence) and a high-speed growth scenario, which implicitly assumes that the gap with productivity in the US will be closed at a rate of 1 per cent per year. Holding constant the income distribution (at its 2005 value), we proceed to measure the global middle class using household surveys to calculate the cumulative share of the population whose daily per capita expenditure is between $10 and $100 (table 3.1).

Under the *growth-without-convergence scenario,* which we call business as usual for Latin America, the countries with the largest share of their population in the global middle class by 2030 would be Mexico, Uruguay and Costa Rica. Meanwhile, those with the smallest proportion of their population in the middle class would be Bolivia, Paraguay and Honduras, closely reflecting the rankings in 2005. Thus, if income

Table 3.1 Change in the Share of the Middle Class between 2005 and 2030 (in percentage points)

Country	Size of the middle class in 2005 (per cent)	Due to Growth		Due to Redistribution	
		Without convergence	With convergence	Own track record	Progressive
Argentina	52.86	16.47	19.05	−4.21	6.24
Bolivia	13.46	17.04	44.42	0	−0.16
Brazil	33.75	19.55	33.32	18.02	18.02
Chile	46.22	23.07	32.37	7.45	7.45
Colombia	24.85	21.03	39.61	−2.5	0.79
Costa Rica	51.81	23.96	30.1	0	6.84
Dom. Rep.	31.1	32	48.18	−1.95	1.41
Ecuador	27.81	21.05	42.65	−2.51	0.81
El Salvador	46.89	22.12	30.09	0	4.29
Guatemala	33.84	25.48	43.06	5.33	2.77
Guyana	17.43	25.28	60.49	0	−4.04
Honduras	16.49	22.82	22.26	−0.23	−0.09
Jamaica	46.87	22.82	17.65	0	6.84
Mexico	60.12	19.81	26.41	9.43	9.43
Panama	41.62	22.59	44.09	0	4.63
Paraguay	18.65	20.02	52.27	0	12.29
Peru	30.58	28.07	40.62	−1.98	2.72
Uruguay	55.84	21.3	12.7	0	29.77
Venezuela	40	27.89	35.52	51.3	51.3

Source: Authors' calculations.

distribution is assumed to remain at 2005 levels and economic growth does not speed up, the size of the middle class will increase moderately without changes to the current country rankings.

However, if there is *convergence* between Latin America and the US, countries with low and low-middle incomes – such as Bolivia, Honduras and Guyana – would experience considerable gains in the middle-class proportion of the population by 2030. When convergence is assumed, lower-income countries grow much faster – as do their middle classes – relative to countries with higher initial per capita incomes. For countries with higher average incomes, such as Mexico, the share of the middle class will not change considerably between the two scenarios.

Simulations: The Effects of Income Redistribution

Economic growth is not the only way that the Latin American middle classes might grow between 2005 and 2030. Redistributive fiscal policy could shift income from higher-income classes to the middle class (in the extreme case, even in the absence of economic growth). How might this affect the trajectory of the size of the middle classes in the region? We simulate two redistribution scenarios. In the *redistribution based on past performance (or own track record) scenario*, each country is projected to follow its historical redistributive trend (regressive, progressive or neutral). In principle, but not always, countries with a regressive trend are expected to see the size of their middle class reduced, while those with progressive redistribution trends will most likely experience increases in the size of their middle class. Based on past redistributive trends alone, the simulations indicate that Venezuela, Mexico, Brazil and Chile will experience the largest increases in the share of the middle class as a percentage of the population between 2005 and 2030. On the contrary, the countries whose proportion of middle-class population would shrink by 2030 are Honduras, Dominican Republic, Peru, Colombia, Ecuador and Argentina (table 3.2).

For the *progressive redistribution* scenario, we use a redistribution trend that follows very closely the experience of Chile and Mexico – the two countries with the fastest reductions in inequality in the region – during the past two decades. As an illustration, if Peru were to follow a progressive redistribution trend such as the one that took place in Mexico and

Table 3.2 Trends in Income Distribution: Gini Coefficient.

Country	Initial	Mid-Period	Final
Colombia	57.22 (1995)	57.92 (1999)	58.49 (2006)
Brazil	60.97 (1988)	59.23 (1998)	55.02 (2007)
Chile	56.43(1987)	55.74 (1998)	52 (2006)
Costa Rica	47.49 (1981)	45.88 (1997)	47.23 (2005)
Argentina (urban)	44.51 (1986)	49.84 (1998)	48.77 (2006)
Bolivia	42.04 (1990)	57.79 (1999)	58.19 (2005)
Dom. Rep.	47.78 (1986)	49.58 (1997)	51.91 (2006)
Ecuador	50.49 (1987)	53.53 (1998)	54.37 (2007)
El Salvador	48.96 (1989)	52.17 (1998)	49.7 (2005)
Guatemala	58.26 (1987)	55.65 (1998)	53.69 (2006)
Guyana	51.55 (1992)	44.58 (1998)	44.58 (1998)
Honduras	59.49 (1989)	53.05 (1997)	55.31 (2006)
Jamaica	43.16 (1988)	40.47 (1996)	45.51 (2004)
Mexico	55.14 (1989)	48.99 (1998)	48.11 (2006)
Panama	48.74 (1979)	48.53 (1997)	54.93 (2006)
Paraguay	39.74 (1990)	56.85 (1999)	53.24 (2007)
Peru	45.72 (1985)	46.24 (1996)	49.55 (2006)
Uruguay	43.65 (1981)	42.33 (1989)	42.33 (1989)
Venezuela	55.82 (1981)	48.79 (1996)	43.44 (2006)

Source: Authors' calculations based on data from scenarios.

Latin America's Global Middle Class   57

Chile in the last twenty-five years, its Gini coefficient would decline from 49.6 in 2006 to 45 in 2030. In general, more progressive redistribution scenarios would yield a larger middle class. However, as we will see, this is not always the case. For very poor countries, where individuals who belong to the global middle class have relatively high incomes, progressive redistribution policies raise the income of individuals in the far left of the distribution at the expense of those with higher incomes, including the middle classes. Thus, for the poorest Latin American countries, redistribution implies a reduction in the share of individuals who belong to the global middle class in favor of those that earn and spend less than $10 per day.

In fact, under this *progressive redistribution* scenario, Honduras, Bolivia and Guyana experience a *reduction* in the proportion of individuals that belong to the global middle class in 2030, compared to 2005. We call this the 'global middle-class paradox'. In countries where mean and median incomes are well below the global middle class income threshold, [redistribution decreases] the size of the group [...]. In contrast, in countries [where incomes are relat]ively higher, progress[ive redistribution yields l]arger middle classes. [If these countries y]were to implement [the redistribu]tion trends observed [over the last twenty-f]ive years, the propor[tion of the middle] class would go from [... th]is is equivalent to an [increase of o]ne percentage point [...]

[redistributive] policy has a positive [influenc]e in the share of the [... not] totally explained by [redistributive] policies. Under our [... have] greater impacts on [redistr]ibutive policies. The [... in] Latin America will [earn betwee]n $2 to $3 per day), [which will be insufficient to lift] them into the global middle class. However, we are not arguing that redistributive policies hold down the size of the middle class. Rather, only when countries have reached higher incomes and individuals are well above the poverty line can redistributive policies be beneficial for a strong global middle class. This will only happen in Latin America after 2020.

When analyzing the different growth scenarios in the previous section of this chapter, we assumed the income distribution was held constant at 2005 levels; when analyzing the redistribution changes, per capita income was assumed to remain at its 2005 level. Therefore, the numbers presented in the tables ignore possible interactions between trends in growth and equity. This is an important limitation of the exercise, as empirical analysis shows that more egalitarian societies have a greater potential for long-run growth; moreover, societies with higher growth rates can afford higher taxation and more redistribution. In particular, if the interaction from redistribution to growth is taken into account, the share of the population that is part of the global middle class could be even larger under the high growth with redistribution scenario.

These results have several policy implications. Countries should promote policies that will boost their economic growth rates, and by doing so enlarge the proportion of the population with global middle-class living standards. Such policies, amongst others, include those designed to increase the accumulation of human and physical capital, but especially those that accelerate productivity growth. Even if growth is essential to developing a large middle class, it is not always enough. Complementary redistributive policies can play a crucial role, although their impact on this outcome will be of a lower magnitude than that of growth. However, a better distribution of income will further boost economic growth, thus creating a virtuous cycle between redistribution and growth.

Latin America and Asia in the Global Middle Class 2005–30

There are about 180 million middle-class Latin Americans, roughly one-tenth of the global middle class. The numbers are likely to increase substantially by 2030, due to economic growth in most Latin American countries, especially if there is convergence. Given population and growth trends in Latin America, the size of the middle class could grow by about 2.6 per cent per year, much faster than population growth. Not all countries are expected to have a growing middle class – Europe and North America already have a very high share of their population in the middle class. A combination of low population growth and inequality could lead to a hollowing out of the middle class in these regions; some of the present middle class would become rich, and some become poor, while few would enter the middle class. These regions, therefore, could see their middle-class populations stabilize at around 1 billion individuals.

Despite this, Latin America's share in the global middle class will become lower, not higher, over time. This is because Asian countries appear to be on the verge of a dramatic rise in their middle class. Asian countries have been extraordinarily successful in reducing the number of people living in extreme poverty and, assuming that Asian growth rates continue at historical rates, these individuals will soon be entering the global middle class. If this takes place, it would constitute the largest increase in the global middle class in history; an estimated 2.7 billion Asians could join the middle class by 2030, more than the entire size of the middle class today. China and India could each have 1 billion middle-class citizens by 2030, three times the number of all of Latin America.

These trends in the size and composition of the global middle class are important for Latin America. Their export growth strategies will need to be tailored to the new markets of Asia, and product innovations aimed at the middle class will need to satisfy Asian tastes to become globally competitive.

The Global Middle Class in Peru is not so Progressive: Attitudes and Values

From a regional and global perspective, we now turn to the national level of analysis. This section compares values and attitudes of the middle class with those of rich and poor groups. The analysis is limited to the single Latin American country – Peru – for which there are data from the 2008 World Values Survey (WVS). We examine the responses of 1,500 individuals living in various regions and socioeconomic classes in Peru. The questionnaire captures attitudes toward the government, economy and country. Using this database, we analyze the influence of income class on attitudes. Consistent with the rest of this chapter, we define the middle class as the group with daily expenditures between $10 and $100 per person in purchasing power parity (PPP) terms. The lower-income class is defined as those with incomes below $10 per day and the rich as those with incomes above $100.[3] Our approach differs from that of Daude, Gutiérrez and Melguizo in Chapter 9 of this volume, which uses a self-reported rather than absolute measure of middle class based on responses to the WVS from 1981–97. In the case of Peru, the authors' findings are largely consistent with the ones we present below – that is, a preference for market-based rather than redistributive policies and an aversion toward State ownership of businesses. Daude et al. find that the middle class is broadly distrustful of the State, suggesting that government policies to promote the middle class might not translate into improved middle-class perceptions of government. They also usefully point out that there is little commonality in views among the middle class across countries, but this conclusion has to be interpreted in light of the changing definition of the middle class in their study as a result of a reliance on self-reporting rather than on an absolute definition of the middle class as in our chapter.

The survey helps us understand how income levels influence where respondents place themselves on the political left-right scale. Responses to a set of political questions provide a broad look at the relationship between income and political attitudes, including the importance of democracy. We also consider sentiments toward progressive taxation or redistribution from the rich to the poor. This is an important question for understanding the relationship between incomes and the role of government in generating a more equitable distribution of wealth in society. This question is followed up with a look into how income levels influence perspectives on private versus State ownership of business. We also consider two questions about respondents' personal goals and what ought to be the goals of the nation.

To estimate these effects, we use a simple linear regression model where attitudes and values are the dependent variables and income classes are the explanatory variables. In particular, we estimate the following equation:

$$W = \alpha + \beta_m M + \beta_r R + \gamma Z + \varepsilon$$

where W is the attitudinal variable of interest, M is a dummy variable that captures whether the individual belongs to the middle class, R is a dummy variable that captures whether the individual is rich (more than $100 PPP per day) and Z is a vector of controls that includes age, age squared, gender, years of schooling, marital status, employment status, children, weight and ethnicity (black, Quechua-speaking, white and mulatto). The coefficients on M and R reflect the difference in attitudes between those classes and the poor, the omitted class in this analysis (table 3.3). We highlight and interpret the most significant results below.

The WVS asks respondents whether they feel that governments taxing the rich and subsidizing the poor is an essential characteristic of democracy. Respondents indicate how much they agree or disagree with this sentiment by choosing a number on a ten-point scale, where the feeling that governments taxing the rich and subsidizing the poor is not an essential characteristic of democracy equals one and that it is an essential characteristic of democracy equals ten. There is a strong negative coefficient on the middle class, suggesting that individuals in the Peruvian middle class do not believe that taxation of the rich and transfers to the poor are essential characteristics of a democracy (table 3.3). This finding suggests that as the middle class in Peru expands, as our scenarios suggest is possible with convergence in growth, the weight of opinion could swing against progressive tax-and-redistribute policies. While there may be a range of causes for sentiments toward a top-down redistribution of wealth, a deeper understanding is needed to inform tax policy platforms.

Private versus State ownership of business is a contentious issue in any region of the world, perhaps no more so than in Latin America. The WVS asks respondents to state their opinion on whether there should be more private ownership of business or more government ownership of business. Individuals are given a ten-point response category where one corresponds to a preference for more private ownership of business and ten equals more government ownership of business. Being in the Peruvian middle class is highly significantly and negatively related to the preference for public ownership of business. This is consistent with the view of the middle class as a highly entrepreneurial segment of society favoring private ownership.

The WVS also asks whether respondents feel the world is better or worse off due to the advancements of science and technologies. Once again, respondents exhibit their preference on a ten-point scale ranging from one (a lot worse off) to ten (a lot better off). Being a member of the middle class in Peru is strongly associated with feeling that the world is much better off because of advances in science and technology. With the new growth of industry centered on broadband Internet and new technologies, this finding is a positive indicator of the willingness of the Peruvian middle class to adopt technologies as a lever for growth.

Attitudes regarding entrepreneurship among the Peruvian middle class – so important to the country's recent growth – can be discerned from responses to a WVS question that asks respondents to rate whether competition is best defined as good or bad, on a scale from one (competition is good) to ten (competition is bad). Middle-class Peruvians are significantly more likely to feel that competition is good for society (table 3.3).

Two WVS questions focus on priorities of the individual and the nation. The first asks respondents to choose which of four priorities is the most important (fig. 3.1). All groups, including the middle class, have the highest preference for 'maintaining national order'. This

Table 3.3 Peruvian Middle-Class Values and Attitudes (regression results).

Variables	(1) Is the world better or worse off because of science and technology?	(2) Governments should tax the rich and subsidize the poor	(3) Importance of democracy	(4) Private vs. State ownership of business	(5) Individual vs. Government responsibility	(6) Competition good or bad	(7) Trust in neighbors	(8) Importance of politics in life	(9) Self-positioning on political scale
Middle	0.744***	−0.446**	0.228	−0.383**	−0.0877	−0.643***	0.00405	−0.0169	−0.00653
	(0.187)	(0.192)	(0.147)	(0.190)	(0.207)	(0.172)	(0.0832)	(0.0639)	(0.172)
Rich	1.363*	−1.010	−0.537	−0.725	0.0344	−0.556	−0.457	−0.0935	0.476
	(0.700)	(0.715)	(0.553)	(0.703)	(0.776)	(0.663)	(0.314)	(0.240)	(0.594)
Gender	−0.0672	−0.0892	0.132	0.595***	−0.157	0.0801	0.295***	0.169***	−0.00249
	(0.174)	(0.179)	(0.138)	(0.178)	(0.194)	(0.161)	(0.0773)	(0.0593)	(0.157)
Age^2	−0.000316	−0.000620	0.000236	0.000676*	0.000165	0.000548	0.000663***	−0.000235*	0.000361
	(0.000379)	(0.000393)	(0.000302)	(0.000395)	(0.000430)	(0.000359)	(0.000169)	(0.000131)	(0.000349)
Age	0.0345	0.0448	−0.0131	−0.0835**	−0.00847	−0.0601*	−0.0672***	0.0180	−0.0407
	(0.0342)	(0.0354)	(0.0272)	(0.0355)	(0.0387)	(0.0322)	(0.0152)	(0.0118)	(0.0312)
Education	0.206	−0.246*	0.408***	−0.414***	−0.199	−0.295**	−0.132**	−0.178***	−0.139
	(0.135)	(0.139)	(0.106)	(0.137)	(0.149)	(0.124)	(0.0600)	(0.0460)	(0.123)
Marital	−0.115	−0.0122	0.0559	0.0672	−0.0799	0.0275	0.0865	−0.0427	0.144
	(0.203)	(0.211)	(0.161)	(0.211)	(0.228)	(0.190)	(0.0904)	(0.0694)	(0.190)

Employment	-0.299	-0.0650	0.328**	0.568***	0.0229	-0.103	0.00846	-0.0215	-0.0778
	(0.190)	(0.197)	(0.151)	(0.197)	(0.214)	(0.178)	(0.0846)	(0.0650)	(0.176)
Children	-0.123**	0.0907	-0.0149	0.0661	0.0119	0.0461	0.0162	0.0135	0.0617
	(0.0594)	(0.0615)	(0.0472)	(0.0631)	(0.0672)	(0.0556)	(0.0264)	(0.0203)	(0.0558)
Black	-0.473	0.0866	-0.401	-0.0927	0.261	-0.439	0.0290	-0.170	-0.749
	(0.590)	(0.614)	(0.467)	(0.604)	(0.671)	(0.555)	(0.264)	(0.204)	(0.524)
Quechua	-0.0104	0.257	-0.500*	0.684*	-1.167***	-0.222	-0.0408	-0.143	-0.357
	(0.347)	(0.361)	(0.276)	(0.360)	(0.389)	(0.323)	(0.155)	(0.118)	(0.322)
White	0.232	-0.0287	-0.0131	-0.230	0.00361	1.086***	0.187	0.0695	0.516
	(0.457)	(0.463)	(0.351)	(0.473)	(0.502)	(0.419)	(0.199)	(0.152)	(0.432)
Mulatto	-0.165	0.0279	-0.256	-0.104	-0.749**	-0.0819	0.0296	-0.113	-0.0323
	(0.335)	(0.349)	(0.266)	(0.347)	(0.375)	(0.311)	(0.149)	(0.114)	(0.308)
Weight	-0.0259	1.179**	1.301***	1.131*	-1.545**	-0.404	0.515**	-0.0511	0.894*
	(0.562)	(0.580)	(0.443)	(0.577)	(0.625)	(0.521)	(0.250)	(0.191)	(0.496)
Constant	4.268***	5.054***	6.254***	6.873***	8.200***	5.927***	4.054***	2.863***	5.958***
	(0.904)	(0.933)	(0.718)	(0.933)	(1.010)	(0.841)	(0.402)	(0.308)	(0.818)
Observations	1,238	1,214	1,232	1,175	1,217	1,210	1,258	1,245	977
R-squared	0.045	0.034	0.044	0.073	0.022	0.048	0.048	0.035	0.019

Note: Asterisks indicate statistical significance of estimated coefficients at the 99% (***), 95% (**) and 90% (*) levels.

64 *Latin America's Emerging Middle Classes*

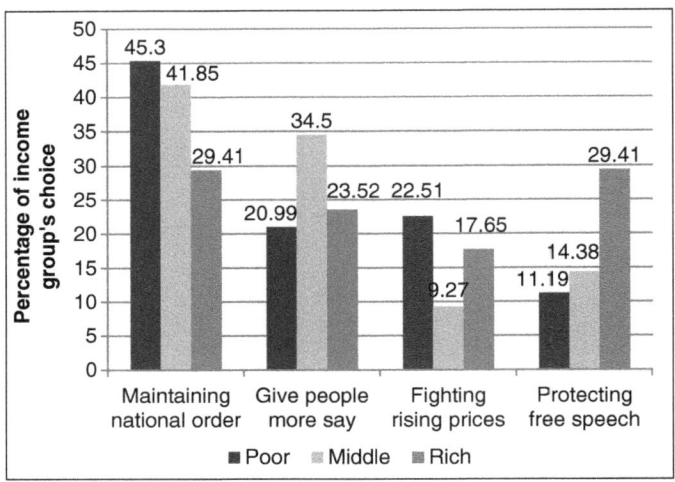

Figure 3.1 Peruvian Individual Top Priorities.
Source: Authors' calculations based on World Values Survey data for Peru 2008.

preference is held by 42 per cent of the population. The next most important category is for 'giving people more say'. In this category, the middle class views are strongest compared to other classes, with 10 per cent more middle class ranking this a top priority as compared to either the poor and rich income groups. These two priorities combined make up for 77 per cent of the middle class's preferences. The other two categories of 'fighting rising prices' and 'protecting free speech' make up the remaining 23 per cent of the middle-class priorities. Only 9.2 per cent of Peru's middle-class citizens consider 'fighting rising prices' a national priority, whereas 22.5 per cent of the poor do. This is consistent with the interpretation of inflation as a direct tax on the poor, not so directly felt by wealthier individuals. Based on the preferences, it appears the Peruvians surveyed are eager for stability and greater participation in their political system. Notably the categories for 'maintaining national order' and 'protecting free speech' appear to be related to income levels. The priority of 'maintaining order' decreases as income level increases, while support for 'protecting free speech' increases as income levels increase.

Finally, we consider what Peruvians underline as the most important aims of the country over the next ten years. There is a dramatic preference by all income categories for two national objectives. The middle class displays the highest preference prioritizing 'a high level of economic growth'. This priority dominates all income levels and resonates with Peru's high levels of economic growth in recent years. These results show that there is clearly a national unity centered on the growth of the country.

The other highly endorsed national priority is for 'people to have more say about how things are done'. This finding echoes the *individual* priority of 'giving people more say', which was strongly preferred by the middle class. The national priority category of 'people have more say about how things are done' appears to have a relationship with income. Preference for this response increases as income levels increase, suggesting that those with higher levels of income feel a greater need to be heard by their government.

Through the lens of our analysis of the 2008 World Values Survey, we see a view of the Peruvian middle class that supports fundamental characteristics of the country's recent rapid economic growth. The Peruvian middle class is firmly supportive of private industry, technology and competition. While we cannot say that the middle class is firmly supportive of weakening progressive tax regimes, the findings show that the middle class does not believe that the redistribution of wealth through taxation is a necessary aspect of democracy.

Policy Discussion and Conclusions

In addition to forecasting plausible scenarios of the size of Latin America's global middle class in the next twenty years, this chapter analyzes the values and attitudes of the global middle class (vis-à-vis other classes) in the case of Peru. We define the global middle class as those households with daily income between $10 and $100 per person in purchasing power parity terms, which implies that we exclude all those individuals who are considered poor in the poorest advanced countries and those who are rich in the richest advanced countries.

Economic growth is the most powerful force in driving the size of the global middle class, of an order of magnitude larger than redistribution. Redistribution contributes relatively anemically to middle-class growth because the global middle-class income threshold is high for most Latin American countries. This means that redistribution tends to favor those who are between the poverty level (say $2 or $3 per day) and the minimum global middle-class income ($10 per day), rather than the relatively affluent members of the global middle class in developing and emerging economies. When modeling progressive redistribution scenarios, many low-income individuals are made better off but not sufficiently well off to enter the global middle class. Economic growth, meanwhile, especially under the assumption of convergence with the US, raises the mean income of the distribution of *all* income groups homogeneously, thus having a larger impact on the size of Latin America's portion of the global middle class.

If economic convergence is assumed with a catch-up rate between the Latin American and Caribbean countries and the US of 1 per cent per year, the share of the middle class in Latin American countries by 2030 will be close to 72 per cent of the region's population. Mexico is forecasted to have the largest share of the middle class by 2030 (86.5 per cent of its population), followed by Panama (85.7 per cent) and Costa Rica (81.9 per cent). Honduras will have the smallest share of the middle class, at 38.8 per cent.

In terms of redistribution, countries with the most progressive trends are projected to have larger middle classes by 2030. This would be the case of Venezuela, Mexico, Brazil and Chile, which will be the regional leaders in the share of the population belonging to the global middle class in 2030. Combining redistribution with income convergence would produce very powerful results: most Latin Americans will be able to join the global middle class by 2030. If productivity growth accelerates and begins a process of convergence with the US level, every decade nearly 60 million Latin Americans will join the group of individuals that consumes between $10 and $100 per day.

Even with relatively rapid growth from now to 2030, the Latin American region's middle class will remain small in global terms. This is the result of a far larger expansion of the middle class expected in countries in Asia, particularly in India and China. If the global middle class provides a major component of global demand, as has been true historically, then it is Asia's middle class that will power the global economy, not Latin America's. This has implications for the region's trade and export promotion policies and consequently for its growth agenda.

The growth agenda is crucial for the expansion of the middle class. Policies promoting equity can play a complementary role, but even under very optimistic scenarios they will not on their own produce a large global middle class. Even if this is so, the speed with which countries reach a large middle class depends on initial conditions, redistribution and the growth rate.

According to the Peruvian data analyzed in this chapter, participation in economics and politics is of great importance to people in the global middle class, who want to have a voice and say in what happens in their country. This has policy implications for the nature of public debate on economic policy, which must be more open and transparent. The consolidation of a middle class will bring along several policy challenges, which need to be addressed in advance. In particular, countries in the region need to avoid future bottlenecks that could potentially undermine structural growth.

The emergence of a large middle class will deliver positive side effects. Among these is the expansion of the tax base, which should result in greater State capacity to deliver public goods, aimed at improving economic efficiency and increased opportunity. In addition, as per capita income is raised above the $10 threshold, fewer individuals require fiscal transfers to support their income. However, demands on the State do not disappear with the enlargement of the middle class. They are simply transformed. There will be a greater need to bring the middle class not only to a given level of income, but also to certain standards in terms of the provision of public goods, such as security and justice, as well as access to high-quality education and health.

Based on the Peruvian surveys, the middle class sees taxes as a redistributive policy from them to the poor and are not inclined to support them. But this may be too narrow an interpretation. Pay-for-service, such as tolls or fees for health and education, may be more acceptable to the middle class than simple taxes. At the same time, the status quo in many Latin American countries is a very low level of income taxation for the middle classes. Given their attitudes and political say, it is very unlikely that the expansion of the middle class will result in greater levels of personal income taxation. This is the main difference between Latin American tax structures and those found in the developed world.

The emerging middle class will likely increase its consumption of housing and durable goods. This effect alone should increase the capacity of the State to collect property taxes, but few countries in the region have developed a good land registry for housing, and therefore miss out on a very important source of potential revenue. A middle-income society is one where property taxation plays a greater role than it currently does in Latin America.

In light of the consumption boom that will likely be boosted by the emerging middle class, the question of whether the durable goods will be imported or domestically produced is relevant and has important implications. Many countries will opt for a productive structure based on exports of natural resource–based products and imports of technologically advanced industrial goods. Conversely, governments can design and implement an industrial policy in which the middle class is used as a leverage point for local manufacturing. Some countries may take advantage of the expansion of the middle class to promote structural change.

The region's global middle-class citizens will be exposed to global trends in information and technology and by definition will aspire to middle-class living standards in other advanced nations. This will make the region's subpar education performance more apparent and expose an inherent contradiction of a class of citizens with global middle-class purchasing power but poor educational standards. Hopefully, this contradiction will trigger greater demands for quality improvements in education in Latin American countries.

Finally, the Peruvian survey results suggest that the middle class has a high affinity for free markets and is supportive of private industry and competition. This is consistent with the negative attitude toward progressive taxation and the lack of support for top-down wealth redistribution. There is a clear primacy of growth policies and relative decline in support for State-owned enterprises and government as the owner of business. This sentiment resonating from the center of the income bracket suggests that the middle class may be optimistic about their own potential but skeptical of the role of the State. When presented with a range of national priorities, the middle class overwhelmingly chooses economic growth over the alternatives. This is positive to the extent that it is consistent with the priorities of the growth agenda. However, global middle classes in Latin America do not seem too keen on strengthening State capacity, which is essential to remove some of the constraints that limit economic growth today.

Notes

1 Chapter 9 of this volume, by Daude, Gutiérrez and Melguizo, analyzes slightly different results regarding middle-class attitudes toward fiscal policy for a larger number of countries in the region. In part, the differences between our results and theirs have something to do with different definitions of the middle class. We will return to the comparison between these results later in the chapter.
2 This definition was established following Kharas (2010).
3 PPP values were calculated by first converting Peruvian income levels into 2008 USD using the average nominal exchange rate (3.0 soles per dollar) and multiplying by the 2008 International PPP Conversion factor (1.64) obtained from the World Bank's *World Development Indicators*.

References

Aghion, P. and P. Howitt (1992) 'A model of growth through creative destruction', *Econometrica*, vol. 60, no. 2, 323–351.

Kharas, H. (2010) 'The Emerging Middle Class in Developing Countries', OECD Development Centre Working Paper no. 285 (Paris: OECD Publishing).

OECD [Organisation for Economic Co-operation and Development] (2010) *Latin American Economic Outlook 2011: How Middle-Class Is Latin America?* (Paris: OECD Publishing).

Ravallion, M. (2009) 'The Developing World's Bulging (But Vulnerable) Middle Class', *World Development*, vol. 38, no. 4, 445–54.

Schor, J. (1999) 'The New Politics of Consumption', *Boston Review*, Summer 1999.

4
Brazil's New Middle Classes: The Bright Side of the Poor[1]

Marcelo Neri

This chapter discusses the new Brazilian middle class, its definition, evolution, profile, attitudes and durability.[2] It describes the methodology used to determine economic classes and reveals that 42 million Brazilians joined the middle class since 2003 due to a combination of economic growth and increased equity. It forecasts different economic classes' paths and calculates individual income risks from longitudinal data.

The chapter is organized in four sections. The first conceptualizes the Brazilian middle class using an income-based measure. The following section uses this measure to chart these income-based classes' past performance through 2014 based on national household and longitudinal employment survey data. The third section addresses the sustainability of the new Brazilian middle class's ascension by measuring stocks of productive assets and of consumption goods. The fourth section traces a somewhat richer profile of different economic classes' actions and perceptions using consumer expenditure survey data and subjective evidence from the international Gallup World Poll. The main conclusions are presented in the end.

Conceptualizing the Middle Class

Our methodology draws upon the literature on social-welfare measurements based on household per capita income. After classifying people in income brackets (explained in the following section), perceptions and assets are incorporated into the analysis. An income-based view of the new middle class is only the beginning. Income assessments are combined with a structural approach that takes into account the roles played by human, physical and social assets. A permanent income measure is then calculated, converting stocks of assets into income flows. Comparing current versus permanent incomes allows us to gauge sustainability aspects of income distribution. The assessment of idiosyncratic earnings risks from longitudinal data also helps to assess the durability of different economic classes.

The structural approach pursued here deals with concrete relations between income flows and stocks of assets by looking at households as producers and consumers. The producer's side is based on the field of labor economics, analyzing wages, employment, but also entrepreneurship. If employers and the self-employed are workers, they are also firms that live off profit. In a sense they are capitalists, though in most cases without capital, and they live with the associated risks of being a capitalist and most likely without wealth.

Our look at households also draws upon the literature of consumption and temporal choice, which is as weak in Brazil as our family savings rates. This perspective helps to go beyond the flat cross-section portraits collected at certain moments in time in favor of visualizing the development of the course of people's lives in a cinematic way. Accordingly, we capture information regarding uncertainties, habits, altruism, capital market imperfections and myopia. If a family does not plan for the future, for example, it will reap the consequences of not doing so over the years.

Of course, flows and stocks of money may or may not bring happiness. In our studies we pair the assessments and expectations of people in relation to their lives as developed in the literature on subjective well-being, which has lately caught the attention of economists.

The Brazilian Income Distribution Parallels the World's

Brazil is a useful example to discuss an income-based middle class in a global perspective because the Brazilian income distribution is relatively close to the world income distribution. This can initially be grasped from fig. 4.1 below (adapted from Milanovic 2011). The figure compares world income distribution within selected individual countries. The poorest US vintile (one-twentieth part) have higher incomes than 60 per cent of the world population. That is, no vintile of the US income distribution touches the world median income. The lines allow us to compare the same relative position among different countries. The US is richer than Russia, which in turn is richer than China, which is richer than India. This is true for any wealth line, or conversely any poverty line, used.

72 Latin America's Emerging Middle Classes

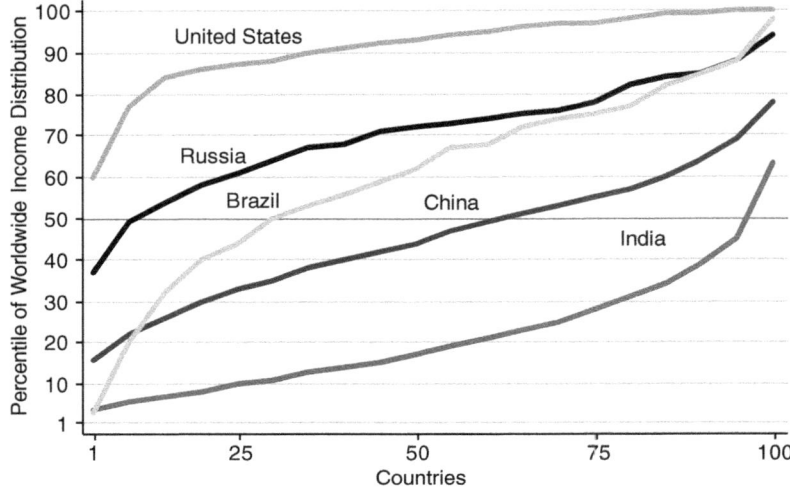

Figure 4.1 World Income Distribution, BRICs and the US.
Source: Adapted from Milanovic (2011).

But where is Brazil? Brazil is everywhere. The poorest Brazilians are as poor as the poorest in India while the richest Brazilians are not far from the wealthiest Russians. Brazilian income distribution is close to an imaginary line with a forty-five–degree slope, where world and Brazilian income distribution move hand in hand. In this sense, Brazil is a 'small world' – a country-sized replica of the global economy.

Branko Milanovic (2005, 2011) also calculates the world Gini coefficient, taking into account the differences in mean income among countries, weighted by country populations. For the purposes of that exercise, zero inequality within each country is assumed. Both worldwide income inequality between countries and Brazilian inequality, illustrated in the same figure, did not move much between 1970 and 1990. Over that period, inequality, whether Brazilian or global, ran more or less parallel to the horizontal axis.

Between countries, inequality started to fall with the growth of China, with the Gini coefficient going from 0.63 in 1990 to 0.61 in 2000. Its downward trend becomes sharper since 2000, when the Indian miracle enters the scene. China and India house more than half of the poor in the global community. Following the growth of 'Chindia' in the 2000s, the world Gini fell to 0.54 by 2009. The level of overall world inequality, which includes within-country inequality that has grown in two-thirds of the world's nations, presents a somewhat milder downward trend in this later period. Its level for the latest year is indicated by the black dot in fig. 4.2 below.

As for the Brazilian decline in inequality, it has taken place only since the 2000s. After thirty years of high inertial inequality following the sharp inequality rise of the 1960s, associated with the so-called Brazilian economic miracle, the Brazilian Gini coefficient began to fall in 2001, going from 0.60 in that year to 0.539 in 2009; in 2012, it reached a level of 0.526, slightly below its early-1960s level. To provide a sense of the changes observed during 2001–12, consider that the poorest 10 per cent in Brazil faced an income growth more than 450 per cent faster than the richest 10 per cent. These changes are quite close to the levels observed worldwide at the same time. The internal scale of distances among Brazilians is once again like a small-scale model of that observed among the different nations of the world.

The Brazilian Gini coefficient, although one of the highest in the world, is close to the global Gini of income inequality between countries. The movement of inequality in Brazil since the beginning of the 2000s is also quite close to that observed on the global scale.[3] So too,

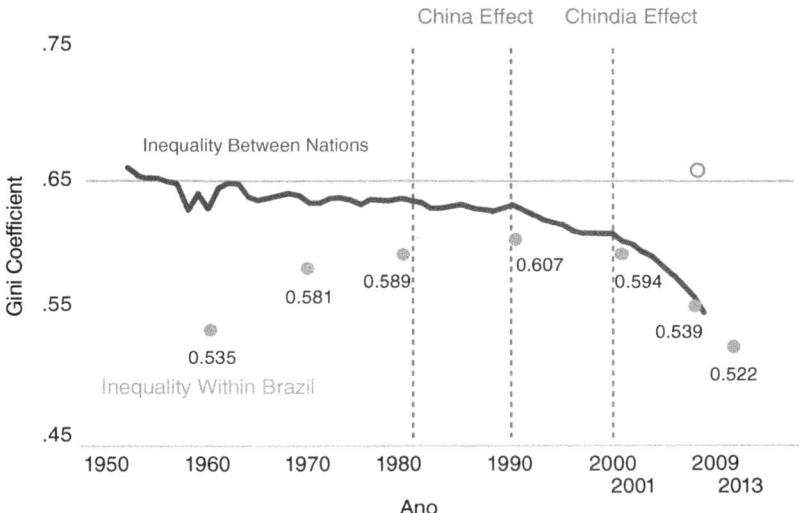

Figure 4.2 Gini Coefficients, Brazil and the World (cross-country).
Source: Adapted from Milanovic (2011) and Neri (2011).

74 *Latin America's Emerging Middle Classes*

Brazilian per capita gross domestic product (GDP) levels and trends in the 2000s mirror global trends. Brazilian GDP per capita (adjusted for purchasing power parity or PPP[4]) in 2012 was 93.7 per cent of the world average. The average GDP PPP growth rate in the 2001 to 2012 period was also reasonably close, 3.49 per cent for Brazil and 3.58 per cent for the world, according to the 2013 World Development Indicators from the World Bank.

If the starting and end points of Brazilian and worldwide inequality and levels are equivalent, Brazil is not just a representative photo, but also a movie of the world at the dawn of the new millennium. The saga of the Chinese and Indians on the way to better living conditions is similar to that of illiterate, black and Northeastern Brazilians.

As a result of the resemblance between the Brazilian and world income distributions, the definition of an income-based Brazilian middle class, or a Latin American middle class for this matter, in fact provides a model for the global middle class. The Brazilian middle class defined here has substantially lower income than the stereotypical definition of the US middle class: namely two cars, two dogs and a swimming pool.

Polarization Measures and the Definition of the Middle Class

This subsection addresses relative and absolute measures of economic classes.

From Relative Income Groups to Absolute Income Classes

Fig. 4.3 presents a simple and straightforward relative measure of economic classes by looking at the performance over time of three income groups: the bottom half (50 per cent), the top decile (10 per cent) and the group in between (the other 40 per cent).

In 1989, the historic peak of Brazilian inequality, the poorest 50 per cent earned 10.56 per cent of total income, while the richest 10 per cent earned 50.97 per cent; the intermediate group earned a little less than its 40 per cent share in the population. During the 1970s, 1980s and 1990s, Brazilian inequality remained steady: the poorest 50 per cent received around 10 per cent of income, mirroring the richest 10 per cent, who received close to 50 per cent of the aggregate income. Group shares began to change systematically only after 2001. In 2011, the share of the 40 per cent intermediate group share overtook the share of the top 10 per cent.

Indeed, Brazil's middle group (intermediate 40 per cent) is bordered on one side by 'India' (the bottom half), and on the other by 'Belgium' (top 10 per cent); for this reason, we can call this middle group 'Brazilian

Brazil's New Middle Classes: The Bright Side of the Poor 75

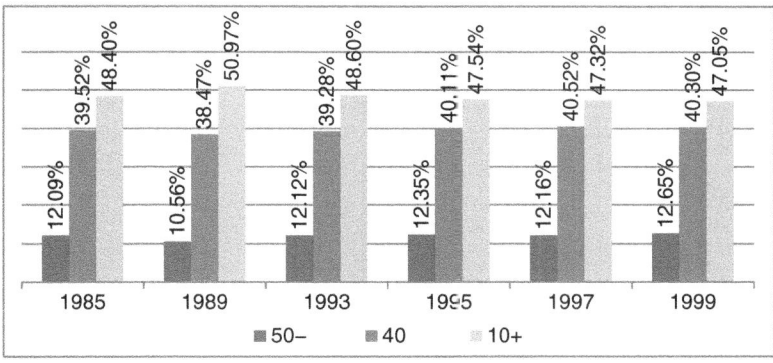

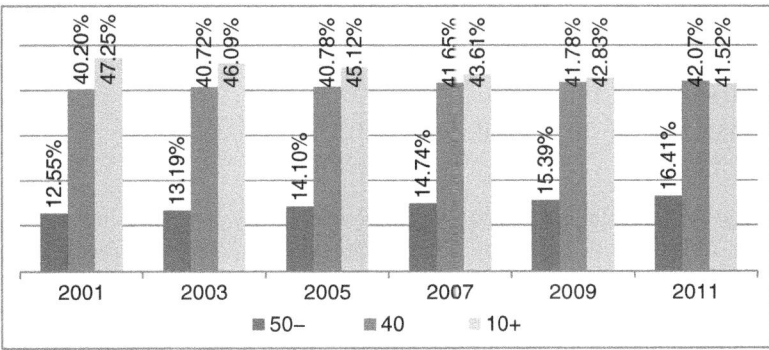

Figure 4.3 Changes in Shares of National Income, Brazil (bottom 50 per cent, mid 40 per cent and top 10 per cent).
Source: PNAD/IBGE microdata.

Belindia', inspired by the acronym created by economist Edmar Bacha. The absolute middle-class definition developed below shares many attributes with this relative definition: both start around the median income and earn on average close to the mean income of Brazilian society.

The categorization of the Brazilian relative income distribution reported above is inspired by earlier studies on Latin American inequality carried out in the second half of the 1990s, coordinated by Sam Morley. There, we also noted the high gross contribution of the top 10 per cent in Brazilian and Latin American income inequality as measured by Theil-T index decomposition.[5] The initial choice of absolute income brackets, the basis of the economic class definition used in this chapter, follow this lead. Income cutoff points were chosen to maximize

Table 4.1 How Much Income Inequality Is Explained by Economic Classes?

	Contribution between income groups in total inequality THEIL-T	
	Economic Classes CPS/FGV	Groups With Equal Sizes
PME 2002–03	76.71%	59.34%
PNAD 2003	79.71%	59.91%
PNAD 2009	74.29%	57.96%
POF 2008–09	71.40%	59.29%

Source: IBGE microdata.

the power of the chosen class stratification to explain inequality, using data from 2002–03. Table 4.1 shows that our economic class categorization (denoted CPS/FGV) has a better explanatory power, using several databases, relative to a definition based on three groups with the same initial size.

We move from a relative to an absolute measure fixing the lines in real terms for later periods. Our definition of middle-class income brackets is theoretically consistent and empirically close to that determined by the extended polarization concept proposed by Gradin and Ray (2007). The Esteban, Gradin and Ray (EGR) strategy generates, in a more general setting of polarization measures, endogenous cuts of the income distribution. The chosen cuts obtained in practice are those that maximize the criterion of 'extended polarization'. That is, they best distinguish the groups in terms of making the internal differences of these income groups as small as possible and as a consequence maximize the differences between these groups.

How does our initial approach using 2002–03 data compare to results derived from the EGR methodology?[6] The combination of our lowest-income economic classes D and E results almost perfectly in the bottom EGR stratum, corresponding to the 52.3 per cent poorest against 52.6 per cent by our criterion, a negligible difference. Second, our central economic class based on national household survey data is four percentage points smaller than the intermediate stratum produced by the EGR methodology (34.95 per cent versus 38.95 per cent). As a result, our highest-income classes A and B differ from the top EGR stratum. We call this residual class B2 to illustrate the move from class C to the EGR middle stratum.

Next, we apply EGR results within these initial classes to further divide them into finer subgroups, in addition to using other institutional parameters, including the official poverty and extreme poverty line income levels. Let us begin with the three large groups (classes AB,

C and DE). Similarly, we applied the EGR methodology of three in our class AB, resulting in classes B1 with 4.31 per cent, A2 with 2.84 per cent and A1 with 1.28 per cent. At the bottom of the EGR stratum, we subdivide classes E and D using the conventional Brazilian poverty line that is close to the highest allowed eligibility value to benefit from the Family Allowance (Bolsa Família) program. We used a similar rationalization adopting the R$70 that corresponds to the lowest reference value of the Family Allowance adopted as a national poverty line in the sphere of the Brazil Without Poverty (Brasil Sem Miséria) program applied to define the boundary between Class E2 and E1. This value corresponded in mid-2011 to the $1.25 a day PPP extreme poverty line referenced in the first of the Millennium Development Goals.

Reconciling Household and Consumer-Expenditure Survey Data

This empirical exercise used the Brazilian National Household Survey (PNAD), correcting for internal differences of cost of living and imputation of unreported (missing) income, estimating for this purpose a separate Mincer equation for each year in the data. In this way, we maintain the proportionality of the sample, keeping it comparable to the population from which it is drawn. We can therefore combine these data with actual changes in population of each class. All calculations are based on household income per capita, excluding non-members (such as domestic servants or their kin living in the household).

The PNAD household survey data is the key reference in studies on the Brazilian income distribution. A better understanding of the economic circumstances of the poor, however, requires building a bridge between the PNAD and the Household Budget Survey (POF), both undertaken by the governmental Brazilian Institute of Geography and Statistics (IBGE). POF is a less-frequent survey, more complete than the PNAD in terms of its income questionnaire, including non-monetary income. The income from real and financial assets that affects to a greater proportion the wealthier segments is also better captured by POF. By a fortunate coincidence, these misreporting problems cancel each other out in terms of income inequality, so that the POF generates levels of inequality very close to those found using PNAD data.[7] Complementarily, the Gini indices of the two surveys are equivalent, with 0.591 for POF and 0.594 for PNAD. A similar result can be found when looking at the Theil-T indexes: 0.7149 for POF and 0.7145 for PNAD. On the other hand, the actual averages of household income per capita (deflated for the same date) are very different – R$697 for POF and R$485 for PNAD – a 43 per cent difference.

Our economic classes were defined by the relative distribution in the initial period, so given the almost identical inequality, we need

Table 4.2 Economic Classes Defined by Total Household Income (R$) (calculated originally from per capita terms).

Economic Classes	Lower Limit	Upper Limit
Class E	0	1254
Class D	1254	2004
Class C	2004	8640
Class B	8640	11261
Class A	11261	0

Source: PNAD and POF/IBGE.

only to multiply the PNAD income brackets by a POF factor, since this basis proves to be a more correct source of the *level* of income. After such adjustments, family income in the middle C bracket lies between R$2,004 and R$8,640, with an average income of R$4,912 at January 2014 prices, adjusted by the local cost of living. Table 4.2 summarizes the upper and lower cut of income levels for each class. Box 4.1 provides further details about the geography of these Brazilian classes, based on data from the 2010 census.

Economic Classes: Past Performance and Forecasts

We forecast the size of the economic classes in Brazil through 2014 by extrapolating the actual data based on the 2003–09 period. During these years, major changes occurred in social welfare, the result of a combination – rare on Brazilian soil – of sustained growth and reduced inequality.

Forecasts of Economic Class Size

We project growth and inequality reduction through 2014 based on trends observed during the 2003–09 period.[8] This allows us to forecast the number of people in each economic class. The last step is to adjust each growth factor applied to include inequalities in recent income expansions within Brazilian states. For each state, people were arranged by income and then divided by fifty brackets. The initial year of reference was 2003. It was observed how each bracket evolved until 2009. The relative (not absolute) pace of change observed between 2003 and 2009 was extrapolated for the forecast period.

Past and Perspectives

Class pyramids, whose height measures population size, can be used to illustrate past and prospective aspects; these are shown for several

Brazil's New Middle Classes: The Bright Side of the Poor 79

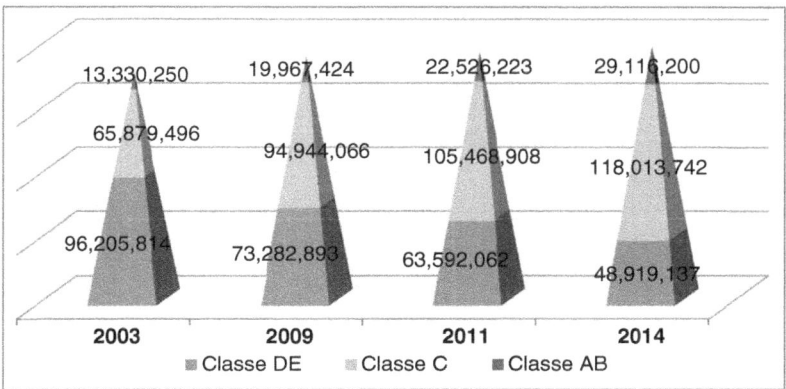

Figure 4.4 The Population Pyramid and Economic Classes 2003–14, Brazil.
Source: PNAD/IBGE microdata.

years in fig. 4.4. If we continue the trend of upward growth and downward inequality observed in each Brazilian state since 2003, we will have around 118 million people in class C by 2014 and 29.1 million in classes AB, compared with the 65.8 million and 13.3 million, respectively, in 2003. This means that over the period 2003–14, 52.1 million people will have joined class C, and another 15.7 million the AB classes. This totals 67.8 million – more than the population of the United Kingdom – new members of the upper classes of the Brazilian income distribution. This is remarkable considering the shrinking consumer markets in the developed countries as a result of the current international crisis. The population of classes A and B will grow proportionately more than class C: the cumulative growth rates are 29.3 per cent and 11.9 per cent, respectively. In the coming years we will be discussing the new A class just as we are discussing the new C class today.

From 2003 to 2014, despite population growth, the absolute population of classes D and E will decrease by 47.3 million, dropping to almost half of their initial size: Brazil in 2003 had around 50 million poor people (class E) and 96.2 million in the D and E classes, compared to 48.9 million in 2014.

Evolution of Population Shares

Our projections take into consideration changes in inequality; namely, we forecast on a differentiated basis the growth found for each sub-group

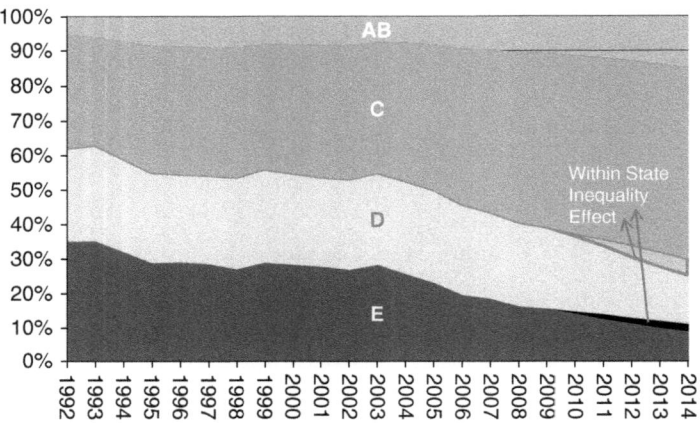

Figure 4.5 Class Composition 1992 to 2014*.

Note: Class growth forecast from 2010 to 2014; 'within-state inequality effects' defined in the text.

Source: PNAD/IBGE microdata.

of income, and regional trends for each of the twenty-seven Brazilian states. In a neutral scenario with no changes in the income distribution within states, the middle class will increase in 2014 to 56.22 per cent of the population. If, however, growth in income were to go hand in hand with the recent drop in inequality, the new middle class will reach 60.19 per cent of the population, a 19.3 per cent rise.

Fig. 4.5 illustrates the broad picture of the evolution of population shares of the various economic classes. The figure shows the composition of the economic classes from 1992 to 2014, adjusted by the changes in inequality. In the same figure we show these same forecasts accompanied by a darker area, indicating the specific effect of maintaining the level of inequality within states and taking into account the different growth rates among Brazilian states. In other words, this is a scenario of balanced state-level growth. That is, we contrast the scenario of uniform income variation within states with one that forecasts changes in inequality within states.

Fig. 4.6 presents state-level maps of the evolution of consolidated ABC classes' population shares, incorporating within-state changes in inequality. The 2014 forecast shows that in all states south of the northeast and north regions, at least three-quarters of the population is in the new middle class or above by 2014.

Brazil's New Middle Classes: The Bright Side of the Poor 81

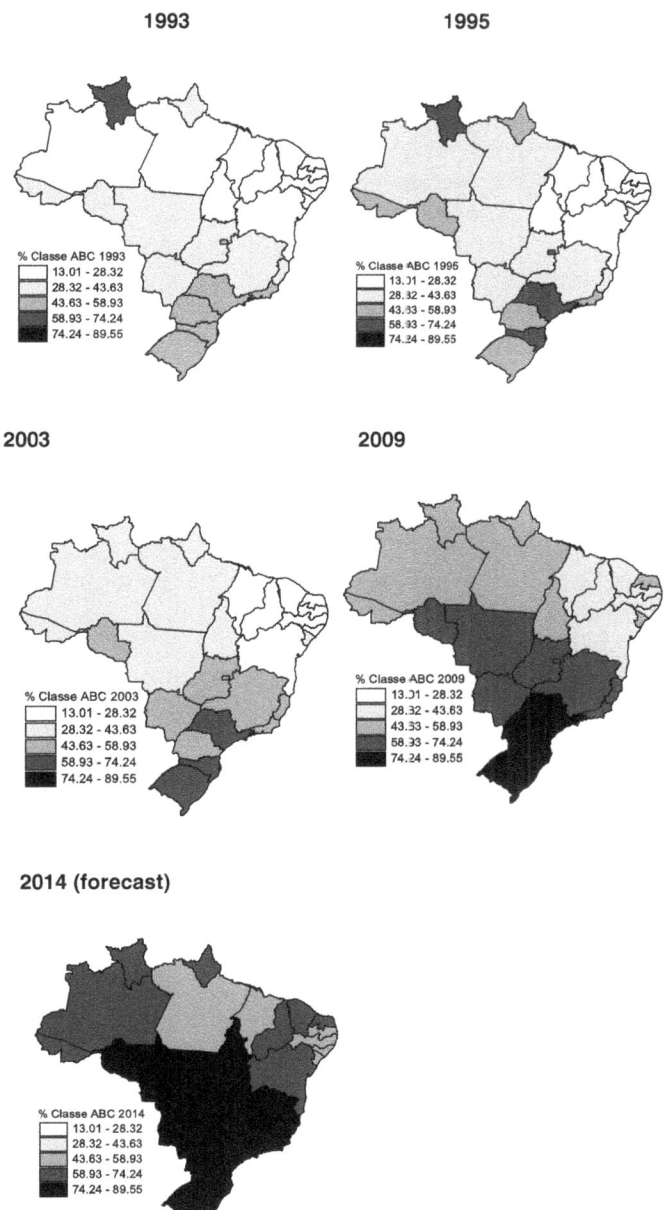

Figure 4.6 Evolution of Class ABC Shares, Brazilian States.
Source: PNAD/IBGE microdata.

Updates Using 2012 Survey Data

After ten years of rapid growth of income, especially in the bottom part of the distribution, it is expected that the aspirations of the middle class will adapt – both in Brazil and globally. At some point we must update the middle-class definition developed above. The strategy adopted is to keep real income brackets constant for long time spans and then recalculate economic classes comparing new and old classifications. The change of aspirations is a key application of subjective data (Neri, 2014).

The reapplication of the EGR methodology to the 2012 PNAD household survey data yield a middle stratum comprising 37.5 per cent of the population, starting in the 49th percentile and ending in the 87th percentile. Ten years earlier, the middle stratum started in the 53rd percentile poorest and ended in the 91st percentile. That is, at both points in time, the middle class starts close to the median income, a useful parameter together with polarization measures to assess middle-class performance. Over the 2003–12 period, the rise of per capita real median income was 78 per cent in the PNAD data,[9] or even 88 per cent if we chain the 2013 median income growth according to monthly employment survey (PME/IBGE).[10]

Updates of the pre-2009 income trends are a test of sustainability of the new middle class itself, given the presence of aggregate shocks associated with the global financial crisis and its effects on macro variables such as GDP growth. The 2012 national household survey, released three years after the calculations reported earlier in this section were made, shows changes relatively consistent with the estimates presented above. The large discrepancy between per capita GDP growth (based on national accounts data) and PNAD's per capita household income growth pointed out in Neri (2011) is increasing even further. Over the period 2003–12, while PNAD data suggest an average per capita growth of 4.7 per cent per year, the per capita GDP rose 2.7 per cent per year. The main cause of this recent divergence is the discrepancy between their respective deflators. Recalculating real GDP growth using people's cost of living would give an average GDP growth of 4.4 per cent per year instead of the 2.7 per cent for the period 2003–12.

A straightforward way to sum up the effects of changes in average income and income inequality is to refer to median income in addition to mean income. Thus, while from 2003–12 the GDP and average PNAD income grew at annual rates of 2.7 and 4.7 per cent, respectively, PNAD median income rose 6.6 per cent per year. In other words, in this period the 'median Joe' in the Brazilian income distribution experienced growth rates similar to those of the Indian economy. In 2013, according to monthly employment survey (PME) data, the median rose 4.7 per cent. This means that the median labor earnings reported by households in the PME increased by around 3.3 percentage points more than observed in the per capita GDP growth rates. In spite of low GDP growth in 2013, if this result is confirmed by the not-yet-released 2013 PNAD data, our class structure projection is relatively on track.[11]

According to PNAD data, labor income corresponds to 76 per cent of household income in national terms and 81 per cent in the six main metropolitan areas covered by the PME survey. Furthermore, social security income was boosted by successive minimum wage increases and by the expansion of the Bolsa Família program by the incorporation of the Brasil Carinhoso program gradually starting in May 2012. From August 2012 to August 2013, with inflation and population growth already deducted, the per capita real benefits paid by the National Social Security Institute (INSS) increased 4.1 per cent (MPS, 2013) and the Bolsa Família benefits increased by 13.1 per cent (Campello and Neri, 2013). In other words, growth estimates restricted to work income are somewhat conservative.

Movements across the Earnings Distribution: Quantile Regression Results

How have per capita incomes grown in the last few years? The answer to this question is important for ensuring that the middle-class definition developed in this chapter has some long-range viability. Fig. 4.7 illustrates estimates of cumulative per capita income growth, based on a quantile regression for the 2011–13 period, controlling for socio-demographic characteristics such as gender, age, race, metropolitan region, position in the household and education, in order to separate the time effects of the changes across the income distribution from those in the observed socio-demographic characteristics. The data in fig. 4.7 show that the rate of change observed between 2011 and 2013 decreases in general as we move from the bottom to the top vintiles of the income distribution. The cumulative real per capita growth rate peaks with a value of 9.46 per cent at the bottom vintile, reaching values above 9 per cent for the bottom half of the income distribution. There is a monotonic fall in these growth rates, reaching 6.19 per cent in the top vintile of the per capita earnings distribution.

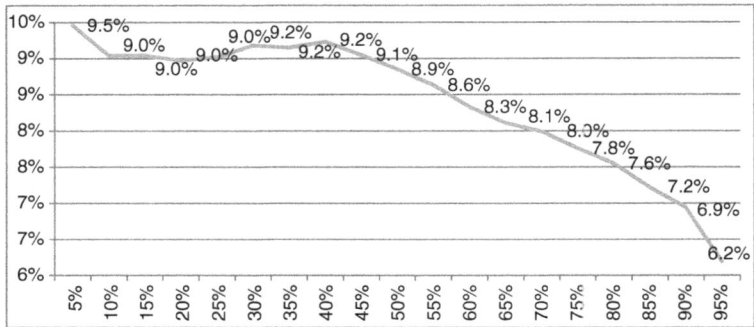

Figure 4.7 Cumulative Income Growth Rates 2011 to 2013, by Vintile.
Note: Quantile regression estimates. The horizontal axis denotes income vintiles.
Source: PME/IBGE microdata.

Family Earnings Risks

How vulnerable are people at different points in the income distribution to experiencing income downturns? The longitudinal structure of the PME, which accompanies the same families over time, permits the measurement of income risks associated with newly improved living standards. In particular, we verified the proportion of people crossing the median per capita income line across a twelve-month period.

The likelihood of crossing the income median in an upward direction, in this period, generally increased from 2002 and 2012 (fig. 4.8), while the risk of a downgrade, measured by the probability of moving downward through the median, is weakening as time goes on. Similar to the quantile regression analysis based on the PME longitudinal data underlying fig. 4.7, we examined the per capita household income analysis above and below the median, controlled by similar socio-demographic characteristics, in order to separate the time effects of these changes from those in the observed socio-demographic characteristics. The controlled results demonstrate even more strongly than the uncontrolled results that the transitions downward across the median income level reached their lowest between 2009–10, 2011–12 and 2012–13, while the upward transitions peaked during the last two-year period.

In short, considering the median as a benchmark, the probability of a drop in income has flatlined in recent years at the bottom line of the PME series, while the probability of rising has never been so high. In addition to being a period of relative stability of reported income for each individual, the passage from 2012 to 2013 has been characterized

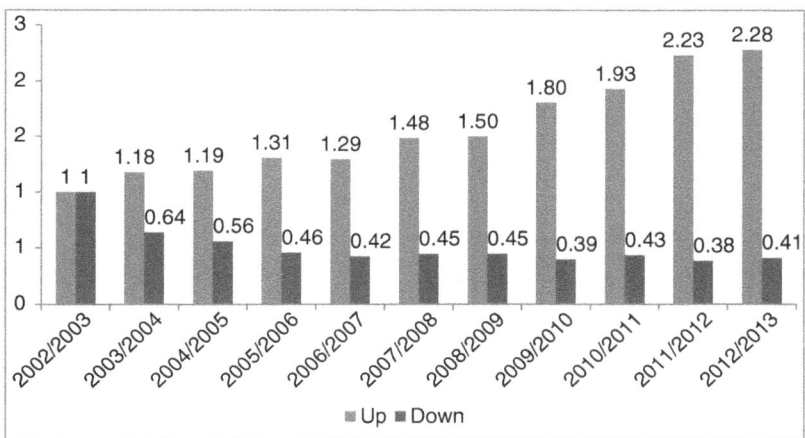

Figure 4.8 Chances of Going Up and Down across the Median – Odds Ratio (2002 = 1).
Source: PME/IBGE longitudinal microdata.

by people having the best chance of moving upward (chances 128 per cent higher than ten years before).

Sustainability of Living Conditions of the middle class

A central question posed by this book – and indeed by members of the new middle class – is to what extent this new economic class can drive economic growth by dint of its consumption potential. This in turn depends on the new middle classes' capacity to generate income in a sustainable way. We address each of these questions here using PNAD household survey data.[12]

Consumption Potential and Income-Generating Ability

Economic classes E, D, C, B and A can be described in terms of their consumption potential. The so-called 'Brazil Criterion' (*Critério Brasil*) compiles information on the number of consumer durables a household owns (TVs, radios, washing machines, refrigerators and freezers, video cassette or DVD machines), as well as the number of bathrooms, having a domestic servant, and other indicators. This criterion estimates the weights based on a classical Mincerian income equation (log of total household income) and classifies people according to point ranges. We thus create a consumption potential index that uses income metrics as a connecting thread and unit of measurement. Income is easy to interpret as a numéraire, because it is part of our daily lives. After defining the model, we quantify the indicator for each characteristic, especially for economic classes based on current income. A reader initiated in economics may relate this approach to the permanent income concept created by Milton Friedman, in 1957, in our consumption potential indicator. Since the seminal work of Robert Hall (1977), we have known that current consumption should contain all the information about future family consumption standards.

People are not intrinsically poor, rich or middle class. They find themselves in these states in different moments of their life cycle. We must test to what extent income and consumption levels will be sustainable in the future. Besides measuring consumption potential based on a large amount of information from household surveys, we propose a complementary conceptualization to measure how the Brazilian middle class evolved from the producer standpoint, using an income equation, a function of productive assets of all the family members. That allows us to observe the ability to maintain a middle-class lifestyle by generating and maintaining an income stream over time. The innovation in our methodology is to observe aspects of middle-class behavior beyond consumption, incorporating elements connected to family income generation. Those aspects include, for instance, the moment when husband or wife finds a formal job, or when a child enters university, or when the family buys a computer. We then connect those social markers to the demand for certain public social services that were at some point a near state monopoly, such as social security, education, health and home financing. We quantify the production side using income metrics from the income equation, which allows us to integrate them with the remaining consumer characteristics and income itself.

Choice of Variables

The family/household is taken to be the basic unit of analysis under the hypothesis of its members' solidarity who, on the whole, share the earnings much like the 'all for one and one for all' of Alexandre Dumas's *Three Musketeers* (this assumption therefore elides for now questions of intrahousehold inequality, which are surely important to the welfare of many individual Brazilians).

We omitted socio-demographic and spatial variables from the explanation of per capita income so that we could afterward infer the equivalent income of households with different characteristics. In terms of statistical significance and explanatory power, the number of toilets, followed by access to mobile telephones, come well before completed years of schooling of the reference person – typically the highest explanatory power in research on income inequality and poverty.[13] Obviously, we are not attempting to establish a causal relation between different variables of stock and income flow, because this is a two-way relation. In our interpretation, we identify variables more closely related to income generation. The exercise helps to gauge the structure of the model that assigns equivalent income and its counterparts in terms of consumption potential and income-generating capacity.

Consumers versus Producers: Sustainable or Not?

Translating the wealth of data about asset inventories, grouped under two perspectives –consumer and producer – the data allow us to divide Brazilians into worker ants and consumerist cicadas, using one of Lafontaine's fables as a metaphor. We showed that, in the picture, Brazilians look more like cicadas, but the movie over the last years depicts a gradual metamorphosis toward ants. The progress in the Brazilian ability to generate income increased, according to our index, 31.2 per cent from 2003 to 2009, and potential consumption increased 22.59 per cent. These data reveal that the producer's side increased 38 per cent faster than the consumer's. During the crisis year 2009, these indexes increased 3.05 per cent and 2.49 per cent, respectively.

As a complement, the survey details the importance of different income sources for the advance in social indicators. Results indicate that, despite the strong growth of income from social programs and retirement payments linked to the minimum wage, the growth of labor income is close to the significant income growth of 4.72 per cent during the 2003–09 period: average work income increased 4.61 per cent per year per Brazilian, which corresponds to 76 per cent of average Brazilian income, providing a sustainable basis for living conditions, in addition to official income transfers.[14]

Middle-Class Perceptions

To better understand the nature of the new Brazilian economy, after the considerable social ascent witnessed during the last decade, we diagnose those aspects of different economic classes' life details that will also determine their durability: in particular, who is the middle class, what do they do and what do they think, using information from the most recent Household Budget Survey (POF).[15]

88　*Latin America's Emerging Middle Classes*

Table 4.3　Individual Characteristics, Education and Work by Economic Classes.

Individual Characteristics by Economic Classes	Total Population	Economic Class					Gradient AB/E
		Class E	Class D	Class C	Classes AB	
Female	51.23%	50.24%	51.07%	51.63%	51.75%	103%
Youth (20 to 29 years)	17.30%	15.79%	17.30%	18.00%	16.98%	108%
Black	7.73%	9.31%	9.59%	6.87%	3.86%	41%
Rural	17.03%	35.99%	19.63%	10.56%	4.14%	12%
Metropolitan Core	23.16%	13.59%	19.46%	24.88%	42.55%	313%
Metropolitan Periphery	12.69%	8.45%	14.38%	13.98%	10.53%	125%
Covered by Bolsa Família	4.99%	12.66%	7.38%	1.54%	0.14%	1%
Attends Private School	6.80%	1.41%	3.07%	8.39%	19.15%	1358%
Attends Public School	24.56%	40.87%	31.26%	17.93%	6.92%	17%
Has College Education	8.76%	0.75%	1.82%	9.89%	36.19%	4825%
Social Security Coverage	37.43%	10.23%	25.58%	44.18%	56.09%	548%
Private Employee	18.64%	7.10%	14.85%	24.60%	23.09%	325%
Public Employee	5.43%	0.98%	2.81%	6.71%	14.63%	1493%
Employer	1.03%	0.08%	0.15%	1.19%	4.38%	5475%

Table 4.4 Public Services Quality and Individual Perceptions by Economic Classes.

Public Services and Standard of Living Perception by Economic Classes	Total Population	Economic Class					Gradient AB/E
		Class E	Class D	Class C	Classes AB	
Standard of Living Perceptions							
Enough family income	21.70%	5.11%	10.58%	26.93%	58.20%	1139%
Always consumes type of food wanted	31.39%	9.83%	19.22%	38.99%	69.24%	704%
Has special checking account	13.66%	0.97%	2.48%	13.18%	52.52%	5414%
Delay in debt payments	33.15%	43.25%	39.45%	29.30%	16.88%	39%
Good overall housing conditions	49.25%	33.46%	39.86%	55.36%	75.78%	226%
Public Services Coverage and Perceived Quality							
Good public transportation services	63.40%	59.81%	60.32%	64.85%	67.86%	113%
No public transportation services	25.18%	45.98%	28.55%	17.76%	10.61%	23%
Good educational services	68.96%	68.64%	66.94%	69.41%	72.76%	106%
No educational services	2.70%	2.61%	2.68%	2.70%	2.85%	109%
Good health services	43.49%	49.58%	39.10%	44.70%	56.39%	114%
No health services	4.03%	5.77%	4.58%	3.14%	3.31%	57%
Good leisure and sports services	51.33%	47.33%	45.51%	51.48%	64.92%	137%
No leisure and sports services	42.85%	56.82%	48.75%	38.20%	22.23%	39%
Good sewage services	77.48%	65.36%	71.20%	80.64%	86.11%	132%
Not covered by sewage services	36.80%	61.98%	43.77%	27.57%	12.95%	21%
Good quality of garbage collection services	86.09%	78.40%	82.61%	88.64%	92.79%	118%
No garbage collection services	13.90%	33.24%	16.08%	7.05%	2.65%	8%
Violence in the neighborhood	31.07%	28.87%	33.08%	30.76%	31.44%	109%

Source: POF/IBGE 2009 microdata.

To make a long story, provided in tables below, short: The middle-class profile in terms of youth and gender is close to that of the overall population. Its education and work profile is generally higher, in particular in terms of access to productive services provided by the private sector. The perceived quality of private aspects of life, such as perceived adequacy of income levels, quality of food consumption and housing conditions, is higher in the middle class than in the overall population. On the other hand, the middle class perceives coverage problems in public infrastructure and public services – including transport, sports and leisure, education and health – to be smaller than quality problems (the exception is sewage). Middle-class attitudes regarding the coverage and quality of publicly provided services may well be critical to the group's support for tax reform; Chapter 9 by Daude et al. provide more details on this 'social-contract' mechanism. In general, quality aspects of life within households are rated more highly than aspects found outside the home, such as public infrastructure and services.

Expectation for the Future

Thomas Friedman, in his best-seller *The World is Flat*, views the middle class as looking beyond its present living conditions toward a better position in the future. This rising social mobility can be seen as the realization of the so-called American Dream, understood as the possibility of social ascent in each country.

According to the Gallup World Poll, Brazilians in 2010 forecast their future life satisfaction in 2015 more optimistically than people in any other country. On a scale from zero to ten, the Brazilian gives an average rating of 8.6 for his expectation of life satisfaction in 2015, overcoming all 154 other countries in the sample, whose average was 6.7. This interpretation helps us understand the expression 'Brazil: the country of the future', created seventy years ago by Stefan Zweig. Before, in the expectations in relation to 2011, 2012, 2013 and 2014, Brazil already stood at the highest place on the podium. Paradoxically, perhaps, this optimism may hinder actions that would corroborate such high expectations like family savings and investment in education.

Conclusions

'Middle class' has not always had positive connotations in Brazilian social commentary. But the new middle class differs in spirit from the term 'nouveau riche', which above all discriminates on the basis of people's socioeconomic origins. The new middle class gives a positive and forward-looking meaning to someone who has achieved better living conditions and continues to move ahead. More important than where you have come from – or are – is where you plan to go. A new middle class is not defined by *having*, but by *being*, and decisions taken today with a view toward tomorrow.

To be sure, consumer credit and official social benefits are part of the Brazilian new middle-class scene, but they play supporting roles. The main role is played by the producer side, formal employment in particular. The miracle of expansion of formal employment (*carteira de trabalho*) is the most potent symbol of social ascent as a consummated act, more than just a platonic object of desire. Many subsistence entrepreneurs have been absorbed into formal jobs (Neri, 2003, 2008). The small entrepreneur with prospects of capital accumulation and growth, on the other hand, is still relegated to the backstage here, given the difficulties of bureaucracy, tax, credit and their respective values and attitudes. Contrary to legend, Brazil is not a granary of little big entrepreneurs, but of large Fordist firms, who after flourishing in a hostile Brazilian business environment, aspire to compete in their respective global segments.

There is a chronic deficiency in public policies supporting productive activities in Brazil, from professional training courses to accessible productive credit. This difficulty strongly counteracts the attitude summed up in the title of a well-known play: *Brasileiro, Profissão Esperança* ('Brazilian, profession: hope'). The key instrument to release the productive potential of our worker is education. And education, while still at a class E level, has improved in quantity, quality (58th among sixty-five countries in the OECD PISA ranking, but among the three with highest growth [OECD, 2013]) and priorities expressed by the population (rising from seventh to second in the list of the Brazilians' concerns – the SIPS survey from IPEA, where the questions from the My World survey were replicated, confirm that education is only second to health in terms of respondents' priorities). Indifference to education policies in the past placed our economic elite in the worst of worlds. A new middle class moreover looks to consume better-quality public services in the private sector, including private schools, health care and private pension funds.

Main Results

The empirical strategy of this chapter was to define an income-based middle class, to measure its level and evolution and then to combine that objective definition with a subjective approach to measure expectations and attitudes of people. This structural approach takes into

account the roles played by different assets in order to assess its sustainability. Our main results are as follows:
- We have shown a clear parallel between income distribution among Brazilians and inequality across countries, both in levels and changes that occurred in the 2000s. For our purposes, the definition of an income-based Brazilian middle class, in fact, delivers a global middle class.
- Between 2003 and 2012, 42.2 million Brazilians joined the so-called new middle class (C class) and 9.6 million joined the A and B classes.
- Using 2003–09 trends of state-level growth and inequality production, we predict that between 2011 and 2014 the C class will have risen by 12.2 million people (while the A and B classes would rise by 7.7 million).
- The new middle class will comprise 60.19 per cent of the population in 2014, substantially up from 37.5 per cent in 2003 and 55.25 per cent in 2012.
- Quantile regressions show that the rate of changes in income between 2011 and 2013 fall as we move from the bottom to the top of the income distribution. The cumulative real per capita growth rate peaks with a value of 9.46 per cent at the bottom vintile reaching values above 9 per cent for the bottom half of the income distribution, compared with just over 6 per cent in the top vintile.
- Using individual longitudinal data, the chances of an individual crossing the income median in an upward direction, in the recent period, increased 128 per cent from 2002–03 to 2012–13, while the risk of downgrade, measured by the chances of moving downward through the median, fell 59 per cent over the same period.
- The progress in Brazilians' ability to generate income increased, according to our synthetic index, 31.2 per cent from 2003 to 2009, and the consumption potential index increased 22.59 per cent. These data reveal that households' 'producer side' increased 38 per cent faster than their 'consumer side'.
- The growth of labor income was close to the significant income growth observed, providing a sustainable basis for living conditions, in addition to official income transfers.
- Middle-class survey respondents are more satisfied with economic indicators of well-being, including adequacy of income and quality of food; they are more concerned with low quality of government-provided services than with low coverage of those services.
- Finally, some authors view the middle class as looking beyond its present living conditions toward a better position in the future.

Brazilians in 2010 forecast their future life satisfaction in 2015 more optimistically than all 154 other countries analyzed.

The Brazilian belief that life will get better helped me to understand what the large databases and my field visits showed regarding the new emerging classes. More than the gold, forest and wood that gave color and name to Brazil, the greatest wealth is their reflection in Brazilians' eyes.[16]

Appendix

Marginal Contribution of Stocks to Inequality of Flows

Table 4.5 provides relevant information regarding the contribution of each variable to the household's income calculated using the microdata from the national household survey (PNAD) by the Brazilian Institute of Geography and Statistics (IBGE). It should be read not considering the magnitude of each category's coefficient, but rather the power of the categories taken together to explain the household income. Thus, when looking at the magnitude of extreme coefficients in each variable, we note for example that the equivalent income of a person who lives in a household with one bathroom, if doubled (that is, two bathrooms for four people instead of one bathroom), increases 27.5 per cent in relation to the baseline scenario. Meanwhile a person with a fixed landline and a mobile telephone at home has, ceteris paribus, an income 38.5 per cent higher than a person with none of these communication technologies at home. The 'spouse's education' variable is more significant than education of the reference person, as it refers not only to the impact of education, but to the composition of family income which is more or less diversified by virtue of more potential income earners. (The education indicator for the reference person does not have this double effect, because each household has at least one reference person.) A household with a spouse with at least partial university (twelve or more years of schooling) has a 28 per cent higher income than one with a spouse with an unknown educational level (regression basis, zero coefficient), which in turn has an income 14 per cent higher than those without a spouse.

Following the order of statistical relevance of the variable selection model, we have a variable on the 'type of family' composition where a family consisting of a couple with all children under fourteen has a per capita income around 30 per cent lower than a family with two adults and no kids. The fifth variable with highest predictive power is the one which captures the nature of the public or private social insurance of the

Table 4.5 Marginal Contribution to Income Inequality.

	Without the respective variable		
	R^2	dif R^2	dif R^2/R^2 orig per cent
All variables (R^2 original)	0.6924	-	
Telephone	0.6813	0.0111	1.60
Spouse's job position	0.6825	0.0099	1.43
Children's school attendance (7 to 14 years old)	0.6860	0.0064	0.92
Washing machine	0.6868	0.0056	0.81
Education of the head of the household	0.6870	0.0054	0.78
Type of family	0.6871	0.0053	0.77
Head's job position	0.6874	0.0050	0.72
Computer	0.6876	0.0048	0.69
Children's school attendance (0 to 6 years old)	0.6884	0.0040	0.58
Type of household (owned, financed and rented)	0.6888	0.0036	0.52
Children's school attendance (15 to 17 years old)	0.6890	0.0034	0.49
Fridge	0.6892	0.0032	0.46
Freezer	0.6896	0.0028	0.40
Spouse's education	0.6897	0.0027	0.39
Head pays social security tax	0.6898	0.0026	0.38
Head belongs to union	0.6916	0.0008	0.12
Per capita number of toilets	0.6919	0.0005	0.07
Per capita number of bedrooms	0.6920	0.0004	0.06
Per capita number of rooms	0.6921	0.0003	0.04
Sewage system	0.6921	0.0003	0.04
Radio	0.6921	0.0003	0.04
Number of members	0.6922	0.0002	0.03
Television set	0.6922	0.0002	0.03
Age when head started working	0.6923	0.0001	0.01

Source: PNAD/IBGE microdata.

household head or none of the above, that is, inactive or unemployed household heads, where the households in which the reference person pays both types of insurance has a family/household per capita income around 30 per cent higher than those where the heads are inactive or unemployed. The remaining variables may be analyzed in the same way.

We explored the contribution of each variable of stock on the variance of inequality in household per capita income. We calculated the marginal contribution of each variable on the total R^2 of the regression, taking them one by one out of the complete regression and calculating the relative difference, such as its contribution to the margin for income inequality.

Class Gradients and Perceptions: An Analysis Based on the Household Budget Survey

Since the overall population mean income is, in general, close to that of the middle C class, we compare the upper A and B classes (the top 10 per cent) and bottom E class (the 15 per cent poorest) gradients to emphasize the contrasts between the Brazilian rich and poor, using the data from the most recent household budget survey (POF).

What do they do?

Education is a luxury asset: 47.46 per cent of the adult elite have at least a full university education and 3.17 per cent have a master's or doctoral degree. Among the poor, this drops to 0.78 per cent and 0 per cent, respectively. Among those who presently attend school, 73.4 per cent of the elite attend private institutions compared to 3.33 per cent of the poor. The Index of Basic Education Development reveals that pupils' learning proficiency in private schools is 66.7 per cent higher than in public schools. Students in private schools have average learning levels similar to those observed in the OECD countries. This is not only a photograph of the Brazilian 'Belindia', but also a preview of the life to be lived on both sides of the Belindia border.

The probability of adults in class AB having a public-sector job is fully 1493 per cent higher than that of the poor, and the probability of AB-class employed people contributing to social security is 548 per cent higher. The probability of a poor person receiving the Continuing Provision Benefit (BPC), a non-contributory benefit for the poor elderly or disabled, is 489 per cent higher for the poorest than in the élite. This class gradient in the Bolsa Família Program is 9022 per cent in favor of the most vulnerable. The reverse is seen in the ownership of a special checking account, a differential of 5414 per cent in favor of class AB. The gradient in the case of the health plan and credit card possession is 4493 per cent and 102 per cent, respectively. Plastic money is the least elitist of those financial instruments.

What do they think?

Let us move on to class perceptions. Note that the poor tend to have a less restricted subjective assessment. However, as Caetano Veloso, a popular Brazilian singer says, 'each one knows the pain and pleasure of being oneself'. The elite have a probability of having their incomes

Table 4.6 Individual Characteristics, Education and Work by Economic Classes.

Individual Characteristics by Economic Classes	Total Population	Economic Class				Gradient AB/E
		Class E	Class D	Class C	Classes AB	
Female	51.23%	50.24%	51.07%	51.63%	51.75%	103%
Youth (20 to 29 years)	17.30%	15.79%	17.30%	18.00%	16.98%	108%
Black	7.73%	9.31%	9.59%	6.87%	3.86%	41%
Rural	17.03%	35.99%	19.63%	10.56%	4.14%	12%
Metropolitan Core	23.16%	13.59%	19.46%	24.88%	42.55%	313%
Metropolitan Periphery	12.69%	8.45%	14.38%	13.98%	10.53%	125%
Covered by Bolsa Família	4.99%	12.66%	7.38%	1.54%	0.14%	1%
Attends Private School	6.80%	1.41%	3.07%	8.39%	19.15%	1358%
Attends Public School	24.56%	40.87%	31.26%	17.93%	6.92%	17%
Has College Education	8.76%	0.75%	1.82%	9.89%	36.19%	4825%
Social Security Coverage	37.43%	10.23%	25.58%	44.18%	56.09%	548%
Private Employee	18.64%	7.10%	14.85%	24.60%	23.09%	325%
Public Employee	5.43%	0.98%	2.81%	6.71%	14.63%	1493%
Employer	1.03%	0.08%	0.15%	1.19%	4.38%	5475%

Source: POF/IBGE 2009 microdata.

lasting until the end of the month 1139 per cent higher than the poor. The elite's perception of having a sufficient quantity of food to eat is 302 per cent higher, while always having food that they want is 704 per cent higher. In general, the requirements associated with the perception of food quality are more biased toward the elite than food quantity.

Owning a decent home is one of the main contributors to people's quality of life. There is a 226 per cent higher probability of living in a good house in class AB compared to class E. The problem of the poor is not only that they have no access to public services, but that the quality of those services for those who do have access is worse. In the worst of all services, sanitation, the probability of someone from class AB having access to a good service is 118 per cent higher than for the poor. Even without taking into account that the poor have less coverage and/or more clandestine connections in supplying a variety of public services, the gradient of the delay in water, electricity or gas bills is 338 per cent higher among the poor. When it comes to public services subject to externalities: to subsidize or not to subsidize, that is the question.

On the matter of perceptions about different public policies, despite the disparities of effective education proficiency mentioned above, the perceived good quality gradient is only 106 per cent higher in the elite vis-à-vis the poor. Between 68 per cent and 73 per cent of these classes consider the quality of education as good. In health services, which occupy the top of the ranking of the concerns of Brazilians,[17] there are problems of coverage and in perceived quality. Despite the supposed universalization of health care in the SUS (National Health System), there is a 174 per cent higher gradient of lack of services for the poor and 142 per cent favorable difference among the elite in assessment of quality considered at least good.

Differentials in coverage and quality are significant in the assessment of collective transportation. The poor perceive a 433 per cent lower access to public transportation than the elite, but with respect to quality the elite who have access perceives at least 113 per cent better quality than that of the poor. Leisure and sports services are 256 per cent less available among the poor and 137 per cent higher in quality among the elite.

Lastly, the probability of a class AB person perceiving problems of violence in the area where they live is 109 per cent more than that of a poor person, consistent with the idea that violence is less associated with poverty and more with inequality itself.

Notes

1. Most of the results presented here derive from work done at the Center for Social Policies (CPS/FGV). I would like to thank Luisa Melo and Samanta Sacramento for their excellent assistance and Jeff Dayton-Johnson for his careful comments.
2. Refer to www.fgv.br/cps for more details; see also Souza and Lamounier (2010); Souza (2010); OECD (2010); SAE (2012); Neri (1990, 2011); and Neri et al. (2012).
3. The same holds for Internet coverage, according to the World Gallup Poll in 2010 and validated by Brazilian National Household Survey: the results were almost the same for the two surveys.
4. For information on PPP, refer to the discussion in Chapter 1.
5. See Neri and Camargo (2000). David Lam's studies make similar observations based on the relative status of income of the highest decile in Brazil vis-à-vis the rest of the distribution, as compared to the US, not a particularly egalitarian country.
6. Cruces, López Calva and Battistón (2009) apply the EGR to six Latin American countries, including Brazil. One difference between their approach and ours is that we use the relative EGR measure to calculate the brackets between classes and then keep the lines constant in real terms over time to generate absolute measures of economic classes.
7. As an illustration of this point, the Lorenz curves of the 2002–03 PNAD surveys and the 2002–03 POF survey overlap almost entirely. Barros and Neri (1995) report a similar result using POFs and PNADs from 1987–88.
8. A few measurement issues regarding historical trends deserve attention. The magnitude of the resumption of growth in the period 2003–09 depends crucially on the database used. Even after upward revisions in gross domestic product (GDP) growth in the national accounts, cumulative growth rates there are more modest compared to those observed in household survey data. This discrepancy will be addressed later in this section.
9. Over the 2003–12 period, the rise of income across deciles starts at 106.6 per cent for the poorest 10 per cent, falling monotonically as we move up in the distribution, to 26 per cent for the top 10 per cent.
10. PME data is limited in the income concepts it surveys and in the geographical coverage it provides: only labor earnings are included, and only in the six main metropolitan regions. Nevertheless, all of the major shifts in Brazilian income distribution over the past thirty years – including the booms after launching the Cruzado and Real stabilization plans, 'Lula's Real' after 2004, the effects of foreign crises and so on – were first detected in the PME data.
11. The discrepancy between GDP growth rates and household income collected by the PME, both per capita, is still occurring as of 2013: while GDP had a 2.3 per cent increase and per capita GDP had a 1.4 per cent growth, the per capita earnings income of households had an increase of 2.04 per cent in the year ending in September 2013.
12. In Neri (2011), I use an approach based on longitudinal data to directly gauge transition probabilities between economic classes. I also propose a decomposition of per capita incomes by income sources and earnings by labor-market components. These alternative approaches are not explored in this chapter.

13 The stepwise procedure selected twenty-eight variables; the fifteen most important are listed below: 1) number of toilets per capita; 2) telephone; 3) spouse's education; 4) type of family; 5) head contributes to social security; 6) washing machine; 7) bedrooms per capita; 8) head's education; 9) position in the head's job; 10) school attendance of child (seven to fourteen years); 11) school attendance of child (zero to six years); 12) computer; 13) refrigerator; 14) school attendance of teenager (fifteen to seventeen years); 15) type of home (own, lease and financing).
14 For additional information on the methodology and results, see technical appendix.
15 For additional analysis on subjective indicators, see technical appendix.
16 In relation to the colors of the Brazilian flag, this is the interpretation of playful meanings. Historically, the colors refer to the green of Don Pedro I's Royal House of Braganza and the golden color of Princess Leopoldina's Royal House of Habsburg.
17 The Brazilian Institute for Applied Economic Research (IPEA), through a household survey entitled 'Social Perception System of Indicators' (SIPS), conducted fieldwork in August 2013, replicating a series of questions from the My World survey (http://www.myworld2015.org). Looking at the priorities chosen by the Brazilian people through the SIPS, the most important was better health care (in 87.64 per cent of the answers, this was among the top six chosen priorities). See Neri and Schiavinato (2014).

References

Barros, R. P. de, M. C. Neri and R. Mendonça (1995) 'An Evaluation of the Measurement of Income and Expenditures in Brazilian Household Surveys: POF X PNAD', *Anais do Encontro da Sociedade Brasileira de Econometria* 17, 1996, 105–159.

Campello, T. and M. C. Neri, eds. (2013) *Programa Bolsa Família: 10 Anos de Inclusão e Cidadania* (Brasília: Ipea).

Cruces, G., L. F. López-Calva and D. Battistón (2011) 'Down and Out or Up and In? Polarisation-Based Measures of Middle Class in Latin America' *Working Papers* 113 (La Plata, Argentina: CEDLAS, Universidad Nacional de La Plata).

Esteban, J., C. Gradín and D. Ray (2007) 'An extension of a measure of polarization with an application to the income distribution of five OECD countries', *Journal of Economic Inequality*, vol. 5, no. 1, 1–19.

Friedman, M. (1957) *A theory of the consumption function* (Princeton, NJ: Princeton University Press).

Friedman, T. (2005) *The World Is Flat: A Brief History of the Globalized World in the 21st Century* (London: Penguin/Allen Lane).

Hall, R. (1978) *The distribution of permanent income* (New York: Halsted).

Milanovic, B. (2005) *Worlds Apart: Measuring International and Global Inequality* (Princeton, NJ: Princeton University Press).

Milanovic, B. (2011) *The Haves and the Have-Nots: A Short and Idiosyncratic History of Global Inequality* (New York: Basic Books).

Neri, M. C. (1990) *Inflação e Consumo: Modelos Teóricos Aplicados ao Imediato Pós-Cruzado* (Rio de Janeiro: BNDES).

Neri, M. C. (2003) *Cobertura Previdenciária: Diagnóstico e Propostas* (Brasília: Ministério da Previdência Social).
Neri, M. C. (2008) *Microcrédito, o mistério nordestino e o Grameen brasileiro: perfil e performance dos clientes do CrediAMIGO* (Rio de Janeiro: Fundação Getúlio Vargas).
Neri, M. C. (2011) *A Nova Classe Média: O Lado Brilhante da base da Pirâmide* (São Paulo: Editora Saraiva).
Neri, M. C. and J. M. Camargo (2000) 'Economic Reforms and Income Distribution', in S. Morley, ed., *Brazil in the 1990: An Economy in Transition* (Santiago: UN Economic Commission for Latin America and the Caribbean).
Neri, M. C., L. Carvalhães and S. Sacramento (2012) *Superação de Pobreza e Nova Classe Média no Campo* (Rio de Janeiro: Fundação Getúlio Vargas).
Neri, M. C. and F. Schiavinato, eds. (2014) *SIPS 2014: Percepções da População sobre Políticas Públicas* (Brasília: Ipea).
OECD [Organisation for Economic Co-operation and Development] (2010) *Latin American Economic Outlook 2011: How Middle-Class Is Latin America?* (Paris: OECD Publishing).
OECD [Organisation for Economic Co-operation and Development] (2013) *PISA 2012 Results in Focus: What 15-year-olds know and what they can do with what they know* (Paris: OECD Publishing).
SAE (2012) *Comissão para a Definição da Classe Média no Brasil* (Brasília: Secretaria de Assuntos Estratégicos da Presidência da República), http://www.sae.gov.br/site/?p=13425, date accessed 1 July 2014.
Souza, A. and B. Lamounier (2010) *A Classe Média Brasileira: Ambições, Valores e Projetos de Sociedade* (Rio de Janeiro: Campus/Elsevier).
Souza, J. (2010) *Os batalhadores brasileiros: nova classe média ou nova classe trabalhadora?* (Belo Horizonte: Editora UFMG).

5
Who Is the Latin American Middle Class? Relative-Income and Multidimensional Approaches

Francesca Castellani, Gwenn Parent and Jannet Zenteno Gonzales

Economic progress in Latin America over the last decade has been undeniable: solid growth rates, macroeconomic stability and fiscal discipline were detained only temporarily by the international financial crisis that began in 2008.[1] The region has made significant progress in its poverty reduction strategy, with poverty rates decreasing from 48 per cent to 29 per cent between 1990 and 2011, and extreme poverty dropping from 23 per cent to 11 per cent (ECLAC, 2013). However, income inequality, despite falling, remains high; the regional Gini coefficient is 0.48. The target groups of social programs remain vulnerable. To address these challenges successfully, a new generation of social programs needs to focus on the quality and relevance of education, protect households against risks, effectively redistribute income and at the same time promote productivity so as to ensure sustainable poverty reduction. Moreover, progress in reducing poverty must also contribute to the prosperity of a solid middle class.

Evidence suggests that the middle class tends to stimulate growth, promote political and economic stability and favor the adoption of progressive political programs. Members of the middle class, it is hypothesized, exhibit a propensity for savings, investment and entrepreneurship, and their consumption habits can be an engine of growth. As a result, a better understanding of the middle class is critical for designing policies to foster and promote their role in society.

This chapter provides a detailed statistical portrait of the Latin American middle class, with special emphasis on the economic behavior that sets middle-class Latin Americans apart from their poorer and richer compatriots. This characterization and measurement is based on household surveys of living standards throughout the region.

The Importance and Measurement of the Middle Class

The middle class is frequently considered an engine of socioeconomic development. Economic research suggests that broad-based income growth and development results from the strengthening of the middle class, as this group tends to favor greater social cohesion, provide skilled and productive labor and demand goods and services, fostering the role of the domestic market as an engine of growth (Easterly, 2001). The middle class is generally associated with higher incomes, higher levels of education, better health outcomes and greater intergenerational mobility. Therefore, understanding the nature of the middle class, and movements into and out of it, is essential for designing and implementing policies to reduce social inequalities. Solimano (2008) shows that countries with greater income inequality have a smaller middle class in relative terms, suggesting a negative relationship between them.

A solid middle class may be the cradle of entrepreneurship and, as such, encourage innovation and capital accumulation. This is the argument of Max Weber in his classic work, *The Protestant Ethic and the Spirit of Capitalism* (1905). The demand of the middle class for quality products encourages investment in production and marketing, with positive effects on income generation (Murphy, Shleifer and Vishny, 1989). But the evidence is mixed. Banerjee and Duflo (2008), looking at the contemporary developing world, do not find that the middle class exhibits greater entrepreneurial propensity than other groups. Nevertheless, in a comparative study, Kantis, Ishida and Komori (2002) find that nearly half of East Asian dynamic enterprises were founded by entrepreneurs from the lower and middle classes, while only 25 per cent were in Latin America. This is consistent with the findings of an OECD survey of Latin America (2010b) that generally demonstrates that business ownership is concentrated among the highest-income groups. The analysis of attitudes toward entrepreneurship points to no significant differences between social groups. Castellani and Lora (2013b) provide a detailed analysis of the linkages between the middle class and entrepreneurship in Latin America. Castellani and Lora (2013b) find that entrepreneurship can be a vehicle for upward social mobility, especially for the middle class, in the region.

Members of the middle class express values and exhibit qualities that might indirectly support policies that promote inclusive growth, encouraging savings and capital accumulation, as they tend to specialize in occupations that require skills and experience (Torche and López-Calva, 2011) and support values such as patience, effort and a strong work ethic (Doepke and Zilibotti, 2008). In addition, the middle class supports political stability and social cohesion (Torche and López-Calva, 2011), which in turn promotes political rights (Barro, 1999) and long-term investment (Alesina and Perotti, 1996). Careful analysis of the nature and role of the middle class is all the more important in the case of Latin America, given the region's low levels of social mobility and high levels of inequality.

Despite recent developments in the research literature, a consensus on the definition of the middle class remains elusive.[2] Though the reference to class stratification is grounded in conventional economics, it is nonetheless difficult to get away from social criteria, such as education, occupational status and consumption patterns. Income-based definitions, in turn, are either 'absolute' or 'relative'. Absolute measures assume fixed income ranges, such as per capita incomes between $2 and $13 a day, correcting for differences in purchasing power across countries. Relative measures consider the relative position in national income distributions (quintiles). Absolute thresholds may suffer from some degree of arbitrariness[3] when applied to heterogeneous levels of development. While usefully providing a common reference, absolute benchmarks might disregard country-specific features. Conversely, relative definitions might provide less homogeneous boundaries, as they are country specific. In general, absolute definitions have been applied to the evolution of the global middle class, while relative boundaries have been used for country-specific investigation. Opinion surveys constitute yet another way to identify members of the middle classes – or rather, to let them identify themselves (see Chapter 8 in this volume, by Lora and Fajardo González). Income-based definitions are objective and perception-based concepts are subjective, and both are debatable.

Among recent studies of developing economies, Ravallion (2009) includes in the middle-income class households with daily per capita income between $2 and $13 (in 2005 US dollars at purchasing power parity);[4] Banerjee and Duflo (2008) use consumption ranges between $2–10 per day (roughly $800–3,600 per year). The lower limit of $2 a day is a widely used international standard for the poverty line. While absolute measures are transparent, it might be challenging to apply them to countries with different levels of economic development. Fajardo and Lora (2011) argue that in Latin America, the perception of social class membership transcends mere financial considerations to include capabilities and personal relationships.

Kharas and Gertz (2010) focus on expenditure in the range of $10–100 per day, as do Cárdenas, Kharas and Henao (Chapter 3 in this volume). Birdsall (2010) uses a mixed definition of income from $10 per day up to the 90th percentile. More recently, Ferreira et al. (2013) propose daily income between $10 and $50 (PPP-2005 dollars), following López-Calva and Ortiz-Juárez (2011). Birdsall (2012) also uses this definition.

As one might expect, the size of the middle class varies according to the definition (relative and absolute) employed. In the case of Latin America, the literature provides estimates by countries as well as for the entire region. Cárdenas, Henao and Kharas (2011) estimate the Latin American middle class at 36 per cent of all households (with daily expenditures between $10 and $100 per person in purchasing power parity terms). Castellani and Parent (2011), using national household data, find that the Latin American middle class ranges between 35 and 50 per cent of all households, when a definition of per capita incomes between 50 per cent and 150 per cent of median income is used, and between 55 and 75 per cent of all households when the definition of $2–20 PPP per day is employed. Lora and Fajardo (2013), using survey data from the 2007 World Gallup Poll, find that size ranges between 40 and 60 per cent ($2–10 per day PPP and $2–13 per day PPP). In the countries studied by Birdsall (2012), the middle class accounts for 15 to 35 per cent of the population ($10 and $100 per person in PPP terms). According to the World Bank study by Ferreira et al. (2013), and based on household surveys, using the $10–50 PPP per day definition, the middle class in Latin America and the Caribbean represents 152 million people, or 30 per cent of the region's population.

This chapter considers several measures to estimate the size of the middle class in selected countries and focuses on a relative definition, anchored around median income,[5] to characterize it.[6] This measurement allows the idiosyncrasies of regional income distribution to be portrayed and considers any improvement as progress toward reducing inequality. In this chapter, households are considered middle class if income per adult is equivalent to between 50 and 150 per cent of the national median income, following the definition of Davis and Huston (1992). Empirical studies on poverty, particularly in high-income countries, often use the 50 per cent threshold as an internationally comparable relative poverty line.[7] The 50–150 per cent range avoids including the poorest and the richest segments in the middle class.[8] Finally, this definition varies with income inequality, unlike other definitions. Households with income per adult equivalent below the 50 per cent threshold will be identified as 'poor', and those with income above the 150 per cent ceiling will be considered 'affluent'. Calculations are based on living standards surveys (LSS) released by the national bureaus of statistics for selected years, using total income adjusted for household composition as a defining variable.[9]

The Evolution of the Middle Class in Latin America, 2000–11

This chapter considers the evolution of the size of the middle class from 2000 to 2011 in Argentina, Bolivia, Brazil, Chile, Colombia, Mexico, Peru and Uruguay. According to the definition of 50–150 per cent of median income, in 2011 around 50 per cent of Latin American households were middle class (ranging from 45 to 55 per cent in the countries studied). Between 16 and 23 per cent belonged to the lower class and around 30 per cent belong to the upper or affluent class (table 5.1). Colombia and Bolivia have the smallest middle class (45–47 per cent of households) in the region, while Argentina, Chile, Mexico and Uruguay had middle classes that exceed 50 per cent of the households.

Table 5.1 Size of the Middle Class in Latin America in or around 2011 (% of households).

	Argentina	Bolivia	Brazil	Chile	Colombia	Mexico	Peru	Uruguay
Poor	16.6	23.0	18.4	17.0	20.0	16.8	20.0	16.3
of which extremely poor	3.9	10.6	4.9	3.5	7.9	3.6	5.4	3.3
Middle class	54.5	44.6	48.6	51.4	46.1	53.4	50.7	55.4
of which lower middle class	17.9	13.7	16.5	18.2	15.4	17.5	15.4	17.7
Upper class	28.9	31.8	31.5	31.0	32.3	29.8	29.3	27.6

Note: Estimations are based on household net incomes adjusted for family composition with OECD adult equivalent scale. Data are for 2009 for Bolivia; 2010 for Colombia, Mexico and Peru; and 2012 for Argentina and Uruguay. Extreme poverty is calculated as the percentage of households earning between 0–25 per cent of median income. The lower middle class is the percentage of households between 50–75 per cent of median income. PPP conversion rates (2005 $US): IMF data.

Source: Authors' calculations based on National Household Survey and Living Standard Surveys.

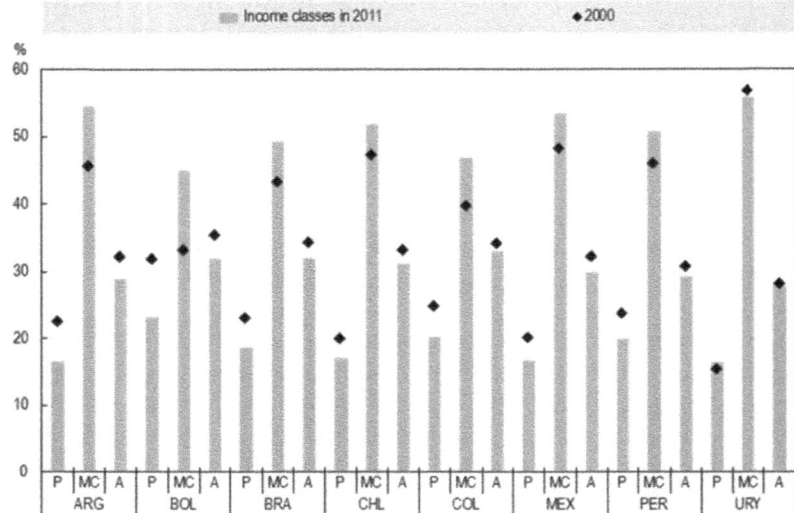

Figure 5.1 Evolution of the Size of the Middle Class, Selected Latin American Countries, 2000–11 (% of households).

Note: P: poor, MC: middle class, A: affluent. Estimations are based on household net incomes adjusted for family composition with OECD adult equivalent scale. For the earlier measure, data are for 2001 for Brazil and 2003 for Colombia. For the later measure, data are for 2009 for Bolivia; 2010 for Colombia, Mexico and Peru; and 2012 for Argentina and Uruguay.

Source: Authors' calculations based on National Household Surveys and Living Standards Surveys.

The evolution of indicators from 2000 to 2011 shows a consolidation of the middle class (fig. 5.1) across all sampled countries. On average, the middle class grew from 44 to 51 per cent of total households. Bolivia, Argentina and Colombia show the strongest consolidation over time, while no evolution is observed in Uruguay.

Compare the size of the middle class according to several alternative measures summarized earlier in the chapter, including: 1) Banerjee and Duflo (2008) (consumption levels of $2–10 PPP per day); 2) Ravallion (2009) (per capita income of $2–13 PPP per day); and 3) López-Calva, Rigolini and Torche (2011) (per capita income of $10–50 PPP per day) (table 5.2).[10] The Banerjee/Duflo measure places a majority (60 per cent) of households in the upper class, confirming the shortcomings of using these measures for middle-income countries. The López-Calva/Rigolini/Torche measure produces a middle class closer in size to ours above. However, its composition is substantially

Table 5.2 Size of the Middle Class According to Relative and Absolute Measures in Selected Latin American Countries, in or around 2000 and 2011 (% of households).

Household level		Argentina		Bolivia		Brazil		Chile		Colombia		Mexico		Peru		Uruguay	
		2000	2012	2000	2009	2001	2011	2000	2011	2003	2010	2000	2010	2000	2010	2000	2012
Median income-based (0.5 to 1.5* median income)	Poor	22.5	16.6	31.7	23.1	22.8	18.7	19.9	17.1	24.6	20.3	20.0	16.8	23.6	20.0	15.2	16.4
	MC	45.5	54.5	33.1	44.9	43.0	49.3	47.1	51.7	39.5	46.9	48.0	53.4	45.8	50.7	56.7	55.8
	Upper class	32.0	28.9	35.3	32.0	34.1	32.0	33.0	31.2	34.0	32.8	32.0	29.8	30.6	29.3	28.1	27.8
PPP-based ($2–10 per day)	Poor	2.1	0.2	22.6	6.8	4.7	2.0	1.7	0.9	10.9	4.8	1.3	0.7	6.3	0.9	0.1	0.4
	MC	35.8	5.7	42.8	33.5	48.1	27.7	28.6	18.4	46.7	36.0	35.4	27.3	49.6	27.1	13.9	9.1
	Upper class	62.2	94.1	34.6	59.7	47.2	70.3	69.7	80.6	42.4	59.2	63.3	72.0	44.1	72.0	86.0	90.5
PPP-based ($2–13 per day)	Poor	2.1	0.2	22.6	6.8	4.7	2.0	1.7	0.9	10.9	4.8	1.3	0.7	6.3	0.9	0.1	0.4
	MC	47.8	10.1	52.3	45.1	58.9	38.0	41.0	30.3	56.3	48.9	47.5	40.8	61.1	38.7	24.2	16.3
	Upper class	50.1	89.7	25.1	48.1	36.4	60.0	57.3	68.8	32.8	46.3	51.2	58.5	32.6	60.3	75.7	83.3
PPP-based ($10–50 per day)	Poor	37.8	5.9	65.4	40.3	52.8	29.7	30.3	19.4	57.6	40.8	36.7	28.0	55.9	28.0	14.0	9.5
	MC	56.0	65.9	31.4	55.1	40.5	56.4	57.5	65.7	37.3	50.7	54.7	63.9	41.5	65.3	73.8	74.0
	Upper class	6.1	28.3	3.1	4.6	6.7	13.9	12.1	14.9	5.1	8.6	8.6	8.1	2.6	6.7	12.2	16.5

Source: Authors' calculations based on National Household Survey and Living Standards Surveys.

Refer to the note accompanying table 5.1 for further details.

different: the absolute Banerjee/Duflo and Ravallion measurements assign more households in the upper class. Given the high level of income inequality in these Latin American countries, these absolute measures have limited relevance.

Who is Middle Class in Latin America and What Do They Think?

Income-based measures may be a flawed or incomplete way to characterize the middle class. Available surveys allow classes to be identified beyond income, by age, occupation and profession of the head of household and household structure. We use our median income-based definition for 2011 to highlight many of these aspects.

Gender

The majority of Latin American middle-class households (more than 60 per cent) are headed by men. By contrast, women more often than men head poor households, except in Bolivia and Mexico.

Age

Heads of households tend to be older in the middle class, except in Argentina. Adults aged forty-one to sixty-five are more likely to be heads of a middle-class household than other age groups. This might be a result of the difficulty of finding a stable job at an earlier stage of life and to the low level of pension payments, pushing many older households into poverty.

Education

Generally, middle-class heads of household have completed secondary education. In the lower class, primary education prevails, while in the upper class, university education prevails. Education is thus highly correlated with income classes.

Family Structure

Middle-class households have mostly nuclear families (parents with children). Couples without children or single heads of households prevail in the upper class, while households with single parents are more often poor. Higher-income households are associated with smaller family size. As well, couples are more likely to be middle class than single heads.

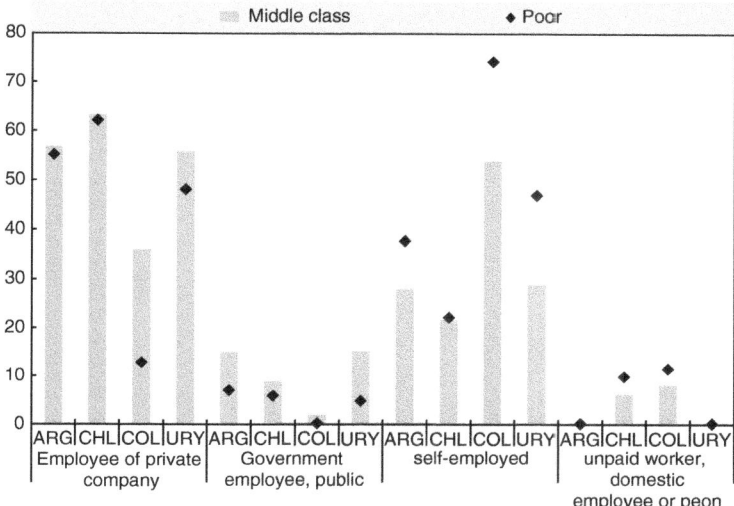

Figure 5.2 Middle Class and Type of Employment, Selected Latin American Countries, 2011.

Note: Share of employed household heads working in the sectors is indicated on the horizontal axis. Estimations are based on household net incomes adjusted for family composition with OECD adult equivalent scale. Data are for 2009 for Bolivia; 2010 for Colombia, Mexico and Peru; and 2012 for Argentina and Uruguay.

Source: Authors' calculations based on National Household Survey and Living Standard Surveys.

Employment

The percentage of self-employed persons is higher in lower-income segments (except in Chile), probably hinting at the difficulty of finding employment for lower skill levels (fig. 5.2). Chapter 6 in this volume, by Daude, de Laiglesia and Melguizo, furthermore, demonstrates that a majority of middle-class workers in the four countries they consider have informal-sector jobs; this is consistent with the information in figs 5.2 and 5.3.

Employment Sector

More than 40 per cent of middle-class household heads are employed in services, followed by trade and industry (17 per cent). In Colombia, Peru and Bolivia, around 20 per cent of the middle class are employed in agriculture.[11] With the exception of Chile, lower-class household heads are

110 *Latin America's Emerging Middle Classes*

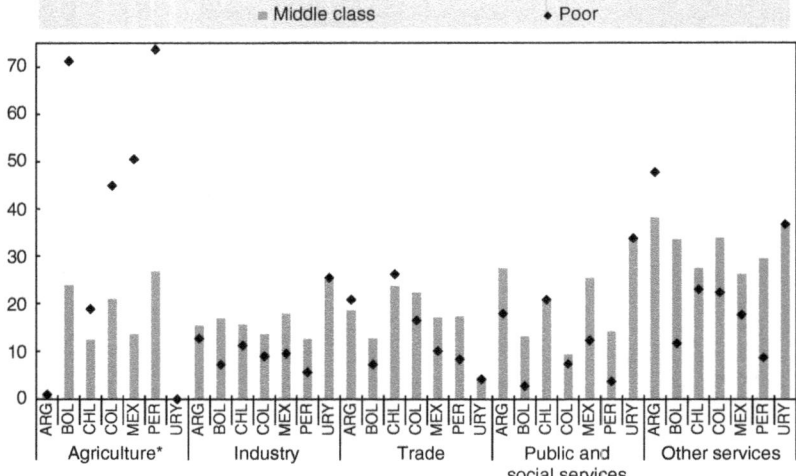

Figure 5.3 Middle Class and Activity Sector, 2011.

Note: Data are only for active occupied heads of household. Data for Argentina and Uruguay are urban. Estimations are based on household net incomes adjusted for family composition with OECD adult equivalent scale. Data are for 2009 for Bolivia; 2010 for Colombia, Mexico and Peru; and 2012 for Argentina and Uruguay.

Source: Authors' calculations based on National Household Survey and Living Standards Surveys.

primarily employed in agriculture, while higher-class household heads are employed in services (fig. 5.3).

Attitudes

The middle class may also be characterized with respect to opinions expressed by its members. For example, the evolution of perceptions in Colombia between 2003 and 2010 shows respondents have more favorable assessments of their economic situation. In 2003, 74 per cent of the middle class considered themselves to be poor, while in 2010, only 49 per cent did. In terms of access to public services (health care, quality of education), the middle class is consistently more optimistic than the poorer and richer segments of the population (table 5.3). Compare these results to Brazilian survey data on perceptions of public services included in Chapter 4 of this volume, by Neri.

Table 5.3 Perceptions of Public Services, Colombia, 2003 and 2010 (% of households).

Household Level		2003			2010		
		Poor class	Middle class	Affluent class	Poor class	Middle class	Affluent class
Considers itself poor		89.5	74.1	41.7	67.3	48.8	23.9
		Attention of public offices					
	better	12.0	15.2	21.6	15.6	18.2	20.6
	equal	28.6	34.7	37.3	52.0	53.2	50.8
	worse	27.2	26.0	23.3	13.8	13.9	16.1
		Security and timely reaction of the police					
	better	26.6	31.7	39.8	25.4	26.3	28.8
	equal	31.3	34.2	31.5	47.0	44.9	39.5
	worse	20.5	21.2	19.1	17.8	22.5	27.2
		Social security and health care					
	better	31.7	35.7	32.9	27.3	29.5	25.1
	equal	33.8	34.6	34.2	46.2	46.1	39.8
	worse	22.0	22.0	27.1	21.3	20.3	31.5
		Public education					
	better	36.6	37.8	31.1	35.3	38.6	31.8
	equal	30.5	30.9	26.0	42.1	40.2	35.1
	worse	13.0	15.1	19.7	8.1	9.2	14.6
		Urban road infrastructure					
	better	31.4	42.9	50.6	22.7	30.5	32.9
	equal	33.8	29.5	24.1	41.1	38.1	28.3
	worse	15.6	18.2	21.0	24.8	25.9	36.5
		Public transportation					
	better	34.8	47.6	54.3	27.6	31.9	33.8
	equal	38.3	32.8	29.3	48.7	45.8	39.1
	worse	14.8	12.9	10.7	16.3	17.8	22.1

Note: Replies of 'do not know' are not included.
Source: Authors' calculations based on LSS 2003 and 2010.

Determinants of belonging to an income class

Clearly, belonging to the middle class is the result of multiple variables. Therefore the statistical analysis of middle-class membership is ideally multivariate. Accordingly, this section presents multinomial probit estimations based on the social class variable (income level) in order to identify, more systematically than the bivariate comparisons of the previous section, which characteristics distinguish income classes in Latin American societies. Like other statistical models, a probit model estimates the contribution of various household characteristics to its situation in the income distribution. The multinomial probit model is appropriate for categorical (that is, not continuous) dependent variables like social class, which takes one of three values: poor, middle class and affluent. In all cases, the estimated parameters reflect the effect of a given characteristic – being a member of an ethnic minority, for example – relative to the so-called reference population, defined as: male household head, forty-one to sixty-four years old, with only primary education, single, belonging to the majority ethnic group, employed in the service sector, not self-employed, living outside the capital region. The Appendix presents complete details on the empirical model used for these estimations and table 5.4 presents empirical results.

Female-headed households are less likely to be affluent. All other things being equal, if the household head is female, the household is more likely to be in the lower income classes: in 2010, being a female household head increased the household's likelihood of being poor by five to six percentage points (in comparison with the middle class and affluent) except in Bolivia and Peru, and the likelihood of being middle class increased by four to nine percentage points. Female heads are therefore less likely to be affluent (by nine to eleven percentage points).

Age has a significant positive effect on income classes. Younger household heads are more likely to be poor or to belong to the middle class; while the older they are, the more likely they are to be affluent. The likelihood of being poor decreases with age. Being less than thirty years old increases the chances of being poor by five to fifteen percentage points compared to the reference population (forty-one to sixty-four years old).

The household head's level of education – whether secondary or tertiary – has a strong positive effect on income classes in comparison with primary-level education only. As expected, the effect of secondary or tertiary education is greater on the chances to be affluent than middle class or poor. Families whose household heads achieved secondary education are ten percentage points and eight percentage points less likely to be poor and middle class, respectively, on average, and are more than eighteen percentage points more likely to be affluent. This confirms that higher levels of education are associated with higher incomes, controlling for other factors. Tertiary education increases the chance of being middle class by twenty-five to forty-six percentage points, depending on the country, in comparison to household heads with primary education.

Being part of a couple increases the chances of being middle class (by three to six percentage points). Belonging to an ethnic minority group, meanwhile, increases the chances of being poor (four to eight percentage points) and reduces the probability of being affluent between three and eleven percentage points, depending on the country. Living in the capital city increases the chances of being affluent in all the countries studied except Bolivia.

Working in agriculture has a significant and negative impact on income class. It enhances the chances of being poor by twelve to thirty percentage points and decreases the chances of being middle class by five to twelve percentage points, except in Chile,[12] where agriculture does not seem to be an impediment to becoming middle class. Working in industry or trade sectors increases the chances of being middle class in Chile and Mexico. Unemployment and being out of the labor force are strongly linked to poverty.

Moreover, being self-employed is generally associated with poverty. It increases the chances of being poor by seven to nineteen percentage points, while decreasing the chances of being middle class. Chile has a very unusual pattern, as self-employment leads to affluence (an increase of eighteen percentage points).

The Multidimensional Middle Class, as Illustrated by the Case of Colombia

This section discusses the relationship between the Multidimensional Poverty Index (MPI) developed by the Colombian National Planning Department (DNP, 2011) and different income classes used throughout this chapter. The MPI, applied in Colombia, measures multiple deprivations in key aspects of human development (fig. 5.4). The Appendix explains the definitions and measurements of the Colombian MPI in greater detail. According to the MPI, a household is in multidimensional poverty if it experiences deprivation in at least five of the fifteen dimensions. Based on this measurement, in 1997, 60.5 per cent of Colombians lived in multidimensional poverty; this figure had decreased to 30.7 per cent by 2010 (table 5.5).

The MPI assesses social and health-related aspects of poverty in five dimensions: household education conditions, childhood and youth conditions, employment, health and access to household utilities and living conditions. In the case of illiteracy, 36.5 per cent of households considered multidimensionally poor in 1997 had at least one person fifteen years and over who could not read and write (table 5.6). In 2010,

Table 5.4 Determinants of Middle-Class Status: Multinomial Probit Estimations around 2010.

Variables	Argentina, 2010 P	MC	A	Bolivia, 2009 P	MC	A	Chile, 2009 P	MC
Male	Ref.	Ref.	Ref.	Ref.	Ref.	Ref.	Ref.	Ref.
Female	0.060*** (0.008)	0.033*** (0.010)	−0.093*** (0.009)	−0.021 (0.021)	0.096*** (0.028)	−0.075*** (0.028)	0.047*** (0.007)	0.040*** (0.010)
Up to 30 years old	0.134*** (0.013)	0.016 (0.013)	−0.150*** (0.009)	0.011 (0.024)	0.108*** (0.028)	−0.119*** (0.025)	0.053*** (0.010)	0.038*** (0.014)
31–40 years old	0.102*** (0.010)	−0.010 (0.011)	−0.092*** (0.009)	0.003 (0.021)	0.085*** (0.026)	−0.088*** (0.023)	0.037*** (0.007)	0.039*** (0.010)
41–65 years old	Ref.	Ref.	Ref.	Ref.	Ref.	Ref.	Ref.	Ref.
More than 65 years old	−0.111*** (0.006)	0.037*** (0.013)	0.074*** (0.014)	−0.056*** (0.020)	−0.001 (0.035)	0.058 (0.035)	−0.077*** (0.004)	−0.027** (0.013)
Primary education	Ref.	Ref.	Ref.	Ref.	Ref.	Ref.	Ref.	Ref.
Secondary education	−0.094*** (0.006)	−0.062*** (0.010)	0.156*** (0.010)	−0.090*** (0.016)	−0.039 (0.026)	0.129*** (0.026)	−0.096*** (0.004)	−0.120*** (0.009)
Technical education or university	−0.196*** (0.005)	−0.243*** (0.011)	0.440*** (0.010)	−0.144*** (0.018)	−0.198*** (0.028)	0.342*** (0.028)	−0.149*** (0.004)	−0.466*** (0.010)
Single	Ref.	Ref.	Ref.	Ref.	Ref.	Ref.	Ref.	Ref.
Couple	−0.041*** (0.008)	0.024** (0.010)	0.017* (0.010)	0.031 (0.021)	0.064** (0.028)	−0.095*** (0.030)	−0.029*** (0.006)	0.011 (0.010)
Majority group				Ref.	Ref.	Ref.	Ref.	Ref.
Ethnic group	N.A.	N.A.	N.A.	0.076*** (0.016)	0.040* (0.021)	−0.116*** (0.020)	0.048*** (0.008)	−0.015 (0.014)
Other provinces/regions	Ref.	Ref.	Ref.	Ref.	Ref.	Ref.	Ref.	Ref.
Capital	−0.053*** (0.005)	−0.021*** (0.007)	0.074*** (0.007)	0.103*** (0.020)	0.033 (0.022)	−0.135*** (0.020)	−0.031*** (0.005)	−0.039*** (0.008)
Number of other occupied household members	−0.065*** (0.004)	−0.002 (0.005)	0.066*** (0.005)	−0.049*** (0.009)	−0.012 (0.010)	0.061*** (0.010)	−0.136*** (0.004)	0.005 (0.005)
Number of other unemployed household members	0.094*** (0.008)	0.060*** (0.015)	−0.154*** (0.017)	0.005 (0.024)	0.065** (0.031)	−0.070** (0.030)	0.081*** (0.005)	0.050*** (0.010)

Who Is the Latin American Middle Class? 115

			Colombia, 2010			Mexico, 2010			Peru, 2010
A	P	MC	A	P	MC	A	P	MC	A
Ref.	Ref.	Ref.	Ref.	Ref.	Ref.	Ref.	Ref.	Ref.	Ref.
−0.087***	0.060***	0.054***	−0.114***	0.044***	0.006	−0.050***	0.010	0.037**	−0.047***
(0.011)	(0.012)	(0.016)	(0.015)	(0.010)	(0.014)	(0.013)	(0.010)	(0.015)	(0.014)
−0.092***	0.054***	0.109***	−0.163***	0.157***	0.029**	−0.186***	0.070***	0.046***	−0.116***
(0.013)	(0.015)	(0.017)	(0.014)	(0.014)	(0.014)	(0.009)	(0.015)	(0.017)	(0.014)
−0.076***	0.023**	0.110***	−0.133***	0.097***	0.054***	−0.151***	0.058***	0.034***	−0.093***
(0.010)	(0.011)	(0.015)	(0.014)	(0.010)	(0.011)	(0.009)	(0.010)	(0.012)	(0.011)
Ref.	Ref.	Ref.	Ref.	Ref.	Ref.	Ref.	Ref.	Ref.	Ref.
0.104***	−0.040***	−0.054***	0.094***	−0.026***	−0.033**	0.059***	−0.031***	−0.062***	0.093***
(0.015)	(0.011)	(0.020)	(0.021)	(0.008)	(0.014)	(0.014)	(0.008)	(0.015)	(0.016)
Ref.	Ref.	Ref.	Ref.	Ref.	Ref.	Ref.	Ref.	Ref.	Ref.
0.216***	−0.128***	−0.075***	0.203***	−0.106***	−0.119***	0.225***	−0.086***	−0.076***	0.162***
(0.010)	(0.008)	(0.014)	(0.015)	(0.005)	(0.012)	(0.012)	(0.006)	(0.013)	(0.013)
0.615***	−0.181***	−0.377***	0.559***	−0.169***	−0.357***	0.526***	−0.155***	−0.271***	0.427***
(0.010)	(0.007)	(0.016)	(0.016)	(0.005)	(0.011)	(0.011)	(0.006)	(0.015)	(0.015)
Ref.	Ref.	Ref.	Ref.	Ref.	Ref.	Ref.	Ref.	Ref.	Ref.
0.018*	−0.016	0.034**	−0.017	0.023***	0.046***	−0.069***	0.014	0.033**	−0.047***
(0.011)	(0.011)	(0.016)	(0.016)	(0.008)	(0.014)	(0.013)	(0.009)	(0.014)	(0.015)
Ref.	Ref.	Ref.	Ref.	Ref.	Ref.	Ref.	Ref.	Ref.	Ref.
−0.033**	0.041***	−0.029*	−0.013	0.084***	−0.014	−0.071***	0.068***	0.011	−0.079***
(0.015)	(0.012)	(0.017)	(0.018)	(0.007)	(0.010)	(0.009)	(0.007)	(0.010)	(0.009)
Ref.	Ref.	Ref.	Ref.	Ref.	Ref.	Ref.	Ref.	Ref.	Ref.
0.070***	−0.097***	−0.046***	0.143***	−0.045***	0.012	0.034***	−0.113***	−0.081***	0.193***
(0.009)	(0.011)	(0.018)	(0.018)	(0.006)	(0.009)	(0.009)	(0.008)	(0.012)	(0.012)
0.130***	−0.092***	−0.001	0.093***	−0.044***	0.002	0.042***	−0.036***	−0.005	0.041***
(0.005)	(0.005)	(0.007)	(0.007)	(0.003)	(0.005)	(0.005)	(0.003)	(0.004)	(0.004)
−0.131***	0.057***	0.035*	−0.092***	0.059***	0.035**	−0.093***	0.023***	0.051***	−0.074***
(0.011)	(0.012)	(0.019)	(0.020)	(0.010)	(0.016)	(0.015)	(0.006)	(0.009)	(0.009)

Table 5.4 (Continued)

Variables	Argentina, 2010			Bolivia, 2009			Chile, 2009	
	P	MC	A	P	MC	A	P	MC
Number of other inactive household members	0.083*** (0.003)	0.068*** (0.005)	−0.150*** (0.006)	0.024** (0.010)	0.046*** (0.013)	−0.070*** (0.012)	0.048*** (0.002)	0.046*** (0.004)
Active occupied, agriculture	0.122*** (0.034)	−0.096** (0.039)	−0.026 (0.037)	0.365*** (0.029)	−0.121*** (0.030)	−0.244*** (0.022)	0.068*** (0.009)	0.048*** (0.011)
Active occupied, industry	−0.016 (0.012)	0.020 (0.015)	−0.004 (0.013)	0.039 (0.031)	−0.007 (0.034)	−0.032 (0.030)	0.013 (0.010)	0.067*** (0.014)
Active occupied, trade	0.085*** (0.013)	0.023 (0.016)	−0.107*** (0.013)	0.014 (0.031)	−0.072** (0.035)	0.059* (0.035)	0.002 (0.009)	0.048*** (0.013)
Active occupied, public and social services	0.022** (0.010)	−0.029** (0.012)	0.006 (0.011)	−0.005 (0.036)	−0.012 (0.037)	0.018 (0.033)	0.015* (0.008)	0.028** (0.012)
Active occupied, other services	Ref.	Ref.	Ref.	Ref.	Ref.	Ref.	Ref.	Ref.
Active unemployed	0.277*** (0.027)	−0.149*** (0.025)	−0.128*** (0.020)	0.475*** (0.067)	−0.189*** (0.065)	−0.286*** (0.016)	0.450*** (0.021)	−0.194*** (0.021)
Inactive	0.176*** (0.012)	0.013 (0.013)	−0.189*** (0.010)	0.330*** (0.048)	−0.142*** (0.043)	−0.188*** (0.027)	0.220*** (0.012)	−0.006 (0.013)
Not self–employed	Ref.	Ref.	Ref.	Ref.	Ref.	Ref.	Ref.	Ref.
Self–employed	0.126*** (0.011)	−0.017 (0.012)	−0.110*** (0.009)	0.193*** (0.020)	−0.047** (0.024)	−0.146*** (0.021)	−0.040*** (0.005)	−0.147*** (0.010)
Observations	43,609	43,609	43,609	4,006	4,006	4,006	70,702	70,702

Standard errors in parentheses
***p < 0.01, **p < 0.05, *p < 0.1

Note: Marginal effects are presented, in comparison with the reference population: Male, forty-one to sixty-four years old, primary education, single, belonging to the majority ethnic group, active employee the service sector, not self-employed, living outside the capital region.
Standard errors in parenthesis
*significant at 10%;
**significant at 5%;
***significant at 1%.

Source: Authors' calculations based on household surveys.

	Colombia, 2010			Mexico, 2010			Peru, 2010		
A	P	MC	A	P	MC	A	P	MC	A
-0.094***	0.029***	0.086***	-0.115***	0.045***	0.045***	-0.090***	0.024***	0.023***	0.046***
(0.005)	(0.005)	(0.008)	(0.008)	(0.003)	(0.005)	(0.005)	(0.005)	(0.007)	(0.007)
-0.117***	0.203***	-0.050***	-0.154***	0.233***	-0.102***	-0.131***	0.288***	-0.119***	-0.169***
(0.010)	(0.017)	(0.018)	(0.016)	(0.016)	(0.017)	(0.016)	(0.015)	(0.015)	(0.012)
-0.080***	0.009	-0.022	0.013	-0.020**	0.059***	-0.038***	0.058***	-0.036*	-0.022
(0.013)	(0.018)	(0.022)	(0.022)	(0.010)	(0.016)	(0.015)	(0.017)	(0.019)	(0.016)
-0.050***	-0.011	-0.013	0.024	-0.022**	0.040***	-0.013	0.031**	-0.014	-0.017
(0.012)	(0.015)	(0.020)	(0.020)	(0.010)	(0.015)	(0.014)	(0.015)	(0.017)	(0.016)
-0.043***	0.013	-0.106***	0.093***	-0.033***	-0.005	0.038***	0.046**	-0.019	-0.027*
(0.011)	(0.020)	(0.023)	(0.024)	(0.009)	(0.014)	(0.013)	(0.019)	(0.019)	(0.015)
Ref.	Ref.	Ref.	Ref.	Ref.	Ref.	Ref.	Ref.	Ref.	Ref.
-0.256***	0.305***	-0.184***	-0.121***	0.246***	-0.089***	-0.158***	0.302***	-0.145***	-0.157***
(0.010)	(0.031)	(0.028)	(0.022)	(0.030)	(0.029)	(0.019)	(0.029)	(0.027)	(0.015)
-0.213***	0.272***	-0.111***	-0.161***	0.045***	-0.058***	0.013	0.138***	-0.095***	-0.043**
(0.012)	(0.023)	(0.022)	(0.018)	(0.013)	(0.016)	(0.015)	(0.024)	(0.023)	(0.019)
Ref.	Ref.	Ref.	Ref.	Ref.	Ref.	Ref.	Ref.	Ref.	Ref.
0.187***	0.170***	0.003	-0.173***	0.075***	-0.068***	-0.007	0.144***	-0.028**	-0.116***
(0.011)	(0.011)	(0.014)	(0.013)	(0.008)	(0.011)	(0.011)	(0.008)	(0.011)	(0.011)
70,702	14,531	14,531	14,531	27,652	27,652	27,652	21,495	21,495	21,495

118 *Latin America's Emerging Middle Classes*

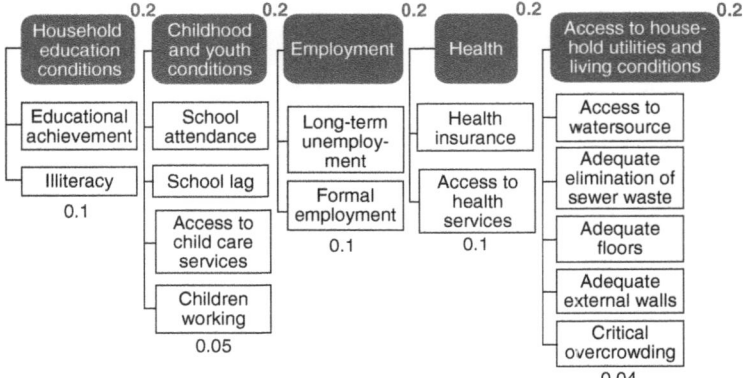

Figure 5.4 Dimensions and Variables of Multidimensional Poverty Index (MPI).
Note: Numbers show the weight given to each dimension.
Source: DNP (2011).

Table 5.5 Multidimensional Poverty Rates for Different Numbers of Deprivations in Colombia (%).

Number of deprivations	Percentage of poor households				1997–2010 (percentage point change)
	1997	2003	2008	2010	
4	71.6	62.5	49.1	45.7	25.9
5	60.5	49.3	35	30.7	29.8
6	44.7	34.5	21.7	17.7	27.0

Source: Authors' calculations based on DNP (2011).

this figure increased to 44.4 per cent. Among non-multidimensionally poor households, only 1.9 per cent had this deprivation in 1997; this figure increased to 3.5 per cent in 2010. In the case of school attendance, in 2010, 20.8 per cent of poor households had at least one child between six and sixteen years who was not attending an educational institution. In non-poor households, the figure is 1 per cent.

Regarding child labor, 25 per cent of poor families had at least one child working in 2010, compared to only 3.1 per cent among non-poor families. Differences in living conditions between the two groups are noticeable: 27.3 per cent of poor households lacked public water system, compared to 6.4 per cent among non-poor households. Illiteracy and school lag[13] become more important over time to the poor.

Table 5.6 Deprivations of Multidimensionally Poor and Non-poor Families in Colombia (% of households).

Deprivations	Multidimensionally poor				Non-multidimensionally poor			
	1997	2003	2008	2010	1997	2003	2008	2010
Educational achievement	94.4	93.3	95.8	94.0	40.1	38.5	44.9	43.0
Illiteracy	36.5	36.8	42.9	44.4	1.9	1.9	3.7	3.5
School attendance	23.7	18.9	20.5	20.8	1.2	1.4	1.3	1.0
School lag	69.3	63.9	71.4	72.8	31.9	22.9	31	35.6
Access to child care services	47.5	43.7	26.6	24.6	18.5	17.1	9.6	10.4
Children working	24.6	25.0	25.8	25.0	4.3	4.6	3.9	3.1
Long-term unemployment	19.2	12.6	10.2	10.5	7.6	7.2	4.8	4.9
Formal employment	98.2	98.6	98.9	99.1	70.1	76.7	75.5	76.7
Health insurance	86.0	82.3	52.8	47.5	36.7	31.2	14.2	14.1
Access to health services	22.4	20.9	23.6	17.2	4.1	4.4	4.5	4.1
Access to water source	22.8	23.1	29.9	27.3	3.0	3.2	6.3	6.4
Adequate elimination of sewer waste	31.7	31.9	31.8	29.1	7.1	6.7	7.0	6.4
Adequate floors	16.1	17.0	23.0	20.6	0.8	1.8	1.8	2.0
Adequate external walls	4.4	5.3	7.8	7.6	1.0	0.8	1.1	1.3
Critical overcrowding	42.8	40.4	39.8	38.1	13.4	13.9	12.7	13.1

Source: Authors' calculations based on DNP (2011).

For the other variables, the differences between the poor and non-poor are not so marked. For example, regarding the rate of formal employment, both the poor and the non-poor have high levels of informality, and no significant changes occurred between 1997 and 2010.

Inspired by Colombia's MPI, we consider the middle class – defined, as earlier in this chapter, as households with per capita incomes between 50 per cent and 150 per cent of the national median – in the light of these additional dimensions of welfare. A significant overlap of middle-class income with multidimensional poverty could be taken as evidence of the vulnerability of the Colombian (and by extension, Latin American) middle class: just being 'in the middle' of the income distribution does not protect a household from the difficulties associated with, for example, informal-sector jobs.

Not surprisingly, income-poor households are most likely to be poor in other dimensions (fig. 5.5). Eighty-two per cent of poor households (based on income alone) were multidimensionally poor in 1997, in the sense that they experienced deprivation in at least five of the fifteen dimensions. This figure decreased to 46 per cent in 2010.

Households can be considered middle class with respect to income, but at the same time suffer from other types of deprivations (in such areas as education, access to health and informality) and therefore be simultaneously considered multidimensionally poor. As it happens, the percentage of middle-class families with some aspects of multidimensional

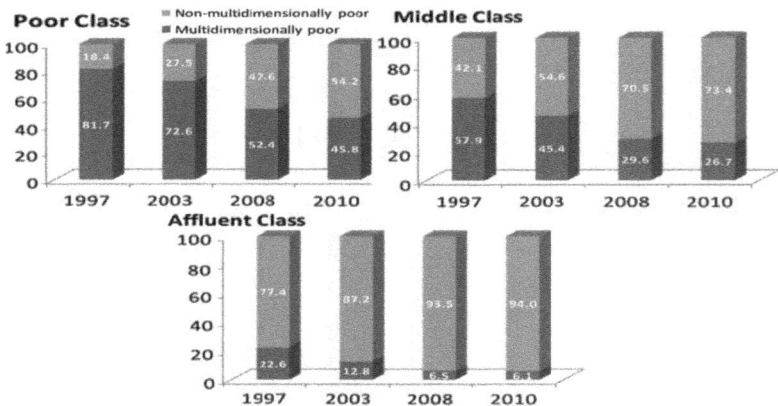

Figure 5.5 Multidimensional Poverty Index and Income Classes in Colombia (% of households).

Source: Authors' calculations based on DNP (2011) and LSS 1997, 2003, 2008 and 2010.

poverty has been declining. In 1997, among middle-class families, 58 per cent were in multidimensional poverty, a proportion that had fallen to 27 per cent in 2010 (fig. 5.5). These results show that in recent years, the Colombian middle class has begun to emerge from multidimensional poverty. This improvement in well-being among middle-class households suggests that our relative-income–based measure is a meaningful one for identifying this stratum.

In what ways are middle-class households most like the poor? The main deprivations afflicting the middle class are lack of formal employment, low educational achievement, a high rate of illiteracy for those over fifteen years old, school lag for the population from seven to seventeen and lack of health insurance (fig. 5.6). Between 1997 and 2010, the most significant advances in terms of reducing deprivations occurred in the area of health insurance: while in 1997, 67 per cent of middle-class families lacked health insurance, this figure had dropped to 24 per cent by 2010. Also, there have been significant improvements in early childhood care, health care access and school attendance.

The main differences in deprivation among poor and middle-class households are illiteracy, school attendance, child labor, health care, access to water source and adequate floors. Still the middle class (by our relative income definition) suffers deprivations in several dimensions

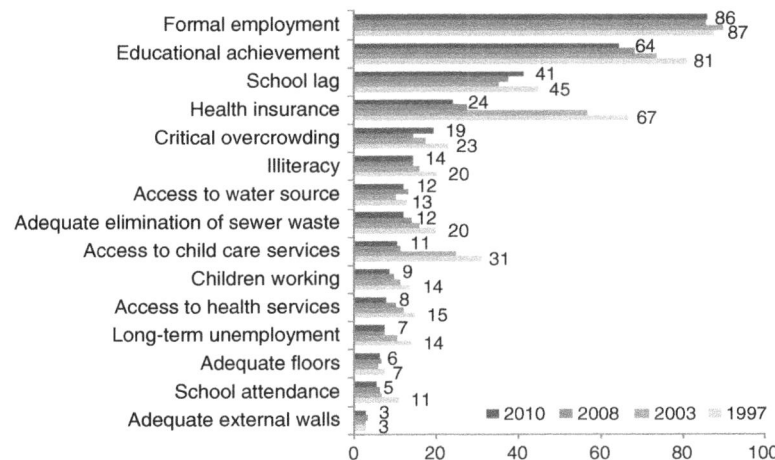

Figure 5.6 Deprivations and Middle Class in Colombia (% of middle-class households deprived).

Source: Authors' calculations based on DNP (2011) and LSS 1997, 2003, 2008 and 2010.

Table 5.7 Colombian Middle Class and Their Deprivations (% of households).

Deprivations	Middle class – Multidimensionally poor				Middle class – Non-multidimensionally poor			
	1997	2003	2008	2010	1997	2003	2008	2010
Educational achievement	95.8	93.4	95.5	94.6	59.9	56.7	56.7	53.1
Illiteracy	32.6	31.8	38.6	42.7	2.8	2.8	4.4	4.0
School attendance	17.7	13.0	17.1	17.7	1.1	1.4	1.5	0.9
School lag	59.2	52.0	62.5	65.7	24.5	20.8	27.0	32.2
Access to child care services	41.3	38.9	21.9	18.4	16.2	12.8	7.1	7.8
Children working	20.6	19.8	23.4	23.1	4.1	3.8	3.7	3.3
Long-term unemployment	16.9	13.1	10.6	9.5	9.6	8.0	5.9	6.7
Formal employment	97.7	98.1	98.5	98.9	72.9	82.7	79.9	81.2
Health insurance	87.1	83.6	55.7	49.8	38.4	34.3	15.3	14.5
Access to health services	22.8	21.1	23.4	17.7	3.7	4.3	4.7	4.2
Access to water source	19.3	18.1	27.4	25.2	3.5	3.7	7.1	7.5
Adequate elimination of sewer waste	28.4	26.2	28.1	25.9	8.2	7.3	7.8	7.0
Adequate floors	11.9	10.6	17.3	17.1	0.9	2.0	2.1	2.2
Adequate external walls	3.7	5.0	7.5	6.6	1.4	1.2	1.5	1.6
Critical overcrowding	32.3	26.8	27.8	31.1	9.9	9.5	8.7	14.8

Source: Authors' calculations based on DNP (2011) and LSS 1997, 2003, 2008 and 2010.

(table 5.7). This vulnerability, while it mitigates over time, involves low education achievements, school lags and lack of formal employment. Access to education and health services is crucial to define the transition for a middle class which is dimensionally poor to one which is not.

Conclusion

The analysis of the evolution of the middle class in Latin America since 2000 shows a solid process of consolidation – although it has been sounder in some countries than others. The analysis reveals a higher proportion of older people with higher levels of education in the middle class. Gender, education and employment in the service sector are factors associated with membership in the middle class. The use of different measures to gauge middle class is still debatable. Our choice of a relative definition based on income distribution brings size estimations consistent with several others, still it falls short of accounting for the vulnerability of the group. The case of Colombia, where we compare an income-based and a multidimensional definition, provides this evidence that monetary measures might conceal deprivations that an 'ideal' middle class would not be exposed to. If a significant share of middle-class households are poor in many other dimensions – as is often the case in several Latin American countries, say, for instance, with respect to job informality – should they be considered poor after all?

Appendix

Multinomial Probit Estimations

Multinomial probit estimations enable researchers to identify which characteristics determine the likelihood of being poor, middle class or affluent (each class is compared with the other two). In the case of this study, multinomial or ordered logit were not adequate solutions.[14] In general, multinomial probit has been preferred to the ordered probit, as it enables different vectors of coefficients for all variables in each class estimation. By contrast, ordered probit considers a unique vector of coefficients, assuming a linear effect between each category. Results presented in our estimations verify nonlinear effects for some variables, with quadratic effects, justifying the selected model of multinomial probit.

The social class variable can take the following values: '0' if poor (households with total income adjusted for family composition below 50 per cent of the median household income); '1' if middle class (households with income between 50 and 150 per cent of the median household income); and '2' if affluent (households with more than 150 per cent of median income).[15] Total income is adjusted for family composition: that is, 'equivalized' to enable comparison between households with distinct sizes and compositions. Household size is adjusted as follows: head of household has a weight of 1; each additional adult (over fourteen years old) has a weight of 0.5; and each additional child below fourteen years old has a weight of 0.3.

The multinomial probit model includes a multivariate analysis of households' determinants for each income class in comparison with the two others. Data sources are the Living Standards Measurement Study Survey (2010) for Colombia and the national household surveys (2009–10) for the other countries.

The model can be specified as follows:

$$Class_i = \alpha_i X_i + \beta_i H_i + \varepsilon_i \quad (1)$$

where:

$Class_i$ = Income class of household i (either poor, middle class or affluent),

X_i = Vector of exogenous individual characteristics of the head of household i,

H_i = Vector of employment, occupational and economic characteristics of the head of household i.

Individual characteristics of heads of household X_i include: age categories, gender, level of education (primary, secondary and university or technical education), matrimonial status and ethnic group.

Employment, occupational and economic characteristics H_i include: region of residence, an independent worker dummy and a variable gathering occupation status and sector of activity – an individual can be either active occupied in agriculture, industry, trade, public or social services or other services; active unemployed; or inactive.

The reference population considers a man between forty-one and sixty-four years old, with primary education (completed or not), who is single, belongs to the majority ethnic group, is active and works in the services sector, who is not an independent worker and who lives outside the capital region.

Multidimensional Poverty Index for Colombia (MPI)

MPI Dimension (weight in brackets)	MPI Variable (weight in brackets)	MPI Indicator
Education conditions (for households) (0.2)	**Educational achievement** (0.1)	Percentage of household with any members aged 15 or older who have less than an average of 9 years of schooling
	Illiteracy (0.1)	Percentage of household members aged 15 and older who cannot read and write
Childhood and youth conditions (0.2)	School attendance (0.05)	Percentage of children between the ages of 6 and 16 who do not attend school
	School lag (0.05)	Percentage of children and youths (7–17 years old) within the household subject to school lag (according to the national norm)

	Access to child care services (0.05)	Percentage of children between the ages of 0 and 5 who simultaneously do not have access to health, nutrition and education
	Children working (0.05)	Percentage of children working (engaged in child labor)
Employment (0.2)	Long-term unemployment (0.1)	Percentage of household members from the economically active population (EAP) who face long-term unemployment (more than 12 months)
	Formal employment (0.1)	Percentage of household members from the economically active population (EAP) not employed or affiliated with a pension fund (this indicator is used as a proxy for whether people are formally or informally employed)
Health (0.2)	Health insurance (0.1)	Percentage of household members over the age of 5 who are not insured by the Social Security Health System
	Access to health services (0.1)	Percentage of people within the household that do not have access to a health institution in case of need
Access to public utilities and housing conditions (0.2)	Access to water source (0.04)	Urban household: considered deprived if lacking public water system Rural household: considered deprived when the water used for the preparation of food is obtained from wells, rainwater, springs, water tank, water carrier or other sources

	Adequate elimination of sewer waste (0.04)	Urban household: considered deprived if lacking public sewer system Rural household: considered deprived if uses a toilet without a sewer connection, a latrine or simply does not have a sewage system
	Adequate floors (0.04)	Lacking materials (dirt floors)
	Adequate external walls (0.04)	Urban household: considered deprived when the exterior walls are built of untreated wood, boards, planks, guadua or other vegetable matter, zinc, cloth, cardboard, waste material or when no exterior walls exist Rural household: considered deprived when exterior walls are built of guadua or another vegetable material, zinc, cloth, cardboard, waste materials or if no exterior walls exist
	Critical overcrowding (0.04)	Urban household: 3 or more individuals per room Rural household: more than 3 individuals per room

Source: DNP (2011).

Notes

1 This document reflects the opinions of the authors and not those of the Inter-American Development Bank or its Board, nor of the OECD or its Council.
2 Refer also to the discussion in Chapter 1 in this volume, by Dayton-Johnson.
3 The lower threshold for the middle class can reasonably be considered to be the poverty line. Even so, several ways of defining poverty coexist: a relative poverty line of 50 per cent of median income, used by many OECD countries, or an absolute poverty line based on the cost of a nutritional basket considered minimal for the healthy survival of a typical family, used by the

national bureau of statistics in the country in question. This leads to different ways of defining the lower boundary of middle class. The upper boundary for middle class is even more complicated and likewise relies on arbitrary limits.

4 All dollar amounts are in US dollars.
5 The median household income is not subject to the same distortions as the average, which can be biased upward by a small number of households with very high incomes.
6 Our definition largely follows the spirit of the classic definition of MIT economist Lester Thurow (1987), who defined the middle class in the US as the group of people with incomes between 75 per cent and 125 per cent of median income.
7 OECD statistics tend to set the poverty line for member countries at 50 per cent of median income.
8 See Torche and López-Calva (2011) for a complete description of all measurements.
9 Importantly, the use of income variables discriminates between groups and does not allow direct comparison with the official national poverty figures, which usually are based on consumption, and use an absolute poverty line based on the cost of a basket of goods covering basic needs.
10 All these definitions are applied to adult equivalent daily income in 2005 dollars at purchasing power parity (using IMF's index of PPP).
11 Because data for Argentina and Uruguay are for urban households only, these countries cannot be compared to the others with respect to sectors, especially agriculture.
12 This finding is likely linked to the presence of high value-added and export-oriented agriculture in Chile.
13 *School lag* refers to the prevalence of children in a given grade that are older than the average age in a given school year. It is measured here as the percentage of children and youths (seven to seventeen years old) within the household subject to school lag (according to the national norm).
14 Ordered logit models are used in cases where the dependent variable consists of a set of categories (more than two) that can be ordered in a meaningful way. This would be the case with the income classes studied here, but the ordered logit model can be applied to data that meet the proportional odds assumption, meaning that the relationship between any two pairs of outcome groups is statistically the same. There is then only one set of coefficients, implying that the relationship between the poor and middle classes would be the same as the relationship between the middle and affluent classes, which is not likely to be the case. The multinomial probit estimations presented in this chapter confirm that the coefficients differ between different categories of the outcome variable.

Multinomial logit models assume the independence of irrelevant alternatives (IIA) assumption. This is due to the fact that the ε's are assumed to be independent distributed from each other: that is, the covariance matrix E (ε ε') is restricted to be a diagonal matrix. Although this independence has the advantage that the likelihood function is quite easy to compute, in most of the cases the IIA assumption leads to unrealistic predictions. One alternative to breaking down the IIA assumption therefore consists in allowing the ε's to

be correlated with each other – and that is exactly what the multinomial probit model does. Technically, these models are very similar: they differ only in the distribution of the error terms.
15 This variable is built on total household income adjusted for family composition, with the OECD's equivalent scale that has been used by the European Commission, among others. Other scales used in international comparisons include household size squared (used in many OECD studies since the 1990s). The difference between one or another scale does not change our results. See Castellani and Parent (2011) for more details.

References

Alesina, A. and R. Perotti (1996) 'Income Distribution, Political Instability and Investment' *European Economic Review*, vol. 40, no. 6, 1203–28.

Banerjee, A. and E. Duflo (2008) 'What Is Middle Class about the Middle Classes around the World?' *Journal of Economic Perspectives*, vol. 2, no. 2 (Spring), 3–28.

Barro, R. J. (1999) 'Determinants of Democracy' *Journal of Political Economy*, vol. 107, no. 6, 158–83.

Birdsall, N. (2010) 'The (Indispensable) Middle Class in Developing Countries; or the Rich and the Rest, Not the Poor and the Rest', Working Paper 207 (Washington, DC: Center for Global Development).

Birdsall, N. (2012) 'A Note on the Middle Class in Latin America', Working Paper 303 (Washington, DC: Center for Global Development).

Cárdenas., M., C. Henao and H. Kharas (2011) *Latin America's Global Middle Class* (Washington, DC: Brookings Insititution).

Castellani, F. and E. Lora (2013a) *The Role of Entrepreneurship in Promoting Social Mobility in Latin America*, Latin American Development Forum Series (Washington, DC: World Bank and Inter-American Development Bank).

Castellani, F. and E. Lora (2013b) 'Is Entrepreneurship a Channel of Social Mobility in Latin America?' IDB Working Paper 425 (Washington, DC: Inter-American Development Bank).

Castellani, F. and G. Parent (2011) 'Being Middle Class in Latin America', OECD Development Centre Working Paper 305 (Paris: OECD Publishing).

Davis, J. C. and J. H. Huston (1992) 'The Shrinking Middle-Income Class: A Multivariate Analysis', *Eastern Economic Journal*, vol. 18, no. 3, 277–85.

DNP [National Planning Department, Colombia] (2011) *Índice de Pobreza Multidimensional*, (principal authors: R. Angulo, R. Pardo, Y. Diaz and Y. Riveros) (Bogotá: Dirección de Desarrollo Social, Subdirección de Promoción Social y Calidad de Vida, Departamento Nacional de Planeación).

Doepke, M. and F. Zilibotti (2005) 'Social Class and the Spirit of Capitalism', *Journal of the European Economic Association*, vol. 3, no. 2–3, 516–24.

Doepke, M. and F. Zilibotti (2008) 'Occupational Choice and the Spirit of Capitalism', *Quarterly Journal of Economics*, vol. 123, no. 2, 747–93.

Easterly, W. (2001) 'The Middle Class Consensus and Economic Development', *Journal of Economic Growth*, vol. 6, no. 4, 317–35.

ECLAC (2009, 2010) *Anuario Estadístico de America Latina y el Caribe* (Santiago: United Nations Economic Commission for Latin America and the Caribbean).

ECLAC (2013) *Economic Survey of Latin America and the Caribbean 2013: Briefing paper* (Santiago: United Nations Economic Commission for Latin America and the Caribbean).

Ferreira, F. H. G., J. Messina, J. Rigolini, L. F. López-Calva, M. A. Lugo and R. Vakis (2013) *Economic Mobility and the Rise of the Latin American Middle Class* (Washington, DC: World Bank).

Kantis, H., M. Ishida and M. Komori (2002) *Entrepreneurship in Emerging Economies: The Creation and Development of New Firms in Latin America and East Asia: Summary Report* (Washington, DC: Inter-American Development Bank).

Kharas, H. and G. Gertz (2010) *The New Global Middle Class: A Cross-Over from West to East* (Washington, DC: Brookings Institution).

López-Calva, L. F. and E. Ortiz-Juarez (2011) 'A Vulnerability Approach to the Definition of the Middle Class', Policy Research Working Paper 5902 (Washington, DC: World Bank).

López-Calva, L. F., J. Rigolini and F. Torche (2011) 'Is There Such a Thing as Middle Class Values? Class Differences, Values and Political Orientations in Latin America', Policy Research Working Paper 5874 (Washington, DC: World Bank).

Lora, E. and J. Fajardo (2013) 'Latin American Middle Classes: The Distance between Perception and Reality', *Economía*, vol. 14, no. 1, 33–60.

Murphy, K., A. Schleifer and R. Vishny (1989) 'Industrialization and the Big Push', *Journal of Political Economy*, vol. 97, no. 5, 1003–26.

OECD [Organisation for Economic Co-operation and Development] (2010a) 'Family Affair: Intergenerational Social Mobility across OECD Countries', in *Economic Policy Reforms: Going for Growth* (Paris: OECD Publishing).

OECD [Organisation for Economic Co-operation and Development] (2010b) *Latin American Economic Outlook 2011: How Middle Class Is Latin America?* (Paris: OECD Publishing).

Ravallion, M. (2009) 'The Developing World's Bulging (but Vulnerable) Middle Class', *World Development*, vol. 38, no. 4, 445–54.

Solimano, A. (2008) 'The Middle Class and the Development Process', *Serie Macroeconomía del Desarrollo* 65 (Santiago: United Nations Economic Commission for Latin America and the Caribbean).

Thurow, L. (1987) 'A Surge in Inequality', *Scientific American*, no. 256, 30–37.

Torche, F. and L. F. López-Calva (2011) 'Stability and Vulnerability of the Latin American Middle Class?', in K. Newman, ed., *Dilemmas of the Middle Class around the World* (Oxford and New York: Oxford University Press).

Weber, M. (1905) *The Protestant Ethic and the Spirit of Capitalism* (New York: Routledge).

6
Covering the Uncovered: Labor Informality, Pensions and the Emerging Middle Class in Latin America

Christian Daude, Juan R. de Laiglesia and Ángel Melguizo

Innovative social policy instruments, notably conditional cash transfers, have been effective in reducing poverty in many Latin American countries.[1] As a result, many households have recently succeeded in moving out of poverty and joining the ranks of the so-called *emerging middle classes*. This chapter will demonstrate, however, that many of these middle-class workers are still vulnerable to significant downward mobility if they are hit by negative shocks, such as illness, disability, job loss or a significant decline in income after retirement.

From an occupational viewpoint, the middle class is often characterized as the group within society that has a stable job, either as a white-collar employee, a qualified independent worker or a small business owner (Banerjee and Duflo, 2008). In developed countries, people with these employment profiles are generally less vulnerable to falling into poverty because of sufficiently high levels of income and assets (financial and non-financial), but also due to access to social-protection networks. However, it is far from obvious that this situation is the same for the emerging middle classes in developing countries, such as Latin America.

Defining the middle class is not an obvious task. While sociologists and political scientists generally approach this issue from a multidimensional viewpoint that combines social status, occupation and other characteristics beyond income, economists traditionally use a single-dimensional monetary metric based on some definition of household income to define the middle class.[2] Furthermore, even when restricting the criteria to income, there are many important differences in establishing the relevant thresholds to classify the population into a middle class and those below and above. For example, while some studies focus on the relative position within the countries' income distribution, others define lower and upper income boundaries for the middle class based on absolute monetary values of income.

Each relative or absolute definition has its advantages and disadvantages, depending on the particular subject of analysis. Some papers in the literature loosely associate the middle class to the households in the middle of the income distribution. For example, Easterly (2001), followed by Bosch, Melguizo and Pages (2013), use the middle three quintiles of the income distribution, while Birdsall et al. (2000) use the households that have incomes above 75 per cent and less than 125 per cent of the country's median income (see Castellani and Parent, 2011, and Castellani, Parent and Zenteno, Chapter 5 of this volume). Of course, these definitions have the advantage of being easy to implement across countries, but also the disadvantage that the resulting middle class might include households that have income levels below the relevant national poverty lines: that is, 50 per cent of median household income could well lie below a relatively poor country's poverty line, and some households would then be simultaneously classified as both middle class and poor. Other studies use absolute income levels to define the middle class in developing countries. Most of these studies try to justify these income thresholds, especially the lower bound, in terms of some measure of poverty.[3] For example, Banerjee and Duflo (2007) use between $2–10 per day and Ravallion (2009) uses $2–13 per day, adjusted for purchasing power parity (PPP).[4] Clearly, these income levels are very low boundaries for middle-income countries, such as most Latin American economies, where national poverty lines often imply a significantly higher level of income. One shared problem of these definitions is that they are somewhat arbitrary. A recent study by the World Bank tries to address some of these problems by defining the lower boundary of the middle class in Latin America based on the household probability of falling back into poverty (Ferreira et al., 2013). Using panel household data for a few countries in the region where this information is available, they estimate $10 per day of per capita income to be the income threshold above which the probability of falling back into poverty is sufficiently low. They also define a group of the population as the 'vulnerable' (*strugglers* in their terminology), which includes those who are not poor (above $4 per day) but have incomes below $10 and therefore have a higher likelihood of falling back into poverty.

Throughout this chapter, the middle classes are defined as consisting of all individuals living in households with adult-equivalent per capita incomes comprised between 50 per cent and 150 per cent of the median for the country (as in OECD, 2010). The lower threshold can be interpreted as a relative poverty line. Indeed, given the diversity of approaches in setting national poverty lines, using them to identify middle-class thresholds would make cross-country comparisons difficult. Moreover, a number of countries in Latin America use multiple poverty lines, corresponding to different consumption baskets. Conversely, 50 per cent of median income is a commonly used relative poverty line more adapted to middle-income countries than international poverty lines such as the one- or two-dollar-a-day lines.[5] In Latin American countries, the thresholds defined by 50 per cent of median per capita income typically lie between the extreme and moderate national poverty lines. Finally, this lower threshold is not far from the $10 per day boundary used by Ferreira et al. (2013). In the case of Peru, it is slightly below S6, around $7 for Colombia and Mexico, and in Chile it implies a lower boundary of $9.

The data used in this chapter are drawn from recent, nationally representative household surveys from Chile, Colombia, Mexico and Peru. Specifically, we covered urban workers' data drawn, respectively, for Chile, from the Encuesta de Caracterización Socioeconómica Nacional (CASEN) for 2009; for Colombia, from the Gran Encuesta Integrada de Hogares (GEIH) for 2009; for Mexico, from the Encuesta Nacional de Ingresos y Gastos de los Hogares (ENIGH) for 2010; and for Peru, from the Encuesta Nacional de Hogares (ENAHO) for 2010.

The following section discusses relevant conceptual and measurement issues of informality in developing countries and analyzes the labor-market characteristics of middle-class workers in Latin America. In particular, we show that informal employment is not composed only of disadvantaged workers; labor informality is also a middle-class issue. In fact, there are more informal than formal workers among the middle classes in all of these countries except Chile. The next section focuses on pension coverage among middle-class workers in Latin America. We show that social protection systems fail to reach even half of middle-class workers, leaving them at a high risk of significant downward income mobility should they get sick, lose their job or retire, which bodes ill for inequality and poverty in the decades to come. In the following section, we discuss different policy options, both ex-post (targeted at people after they retire) and ex-ante (for workers in the labor force) for middle-class workers in Latin America according to their capacity to save and their labor-market characteristics.

Try this additional measure

50 -150 % of median income for the country.

(OECD, 2010)

more
Middle class workers
are informal than
~~not~~ formal
___

Use last 4 surveys and
compare middle class
with multidimensional
vulnerabilities.

Formality and Informality Among Latin American Middle Classes

For some authors, a secure, steady job is a defining characteristic of the middle class (Banerjee and Duflo, 2008). If the middle classes are instead identified through their standard of living relative to their compatriots, many whose incomes allow them not to live hand to mouth, members of the middle class might actually hold jobs which are neither secure nor provide steady incomes.

This section shows that despite their income levels, the majority of middle-class workers in Latin America can be considered vulnerable, as they have neither a formal job nor social insurance. About half of urban workers in Chile (49 per cent), Colombia (50 per cent), Mexico (54 per cent) and Peru (41 per cent) are middle class (as defined in this chapter). Indeed, very low incomes tend to be concentrated among agricultural workers, who are largely rural, and among households with no income earners. However, being part of this middle-income group in Latin America is not synonymous with low vulnerability in the labor market.

In general, informality plays an important role in the vulnerability of workers in Latin America. Indeed, attempts to explain the limited coverage of Latin America's social protection schemes often point to the duality of its labor markets. A number of authors equate formal employment with job-linked entitlements to social security (including Gasparini and Tornarolli, 2007; IDB, 2013; and Bosch, Melguizo and Pages, 2013).

Broadly speaking, informality refers somewhat loosely to the set of activities that are carried out outside the legal or regulatory framework. Such a generic term spans very different realities, from outright illegal exchanges to very common transactions that nonetheless take place outside formal and contractual environments. In terms of employment, a job is considered informal when 'the employment relationship . . . is not subject to national labor legislation, income taxation, social protection or entitlement to certain employment benefits' (ILO, 2003); in other words, when the employment relationship is neither observed nor protected by the state.

Informality is a defining characteristic of labor markets in most developing countries. In fact, across the world, over two-thirds of non-agricultural workers are estimated to be informal. Simply put, 'informal is normal' (Jütting and de Laiglesia, 2009). Latin American labor markets exhibit relatively high degrees of informality. According to ILO estimates for the end of the first decade of the 2000s (ILO, 2012), over half of workers outside of agriculture were informal in Mexico (54 per cent), Ecuador (61 per cent), Colombia (61 per cent), El Salvador (68 per cent), Nicaragua (69 per cent), Paraguay (71 per cent), Peru (71 per cent), Honduras (75 per cent) and Bolivia (76 per cent).

Next, we briefly discuss the alternative definitions and measurements of informal work. In the second part of this section, we provide evidence on the degree of informality of middle-class workers and discuss also some of the possible drivers of it.

Defining and Measuring Informal Work

Informality is most often defined by exclusion: what it is not. The term 'informal sector' was coined by the Kenya report of the ILO's World Employment Programme in 1972 (ILO, 1972) with reference to the context of urban Kenya. As a consequence, informal production units and workers are different from one economy to the next and are very heterogeneous between countries.

The most comprehensive internationally agreed framework for defining and measuring informal employment defines informal employment based on job and production unit characteristics.[6] Employees are in informal jobs if the employment relationship is not subject to labor law, taxation, social protection or entitlement to certain benefits. Self-employed workers are in informal jobs if the production units they work in are in the informal sector[7] or if they are in households producing for their own final consumption. In turn, the informal sector[8] comprises private unincorporated enterprises with some market activity that are small (in terms of employment) and/or unregistered and/or whose employees are unregistered. This definition leaves a number of indeterminacies to be determined by individual countries. Indeterminacies in the identification of informal enterprises arise because they can be identified through size, regulatory status or the status of their employees, depending on country circumstances. Indeterminacies also exist when using the employment relationship to identify informal salaried jobs, since coverage by labor law, taxation and social security are linked but do not automatically follow from one another. The original definition excluded agricultural activities, largely for practical reasons. In this chapter, we use the urban samples of nationally representative surveys, such that the exclusion of agriculture has only limited impact on the results.

For the purpose of our analysis, we define formal employment as that which is subject to written contract or a document that certifies social protection entitlement through employee status. Using the existence of a labor contract to determine formality facilitates comparability since it echoes a form of regulation that is common to the countries of Latin America – the obligation to formalize and register an employment relationship (Kanbur, 2009). However, this means of identifying formal workers is not without limitations. First, labor law in some Latin American countries allows for verbal labor contracts. That is the case in Colombia and Mexico; Chilean law, meanwhile, requires labor contracts to be written. Written contracts are therefore more formalized than is required for workers to be under the protection of labor law, so that the measures in this chapter may overstate the degree of informality in labor markets in these countries. However, in practice, given the burden of proof it would place on the worker in a court of law, rights are unlikely to be enforceable without a written contract. Second, the use of written contracts does not allow us to identify informal production units.

An alternative often applied in the literature is to count workers covered by contributive social protection schemes as formal. This approach is less comparable between countries and suffers from potential indeterminacies as a result of unbundling of benefits. Coverage against risks such as health, occupational hazards, old age, maternity and unemployment may be provided separately, with entitlements being different across dimension, so that workers could be formal by one measure while being informal on others.

It is also necessary to distinguish, as typically social security regulations do, between dependent workers and the self-employed. Dependent workers are those who receive a wage or salary for their work; they are typically obligated to register with and contribute to social security, and their employers also have to contribute to social security on their behalf. Self-employed workers are those whose income depends on the profits of the enterprise (own-account workers, entrepreneurs and workers in a family firm). In half of the countries, self-employed workers are not obligated to register with or contribute to social security. In the case of pensions, Latin American countries with defined-contribution pension systems have typically not required independent workers to contribute (see, for instance, Bosch, Melguizo and Pages, 2013, table 3.1). This includes three of the countries examined in this chapter: Chile, Mexico and Peru. Recent reforms have made contributions to the pension system compulsory for independents in Chile and Peru, although in both cases the provisions are not in force in the years under study in this chapter.[9] Conversely, contributions are compulsory in Colombia for all workers, including independent workers, since the 2003 reforms.

In what follows, we subdivide the group of independent workers by their education level to identify independent professionals.[10] Finally, we exclude workers whose primary occupation is in agriculture, given that the chapter relies on urban subsamples. We classify workers into four groups following these considerations: formal employees, self-employed workers with post-secondary education, other self-employed workers and informal employees. Classifications are based on survey responses to personal and job characteristics.

Informality: Not Only an Issue for the Poor

The composition of the urban workforce partly reflects the degree of inequality across countries and their level of development. The majority of workers in the sample are in the middle-income group in all four countries except in Peru, where 41 per cent of them are. In all cases, these are sizeable groups: almost 18 million Mexican workers, 2.5 million Chilean workers, 6.7 million Colombian and 4.6 million Peruvian workers can be classified as middle class with the data at hand.[11]

By and large, the majority of middle-class workers in the four countries considered together are informal. In fact just one-third (10.7 out of 31.2 million) are in formal salaried employment. An assessment of the composition of the middle-class workforce by employment category reveals that only in Chile is formal salaried work the largest group, and even there, approximately one-third of middle-income workers work without a signed contract, a share that rises to two-thirds in Colombia, Mexico and Peru (fig. 6.1).

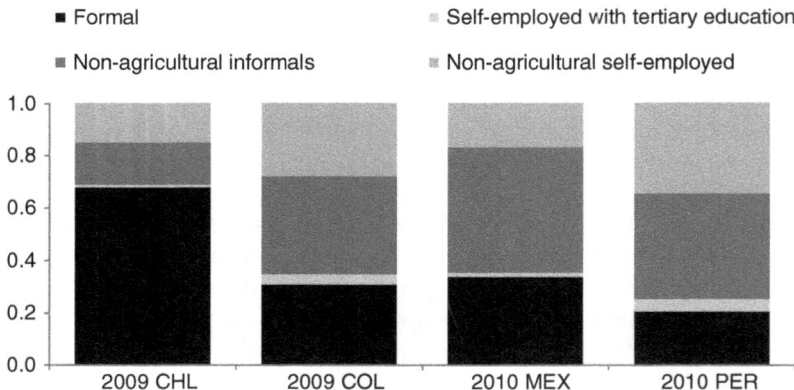

Figure 6.1 Non-agricultural Middle-Income Workers in Colombia, Chile, Mexico and Peru by Occupation (Percentage of workers – 14 to 64 years old).

Source: Carranza et al. (2012) and authors' calculations, based on household surveys.

Even though they are largely informal, middle-class workers in the countries considered are also predominantly salaried (over 80 per cent of them in Chile and Mexico, 79 per cent in Brazil, as found by da Costa et al., 2011). In fact, in a number of countries, it is in that income group that salaried workers are most present, partially reflecting conceptualizations of the middle class that focus on regular income streams and security (Banerjee and Duflo, 2008), even though the prevalence of informality makes those incomes uncertain.

The rate of formalization of dependent employment is strongly and positively related to the income group households belong to. This is striking in Mexico, where only 17 per cent of employees among the poor are formal, compared to 42 per cent among middle classes and 69 per cent of the affluent. Minimum wages are often considered obstacles against formalization, especially when paired with high payroll taxes, because together they raise the minimum cost of employing a salaried worker. This would suggest that low-wage workers will be informal because they are low-productivity workers – it is the only way to employ them profitably. This argument is consistent with the prevalence of informality in Colombia, where the minimum wage, at 51 per cent of the average wage, is relatively high and binding.[12] In the Mexican case, however, we find that average labor incomes of the lowest income group are above the minimum wage, which is largely considered non-binding. Rather than the chosen form of low-wage contracts, informality of salaried work appears to be a more complex phenomenon, where deprivation of or avoidance of the set of benefits formality entails – including social protection – is at play.[13]

An examination of the composition of the workforce by income group also shows that independent workers are overrepresented among the poorest group. While *a priori* considerations would tend to consider formal salaried jobs as the most desirable, in the Chilean case, independent workers are also overrepresented among the richest income group – with incomes above 150 per cent of the median. As in all countries examined, skilled independents are largely concentrated among the richer households – 85 per cent of them in Chile are in that group, but is also true of other independents, half of which are in the highest income group.

A substantial and growing body of evidence calls into question the view that informal workers are shut out of the formal sector as the sole result of a segmented labor market (the 'exclusion' view). In particular, the finding that mobility between formal and informal employment is relatively large in both directions, at least in some countries, suggests that part of the population chooses to be outside the regulated economy: the 'exit' view (see Jütting and de Laiglesia, 2009, for emerging economies, and Perry et al., 2007, for Latin America).

The patterns in workforce composition by income status underline the heterogeneity of informal work. Indeed, they suggest that informal employment itself should be thought of as consisting of multiple tiers (Fields, 1990 and 2005). Lower tiers comprise occupations traditionally associated with informality as a residual sector, such as petty trade, domestic work and many own-account occupations without growth prospects. However, there are also upper tiers of informal employment consisting of relatively better-off workers, including entrepreneurs with accumulated capital but also certain informal employees able to command above-average pay and possibly to pocket a share of the evaded payroll taxes. Transition costs to these tiers, whether in physical, relational or human capital, exist and are possibly substantial.

Policies that aim to increase coverage of social protection should take into account the diversity of informal employment among the middle classes, including the importance of self-employment and the existence of multiple tiers. There are workers in upper tiers who opt out of the formal economy but who could nonetheless afford the necessary contributions. On the other hand, most workers in the lower tier are not offered the possibility of contributing through payroll taxes and cannot afford to contribute voluntarily as independents.[14] Finally, contribution systems need to recognize the differences between salaried and independent workers.[15] Especially for relatively poor independent workers, regular contributions to multiple institutions of a size comparable to the contributions made by employees and their employers are likely to be overly costly. This diversity calls for differentiated approaches and a multiplicity of instruments.

Pension Coverage Among the Middle Classes

Pension coverage in Latin America is low as a consequence of the low level of contribution during the working years of life. Household survey data show that only 43 per cent of employees contributed to any type of pension scheme during 2010. Low contributions are evident in most countries, although the variation is significant, ranging from 20 per cent in Bolivia, Paraguay and Peru, between 30 and 40 per cent in Colombia and Mexico, up to 70 per cent in Costa Rica and Uruguay (Bosch, Melguizo and Pages, 2013).

Contributions tend to be especially low among self-employed and workers in small firms, where the shares of contributors to pension schemes are below 20 and 30 per cent, respectively. By contrast, half of dependent workers hired in medium firms, and more than 70 per cent of those in big firms, save in some kind of formal pension scheme.[16]

These modest levels of contributions to the pension system are evident not only among the low-income population, but also among the emerging middle class. Only 9 per cent of middle-class workers in Peru, 28 per cent in Mexico and 39 per cent in Colombia contribute to at least one pillar of the pension system, either public or private. These figures are in stark contrast with those of Chile, where almost 65 per cent of middle-class workers are saving for their pensions (fig. 6.2).[17]

The absence of a written contract in the employment relationship therefore strongly limits these workers' participation in the social protection systems, which are based on the assumption of an established formal employment relationship. Social insurance systems in the region were inspired by the schemes developed in continental Europe in the nineteenth century, which were designed to cover labor-related contingencies, despite structural social and economic differences. At present, less than one-fifth (at best) of workers without a written contract contribute to the pension schemes, in sharp contrast to levels of contribution observed among formal workers (dependent workers with a written contract): 56 per cent in Peru, 69 per cent in Mexico, 78 per cent in Colombia and 91 per cent in Chile.

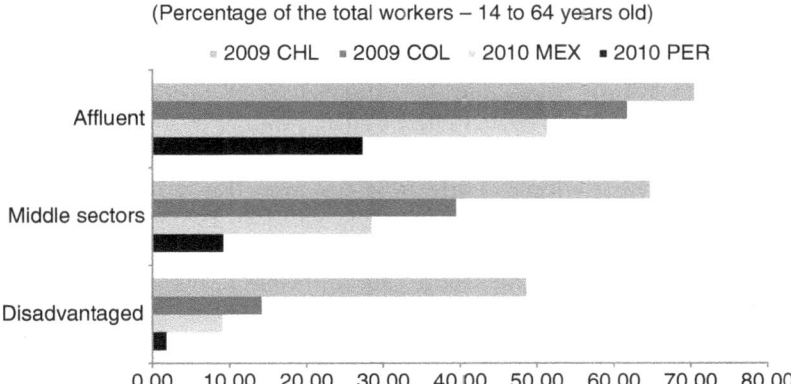

Figure 6.2 Workers Contributing to the Pension System by Level of Income in Colombia, Chile, Mexico and Peru (Percentage of the total workers – 14 to 64 years old).

Note: Mexican data refers to workers affiliated to a pension scheme.

Source: Carranza et al. (2012) and authors' calculations, based on household surveys.

In Colombia, Chile, Mexico and Peru, there are 20.5 million urban middle-class workers who work without a signed contract (4.4 million in Colombia, 0.8 million in Chile, 11.8 million in Mexico and 4.5 million in Peru), compared to 10.7 million in the formal economy. These middle-class workers' incomes significantly exceed their respective national poverty lines (two times in Peru, three times in Colombia and Mexico and five times in Chile), which suggests that they have some saving capacity. However, the average amount of the earnings reported is close to the legal minimum wage in Colombia and Peru (which also establishes the minimum base of contributions). Since a significant portion of middle-class workers in these countries earn less than the minimum wage, establishing it as the minimum contribution base implies a very high contribution relative to their income. This might create an additional hurdle for workers to become formal and have access to pensions in the future. Therefore, instruments that create some flexibility and incentives to contribute on an implicitly lower base might be particularly relevant for these two countries.

Policy Options: Social Pensions and Matching Contributions?

The main goal of a pension system should be to achieve 'adequate, affordable, sustainable and robust pensions, while at the same time contributing to economic development' (Holzmann and Hinz, 2005). Latin America has been a pioneering region in implementing structural pension reforms, mainly by establishing private pension schemes based on individual accounts. These reforms appear to have achieved some of the goals, namely, affordability and financial sustainability, but run the risk of failing to meet others, especially in terms of adequacy and robustness. Challenges are common to both those countries that undertook structural reforms and those that did not. In addition, as discussed above, labor-market informality severely limits coverage of pension systems – even with individual capitalization accounts where incentives to contribute are, in principle, higher than with other systems.

Three key features of Latin America's socioeconomic situation must be taken into account when designing a pragmatic pension reform: the high levels of labor informality, a young (although rapidly ageing) population and the limited fiscal resources (OECD, 2010; OECD-ECLAC-CIAT, 2014). For many people, social insurance will have to be provided by means other than via formal employment. In fact, such policies must encourage participation in contributory systems by informal middle-class workers – people who are both able to save and likely to opt into social protection programs.

Mechanisms to guarantee pension coverage can be categorized as being of two types: those that act at the moment of retirement, called ex-post interventions, or those that act during the working career, called ex-ante interventions (Holzman et al., 2009; Hu and Stewart, 2009). In the following two subsections, we discuss the existing ex-post and exante instruments and main lines of recent reforms in the region, respectively.

Ex-post Pension-Policy Interventions

Ex-post interventions are themselves of two main types: transfers that are not linked to contribution histories, often called 'social pensions', and transfers to guarantee a minimum pension within mandatory contributory pension systems, conditional on a given contribution history. Social pensions can be universal (paid to all individuals who reach eligibility age, sometimes with residency restrictions; this is the case in Bolivia) or means-tested (the case in Argentina, Brazil, Chile, Costa Rica, Mexico, Peru or Uruguay). Another condition imposed in some countries is the absence of formal retirement savings (that is, a pension from the general pension scheme), as in Mexico.

The pervasive levels of informality in Latin America make relying on this ex-post solidarity pillar almost inevitable. Indeed, calls to strengthen it have been made by the UN Economic Commission for Latin American and the Caribbean (ECLAC, 2006) and the IDB (Levy, 2008; Pages, 2010; Bosch, Melguizo and Pages, 2013). These proposals would establish a universal pension at levels sufficient to eradicate extreme poverty during old age but not too high to discourage formal employment. These benefits would be received independently of having formal savings (overcoming the negative conditionalities that some countries implemented in order to save resources) and should be combined with strong fiscal institutions to avoid discretionary decisions in terms of eligibility and generosity, as well as to secure its financing (IDB, 2013b). The ILO has gone even further, by approving a recommendation for the establishment of national social protection floors (ILO Recommendation No. 202). These floors comprise four basic social guarantees, including basic income security in old age, often implemented as a social pension.[18] These proposals could have a significant impact on poverty reduction but should be carefully designed to limit fiscal commitment and minimize the potential disincentives to formalization.

Within the scope of mandatory contributory pensions systems, countries may evaluate reducing the number of years of necessary contributions to qualify for a minimum pension in order to cover informal middle-sector people with spotty contribution records. In general terms, the eligibility is set at twenty to twenty-five years of contributions, a level that many workers do not meet. An increasing minimum pension (that is, increasing with contributions, up to a certain level) of the type adopted in Chile may address this risk at least in part. It also provides some incentives for increasing pension savings for those people who have earnings that would only be marginally above the minimum pension. However, such a reform is still subject to the disincentives critique (Attanasio et al., 2011), and they will not be cheap (estimates put the cost at the order of 1 per cent of GDP).

Ex-ante Policy Interventions

Ex-ante policies (during working life) hold the greatest scope for pension reforms benefiting the middle classes. The most direct policy option is to make affiliation compulsory for the self-employed. Currently, compulsory affiliation is relatively rare; in Bolivia, Mexico, Venezuela and most of the economies in Central America and the Caribbean, the participation of these workers in the social insurance scheme is voluntary. However, it should not be considered a panacea. Some studies show (comparing Brazil and Chile) that the effective implementation of such policy is not a simple matter of passing the necessary legislation (da Costa et al., 2011). By definition, it is difficult to enforce compulsory contributions for those in the informal sector. Furthermore, some informal workers can afford to save just to cover basic needs; compulsory saving may therefore not be optimal for low- or even middle-income households – unfortunately, household-survey data are not useful to address this question, and estimates from alternative databases are not sufficiently accurate to analyze this properly.

Several countries have been considering alternative hybrid approaches, such as 'semi-compulsion', combined with some administrative easing. Under these programs, workers are automatically enrolled but are able to opt out. Also, a greater flexibility regarding contributions with respect to both amounts and timing, given the higher volatility of revenues, are other policy tools that can benefit workers in the lower-middle sector (Hu and Steward, 2009).

Finally, in recent years the debate has shifted toward the so-called 'matching contributions', which emerge as one of the options to address the challenge of increasing pension savings among the middle classes. Broadly speaking, these incentives increase the pension savings' financial return by: 1) reducing the amount of contributions to access the same level of pension benefits (namely progressive or targeted subsidies on social contributions, financed by general revenues) or 2) increasing the level of pension benefits for the same volume of contributions (by granting a subsidy ex-post). Such instruments can be complemented with improvements in the 'nudging' pension savings regulations, such as reminders, default options and opt-out schemes (for example, schemes to which one contributes by default unless otherwise stated).

These pension savings incentive schemes are promising and seem to be especially useful to increase the urban middle-class workers' level of formality, but the available evidence is far from robust (OECD, 2010; Ribe et al., 2010; Bosch, Melguizo and Pages, 2013). Some experimental evaluations for the US show a greater impact on affiliation than on active contributions and an equivalent or even higher relevance of processes (for example, default options) than those of prices (see the review in Holzmann et al., 2012). According to a pilot Social Protection Survey in Lima-Peru launched by the IDB, more than 50 per cent of the middle class (defined as the second through fourth deciles of the working-age population) would respond to a matching scheme of 1:1 (a subsidy of 50 per cent of social contributions).

In spite of these uncertainties, some countries in Latin America are implementing matching contribution schemes. Two interesting and contrasting examples of matching contribution schemes are being implemented in Colombia and Peru. After several years of analysis, Colombia is implementing the BEPS (*Servicio Social Complementario de Beneficios Económicos Periódicos* in Spanish). This voluntary-base scheme includes an allowance of 20 per cent of the BEPS accounts' cumulated contributions, targeted to low and low-middle–income workers[19] as well as more benefits for fidelity in the short run, such as micro-insurance or administrative cost reductions. In addition to these incentives, the main novelty is that the BEPS allows contributors to make payments below the minimum wage level, thus relaxing the barrier generated for many workers. As for Peru, it will run the *Sistema de Pensiones Sociales*, a voluntary-based scheme for both low-income workers (that is, those receiving up to 1.5 times the minimum wage) and micro-enterprise owners (those hiring up to ten employees) who are not affiliated to any pension scheme. This system yields a progressive reduction of social security contributions in order to access the same amount of pension benefits as in the general system (maximum level of contributions rises to 4 per cent of the minimum wage, compared to 13 per cent in both the national and private systems). Such contributions are partly offset by the government (which contributes the same amount of shares as the workers).

These countries have joined the mixed experiences of Chile and Mexico. Since the start of the international crisis in 2008, Chile has established a couple of programs to support youth employment, which operate as social contribution cuts for younger workers, benefiting both the worker and the firm. The *Subsidio Previsional a los Trabajadores Jóvenes* established a 50 per cent social tax subsidy for low-income (earning less than 1.5 times the minimum wage) workers aged eighteen to thirty-five years, during twenty-four months, benefitting the employer (since 2008) and workers (from 2011). The *Subsidio al Empleo Joven* targets the 40 per cent poorest workers aged eighteen to twenty-five, with an inverse-U subsidy for workers (two-thirds) and firms (one-third). Finally, in the case of Mexico, there is a social contribution equivalent to a 5.5 per cent matching of the minimum wage in Mexico City for affiliates who earn up to fifteen times the minimum wage.[20]

It is probably too early to assess them rigorously, but all four cases raise a series of questions about their effectiveness. First, benefits have been limited to low-income workers (especially in Colombia), a targeting which raises doubts given their limited saving capacity. Second, formality implies a number of other non-wage costs related to health coverage and other labor regulations (firing costs, holidays) which are, once added, in most cases, higher than the pension contribution itself; therefore, even if labor costs were a driving force for informality, these incentives will only be marginally effective. Third, all schemes concentrate mainly on creating financial incentives and do not address information and behavioral barriers. Finally, from an economic perspective, in the case of Peru, the system seems to establish a new *de facto* pension system that might create incentives for firms to remain excessively small.

Summing up, matching contributions are a useful tool, but the policy's design might reduce its effectiveness and even end up creating bad outcomes, especially if such schemes end up creating subsidized parallel systems. In order to avoid the latter outcome, these schemes ought to be fully integrated into the social protection systems as a supplementary benefit component (rather than offering an alternative benefit for informal workers). Furthermore, if fiscal constraints allow it, it would be advisable to eliminate some of the conditionalities to access these incentives and expand the potential beneficiaries to the middle class as a whole, especially in countries with relatively high minimum wages. Moreover, financial incentives could be combined with innovations in the mechanisms based on new technologies and behavioral patterns, such as default options and reminders/payments via cellular phones.

Finally, instruments should be evaluated rigorously to improve their design and move toward universal pension coverage.

Conclusions

This chapter has analyzed labor-market characteristics of the middle classes in four representative Latin American countries – Chile, Colombia, Mexico and Peru – and policies to increase pension coverage among middle-class workers. While it is difficult to define the middle class universally, it is clear that a key element is the labor-market status. Having a steady and secure job is – if not yet a reality – an aspiration of the emerging middle classes in the region. Therefore, expanding social policies to address vulnerabilities of this income group will be an increasingly relevant issue for policymakers and governments in the region. We presented evidence that shows that middle-class workers in Latin America are still very vulnerable to negative shocks such as sickness, job loss and poverty after retirement due to the lack of a robust and well-developed social insurance system. In this chapter, we have emphasized issues of pension coverage of the middle classes, but other social policy areas are often equally important and should be designed in concordance with the pension system, including unemployment insurance and the provision of health services (OECD, 2010).

We showed that labor informality – defined as workers that do not have a formal contract – is a widespread phenomenon not only among the disadvantaged, but also among middle-class urban workers in the region. Around two out of three non-agricultural middle-class workers in Colombia, Mexico and Peru are informal; Chile is exceptional insofar as 'just' one-third of urban middle-class workers are informal. Not surprisingly, this is reflected also in the fraction of urban middle-class workers that contribute to the pension system. However, the differences across countries are significant. For example, while only 9 per cent of middle-class workers in Peru contribute to at least one pillar (either public or private) of the pension system, in Chile almost 65 per cent of middle-class workers are saving for their pensions, with Mexico (28 per cent) and Colombia (39 per cent) being intermediate cases. Clearly, this is a matter of concern for policymakers, as the lack of pensions is a leading indicator of vulnerability and risk of poverty after retirement.

Some policies may be particularly effective in increasing pension coverage among the Latin American middle classes and reducing their vulnerability. In particular, among ex-post instruments, social pensions that provide a minimum income independently of the level of contributions can significantly reduce the risk of falling back into poverty after retirement, especially for the lower middle class. However, progressive social tax subsidies and matching contribution among the ex-ante instruments seems to be the most promising to address the needs of the middle class in Latin America regarding pensions. In general, it is important to design these schemes taking into account a series of criteria that affect the sustainability and effectiveness of these policies. First, they should be fully funded by long-term funds, so that they do not put at risk fiscal sustainability or their own long-term financial viability. Second, they should be designed taking into account the incentives that they provide to workers and employers to opt for formal employment; sometimes the instruments can create an implicit subsidy to stay in the informal sector or for firms to stay small. Furthermore, beyond financial incentives, existing schemes should also incorporate mechanisms such as default options that nudge people toward participating in them as well as formalizing. Finally, making the implementation and design more flexible, in order to allow for evaluations and readjustments that increase the efficiency and effectiveness of schemes, would also be helpful.

A final remark is that this agenda to provide better social protection for the emerging middle classes in Latin America has to go hand in hand with a coherent productive strategy. Labor productivity is still very low in the region, holding back potential growth (see IDB, 2013). Greater productivity growth, and a structural transformation that allows growth to be more inclusive, would create better jobs and higher salaries, relaxing some of the tough trade-offs that policymakers currently face in the region.

Notes

1 The views expressed herein are the sole responsibility of the authors and do not necessarily reflect the opinions of their institutions.
2 The pros and cons of these approaches are similar to those in the literature on poverty measurement. See, for example, Alkire and Foster (2011) and Ravallion (2011) for a multidimensional and an income-based approach, respectively. See Chapter 1 in this volume, by Dayton-Johnson, for an overview. In addition, the perception of the relative status within society might be as important as the individual's situation in defining a sense of belonging to the middle class; the distance between subjective and objective measures of middle-class membership are addressed by Lora and Fajardo in Chapter 8 of this volume.
3 See Castellani and Parent (2011) for a survey.
4 Refer to the discussion in Chapter 1 in this volume, by Dayton-Johnson, for more details about the purchasing power parity adjustment.

5 See Garroway and de Laiglesia (2012) for a discussion of the use of relative poverty lines in development contexts.
6 This framework was adopted by the 17th ICLS (International Conference of Labour Statisticians) in 2003 (ILO, 2003).
7 As defined by the 15th ICLS.
8 As defined by the 15th ICLS in coherence with the System of National Accounts (SNA). The informal sector is therefore not an *economic* sector in the sense of a set of activities with common product lines or technology, it is rather a subsector of the *institutional* sector called 'households' in the SNA 1993 classification.
9 In Chile, independents started contributing with their income tax payments in 2013 and could opt out of contributing until 2015. In Peru, independents will begin contributing in the course of 2014.
10 Identifying formality of independent workers following the ILO definition would require reliable and consistent survey questions regarding firm incorporation and registration, which are not available across all countries.
11 Although this chapter focuses on urban workers outside agriculture, the thresholds were identified using national data, which includes rural areas, except in Colombia. In this case, we used the sample covering the main thirteen cities, which might lead to higher thresholds than would otherwise have been obtained.
12 Calculation based on the ILO Global Wage Database.
13 See Levy (2008).
14 The rate of contribution of independent workers is comparable to the employer and employee shares of contributions in most countries. Mexico is an exception in that independent workers contribute voluntarily and choose the size of contributions. For a survey of special regimes in Latin America, see Bosch, Melguizo and Pages (2013), table 5 1.
15 See Hu and Stewart (2009) for a discussion of specific contribution modalities for independent workers. Furthermore, there are important differences by firm size. Employees in small firms in Latin America tend to exhibit contribution densities similar to independent workers.
16 Small firms are defined as those up to five employees, medium as six to fifty employees and big firms as those over fifty.
17 These rates of contributions should be interpreted cautiously, since they just represent the share of workers who, at a particular point in time, declare themselves as contributors. First, they represent soft data taken from surveys, so they could differ from the official statistics. And second, they cannot be taken as the contribution density, given that these surveys do not follow the same individual over time.
18 The other three guarantees advocated by ILO are access to essential health care, basic income security for children (including access to nutrition, education, care and other necessary goods and services) and basic income security for persons of working age unable to earn sufficient income.
19 Low- and low-middle–income workers are defined as levels I, II and III of the *Sistema de Identificación de Potenciales Beneficiarios de Programas Sociales* (SISBEN).
20 For a review of these cases, and other emerging and developed regions, see Hinz et al. (2012).

References

Alkire, S. and J. E. Foster (2011) 'Counting and Multidimensional Poverty Measurement', *Journal of Public Economics*, vol. 95, no. 7–8, 476–87.

Attanasio, O., C. Meghir and A. Otero (2011) 'Formal Labor Market and Pension Wealth: Evaluating the 2008 Chilean Pension Reform', mimeo (University College of London, Department of Economics).

Banerjee, A. and E. Duflo (2008) 'What Is Middle Class about the Middle Classes around the World?', *Journal of Economic Perspectives*, vol. 22, no. 2 (Spring), 3–28.

Birdsall N., C. Graham and S. Pettinato (2000) 'Stuck in the Tunnel: Is Globalization Muddling the Middle Class?', Center on Social and Economic Dynamics Working Paper 14 (Washington, DC: Brookings Institution).

Bosch, M., A. Melguizo and C. Pages (2013) *Better Pensions, Better Jobs. Towards Universal Coverage in Latin America and the Caribbean* (Washington, DC: Inter-American Development Bank).

Carranza, L., A. Melguizo and D. Tuesta (2012) 'Matching Pension Schemes in Colombia, Mexico and Peru: Experiences and Prospects', in R. Holzmann, R. Hinz, N. Takayama and D. Tuesta, eds., *Matching Defined Contributions Schemes: Role and Limits to Increase Coverage in Low and Middle Income Countries* (Washington, DC: The World Bank), 193–213.

Castellani, F. and G. Parent (2011) 'Being "Middle Class" in Latin America', OECD Development Centre Working Paper 305 (Paris: OECD Publishing).

Da Costa, R., J. R. de Laiglesia, E. Martinez and A. Melguizo (2011) 'The Economy of the Possible: Pensions and Informality in Latin America', OECD Development Centre Working Paper 295 (Paris: OECD Publishing).

Easterly, W. (2001) 'The Middle Class Consensus and Economic Development', *Journal of Economic Growth*, vol. 6, no. 4, 317–35.

Ferreira, F. H. G., J. Messina, J. Rigolini, L. F. López-Calva, M. A. Lugo and R. Vakis (2013) *Economic Mobility and the Rise of the Middle Latin American Middle Class* (Washington, DC: The World Bank).

Fields, G. S. (1990) 'Labour Market Modelling and the Urban Informal Sector: Theory and Evidence', in D. Turnham, B. Salomé and A. Scharz, eds., *The Informal Sector Revisited*, OECD Development Centre Seminars (Paris: OECD Publishing), 49–69.

Fields, G. S. (2005) 'A Guide to Multisector Labour Market Models', Social Protection Discussion Paper Series 0505 (Washington, DC: World Bank).

Garroway, C. and J. R. de Laiglesia (2012) 'On the Relevance of Relative Poverty Lines for Developing Countries', OECD Development Centre Working Paper 314 (Paris: OECD Publishing).

Henley, A., G. R. Arabsheibani and F. G. Carneiro (2009) 'On Defining and Measuring the Informal Sector: Evidence from Brazil', *World Development*, vol. 37, no. 5, 992–1003.

Holzmann, R. and R. Hinz (2005) *Old-age Income Support in the 21st century* (Washington, DC: The World Bank).

Holzmann, H., R. Hinz, N. Takayama and D. Tuesta, eds. (2012) *Matching Defined Contributions Schemes: Role and Limits to Increase Coverage in Low and Middle Income Countries* (Washington, DC: The World Bank).

Hu, Y. and F. Stewart (2009) 'Pension Coverage and Informal Sector Workers: International Experiences', OECD Working Papers on Insurance and Private Pensions 31 (Paris: OECD Publishing).

IDB (2013) *Rethinking Reforms: How Latin America and the Caribbean Can Escape Suppressed World Growth*, 2013 Latin American and Caribbean Macroeconomic Report (Washington, DC: Inter-American Development Bank).

ILO (1972) *Employment, Incomes and Equality: A Strategy for Increasing Productive Employment in Kenya* (Geneva: International Labour Organization).

ILO (2003) *Final report of the XVII International Conference of Labour Statisticians* (Geneva: International Labour Organization).

ILO (2012) *Statistical Update on Employment in the Informal Economy*, ILO Department of Statistics, June (Geneva: International Labour Organization).

Jütting, J. and J. R. de Laiglesia, eds. (2009) *Is Informal Normal? Towards More and Better Jobs in Developing Countries* (Paris: OECD Publishing).

Kanbur, R. (2009) 'Conceptualising Informality: Regulation and Enforcement', IZA Discussion Paper 4186 (Bonn: Institute for the Study of Labour).

Levy, S. (2008) *Good Intentions, Bad Outcomes. Social Policy, Informality and Economic Growth in Mexico* (Washington, DC: Brookings Institution).

OECD [Organisation for Economic Co-operation and Development] (2010) *Latin American Economic Outlook 2011: How Middle-Class Is Latin America?* (Paris: OECD Publishing).

OECD-ECLAC-CIAT (2014) *Revenue Statistics in Latin America* (Paris: OECD Publishing).

Perry, G., W. Maloney, O. Arias, P. Fajnzylber, A. Mason and J. Saavedra-Chanduvi (2007) *Informality: Exit and Exclusion* (Washington, DC: World Bank).

Pages, C. (2010) *The Age of Productivity: Transforming Economies from the Bottom Up.* (Washington, DC, and New York: Inter-American Development Bank and Palgrave Macmillan).

Ravallion, M. (2011) 'On Multidimensional Indices of Poverty', *Journal of Economic Inequality*, vol. 9, no. 2, 235–48.

Ribe, H., D. A. Robalino and I. Walker (2010) *From Right to Reality: Achieving Effective Social Protection for All in Latin America and the Caribbean* (Washington, DC: The World Bank).

7
Business Sector Responses to the Rise of the Middle Class
Lourdes Casanova and Henrique Brusius Brust Renck

The Emergence of a New Middle Class in Latin America

It has been (and still is) a prosperous time in Latin America during which, by some estimates, the middle classes have grown by 50 per cent in the past decade or so. Of the 73 million who ceased to be considered poor in recent years, 50 million worked their way up the social ladder and joined the middle class. From 100 million at the turn of the century, this new middle class (see definition below) accounts for more than 150 million Latin Americans and represents one in three of the region's citizens. The economic growth created new jobs and allowed the transformation of many informal jobs into formal ones. The highest growth of the middle class was in Brazil, followed by Colombia, Costa Rica, Chile and Peru. This social mobility stems from a process set in motion at the dawn of the millennium, one which raised living standards in a widespread manner throughout the subcontinent and better positioned Latin American countries in the global economy.

The definition of a middle class varies in different regions of the world. World Bank experts Herrera et al. (2013) and López-Calva et al. (2011) define the middle class in Latin America as those households with less than 10 per cent probability of falling again below the poverty line within five years.[1] In practical terms in Latin America, this means living with a daily per capita income between $10 and $50, adjusted for purchasing power parity, which translates to an annual household income between $14,600 (or $3,650 annual income per person) and $73,000. López-Calva (2012) believes that being middle class in Latin America means, for many, having a job with a regular salary, which means being part of the formal economy. In this chapter, we adopt these definitions and will move beyond the debate of what being middle class means to concentrate on how local companies have profited from the tremendous wealth created by this new middle class.

That economies outside the traditional economic centers would gain ground is not a new idea. Since the early 1980s, emerging markets such as China, Brazil, Mexico, Turkey and India have called attention to their dynamism. No longer seen primarily as sources of cheap labor and undifferentiated commodities, those regions became important sources of new consumers and emerging markets that are now at the heart of retailing and consumer products. This new middle class helped reshape not only trade patterns, but also how the rest of the world sees these countries.

Latin America has been the most dramatic example of this transformation. While Asian countries such as China and India have been at the heart of global growth, the impact on consumer markets has been greater in the Latin American subcontinent. Sustained economic growth since the turn of the twenty-first century, and an upsurge in average earnings with a decrease in poverty levels in nearly every country, has increased the disposable income of Latin Americans. Middle-class growth in Asia is larger in absolute numbers of people, but as more Latin American residents join the cohort of the middle class, according to Boza (2012), they contribute to a proportionally greater surge in demand of consumer goods than in the Asian case.

Such a significant socioeconomic change took time. Latin American economies experienced an economic boom in the 1970s, when consumption improved and multinationals entered the region, and several of the 'multilatinas' that currently rank among the world's largest made their first attempts into foreign markets. In addition, state-led industrialization and the growth of public employment supported the rise of a middle class composed of managers, bureaucrats and a labor aristocracy of skilled workers (*The Economist*, 2007). The currency crisis of the early 1980s, the debt crisis and the consequent strains on public budgets led to a 'lost decade' of economic growth in Latin America. The following two decades witnessed strong economic liberalization under the so-called 'Washington Consensus' policies imposed by the World Bank and the International Monetary Fund and the foundation of free-trade zones such as Mercosur in 1991 and the North American Free Trade Agreement (NAFTA) in 1994. The momentum once again cooled due to the contagion effect of the economic crises in Asia and Russia in 1997–98, and in Argentina in 2001–02 (Casanova, 2009).

Then in 2002, a sharp rise in commodity prices strengthened the resource-based Latin American economies and companies, which triggered a rebound in the economic situation in the region. Steady Gross Domestic Product (GDP) growth has been mostly ubiquitous in the subcontinent ever since, even if not as rapid as the growth experienced by Asian countries in the same period. This process of Latin America's economic rebound culminated in the 2008 financial crisis, which dramatically impacted household consumption throughout the developed world, whereas several emerging economies held more or less steady. Several foreign companies found in the emerging economies a safe harbor during the crisis that eroded their profits in home markets. The emergence of middle classes across most Latin American countries became evident, and the benefits of growth are now more evenly spread over different social strata (*The Economist*, 2007). According to the ILO (2012), growth has reduced the size of the informal economy,[2] generating more formal jobs as well as positive trade balances. These favorable results have enabled public policies of income redistribution and public service improvements throughout the subcontinent, thus affecting in a positive way the quality of life of the people in Latin America.

Economic stability and a widespread increase in income levels have altered consumption patterns in Latin American markets. Companies have responded to those changes. The goal of this chapter is to explore how local multinationals have benefited from – and responded to – the rise of this new middle class in Latin America. The question is posed for different business sectors (retail, financial products, automobiles, consumer goods and services). Case studies of particular businesses' strategic responses to the new opportunities and challenges presented by a growing middle class are highlighted in a series of boxes.

The Growth of Emerging Multinationals

The new power of emerging markets has been widely discussed, but less attention has been paid to the emergence of multinational firms from this part of the world. As consumer habits change with the increase in income, local companies, like global multinationals based in high-income economies, face the challenge and benefit of addressing the new demands of a social stratum that is both quality-demanding and price-conscious, a legacy of tougher economic times not yet forgotten.

The supremacy of US and European multinationals is being challenged in different industries. Two Chinese companies, Huawei and ZTE, are among the five biggest telecom equipment manufacturers in the world. The Brazilian Vale is the number-one iron-ore exporter, the Mexican Cemex is number three in cement and the Chilean Codelco is the biggest copper mining company in the world. A total of 143 – almost one in three – of the companies listed in the 2013 Global 500 ranking of the American business magazine *Fortune* in July 2013 come from emerging economies. In contrast, in 2005, only forty-seven, or 9 per cent, were from emerging markets. Most of these new champions in the private sector come from Asia: ninety-five from China and Taiwan, fourteen from South Korea and eight from India. Thirteen Latin American companies have made it to the top: eight from Brazil, three from Mexico, one each from Venezuela and Colombia.[3]

In 2012, Latin America's 500 largest companies together had sales of $2.67 trillion, equivalent to the combined sales of the fourteen largest companies in the world (*Latin Business Chronicle*, 2013). The global commodities boom explains part of the surge in multilatinas. The three largest companies in the continent – Brazil's Petrobras, Mexico's Pemex and Venezuela's PDVSA – are in the hydrocarbon sector, in a region that concentrates one-fifth of the world's oil reserves. Brazil's Vale, meanwhile, is in the mining sector. The rise of other regional champions, however, is more driven by the emergence of the middle class. Such are the cases of the Mexican telecommunications multinational América Móvil, the Brazilian JBS Friboi in food and the Brazilian retailer CBD (also known as Pão de Açúcar group). The Brazilian banks Banco do Brasil, Bradesco and Itaú-Unibanco have likewise seen their retail and consumer finance businesses increase with the growing ranks of middle-income families.

Nevertheless, the ascent of those companies is not simply due to an increasing demand for their products and services. Until 2000, Latin America's middle class was quite small, and there was barely any middle ground between selling large quantities for the lower-income classes or catering to the upper class. Local businesses therefore had merchandise and marketing tactics specialized for one or the other of these niches. Starting in 2002, products, analytical tools and marketing strategies started being tailored to address the new market opportunities presented by the emergence of middle-income consumers. Companies had to move beyond importing product designs or marketing dogmas and develop innovative business models. In addition to innovating internally, Latin American firms learned to turn the same factors that had long held them back into competitive advantages – that is, making a virtue out of necessity, adopting inventive strategies to cope with the idiosyncrasies of Latin American markets and the institutional environment (Casanova, 2009).

Although multinational firms had been selling their products in Latin America for decades, this turned out to be an advantage to domestic firms who knew their markets much better than traditional multinationals and could seize the opportunities presented by the new middle class earlier. Until then they had targeted the upper classes, a group that emulates the aspirations and consumption habits of their European and North American counterparts. Moreover, affluent Latin American consumers are either willing to pay whatever charged by the few providers or to purchase products abroad, thus barely requiring any marketing effort on the part of multinational suppliers. Multinational companies' offices in Latin American countries had been doing little more than mediating between local suppliers and the offices overseas that handled the core business. On the other hand, the up-and-coming middle social tier in emerging economies not only displays far less homogeneity across countries, but also differs significantly from that of industrialized countries in several dimensions, from income levels to living standards and levels of education. The corporations that managed to tap into the middle-class interest did so by revisiting their modus operandi (López-Calva, 2012).

In short, both local and foreign firms responded to the middle-class boom with innovation in products as well as in strategies. We will focus our attention on the impact of the rise of the middle class on Latin American companies. Some industries have been exceptionally successful in taking advantage of the changes in the socioeconomic environment. In the next section, we will look at some of the companies in these industries, which we believe have been positively impacted.

Industries Most Favored by the New Middle Class in Latin America

Retailing, financial services, the automotive industry and consumer products are particularly illustrative examples of growth being directly impacted by the new middle class. In each of those industries, it is easy to pinpoint companies that not only thrived during recent global economic downturn, but also excelled in boosting revenues by surfing the flowing tide of a growing middle class.

Retail

A. T. Kearney's (2013) Global Retail Development Index shows the most promising countries for retail expansion: Brazil has been the top country worldwide three years in a row, and Chile and Uruguay follow. Four other Latin American countries – Peru, Panama, Colombia and Mexico – also appear among the top thirty. Latin American retail companies have benefitted from the strong growth in middle classes, controlled inflation, sustained economic growth and political stability, which have increased consumer and investor confidence and created a favorable environment for retail development.

In contrast to Europe, Latin America is characterized by geographical dispersion, which favors large, American-style megastores and shopping malls. However, such an opportunity is yet to be fully exploited: The so-called modern retail channels (supermarkets and hypermarkets) in the region account for 45 per cent of net sales, whereas the world average is above 60 per cent. This represents not only an opportunity for real estate development and giant retailers, but also for local chains. For example, in August 2011, the four largest drugstores consolidated in Brazil: Droga Raia and Drogasil merged to form Raia Drogasil and merged later in Drogarias DPSP, forming the second-largest drugstore chain in Latin America (see box 1). However, the five largest drugstore chains in the country still account for only 29 per cent of revenue in an industry in which small and medium shops predominate, with 66 per cent of the revenues (M2Farma, 2013). Similar market consolidations have happened all over the subcontinent. In Colombia, retail chain Almacenes Éxito launched an initial public offering in the Colombian stock exchange to raise funds to acquire Grupo Disco del Uruguay for $746 million in 2011 (*América Economía*, 2011). Also in 2011, the Chilean retailer Cencosud advanced into the Brazilian market by acquiring the local supermarket chain Prezunic for $494 million (*O Globo*, 2011). Local retailers, still small in the global scale, are increasing in size through these mergers and acquisitions.

Although the Asia Pacific region remains the largest market for retail, Latin America has become the most attractive market in recent years because it differs from Asia in relevant aspects. Although both regions have experienced a steady growth of their middle classes, GDP per capita

---

Box 1 Drogarias DPSP

Drogarias DPSP is the second-largest drugstore company in Brazil and in Latin America in sales and number of stores and the seventh-largest retail group in Brazil. The company was founded in 2011 through the merger of Drogaria São Paulo, headquartered in São Paulo, and Rio de Janeiro–based Drogaria Pacheco. Operating under both brands, the company reported net profits of $84.2 million in the first quarter after the merger (*Valor Econômico*, 2012). Currently headquartered in São Paulo, the company has 708 drugstores in five Brazilian states with sales estimated at $2.4 billion in 2013 (RaiaDrogasil, 2013). The company is still private and is expected to go public in the near future.

in Latin America is triple that of China and seven times that of India (McKinsey & Company, 2011). In addition, per capita expenditure is significantly higher in Latin America: $1,700 in 2011, against $900 in Asia in the same year. This means that although Asia Pacific hosts the largest number of middle-class consumers, those not only have less available income than their Latin American peers, but also chose to save rather than to spend the additional income responsible for their upward reclassification (*iEco*, 2012).

Although unemployment in recent years has been at record low levels, formal employment and credit history were still prerequisites to access consumer finance by traditional financial institutions. In order to allow new middle-class shoppers to fulfill their purchase expectations, retailers adjusted to overcome this hurdle by offering credit themselves. Today, the majority of shoppers are on 'managed' credit, or credit granted by retailers themselves and negotiated in-store. This enables retailers not only to diversify profit sources, but also provides invaluable information on shoppers' available incomes and potential to spend. The Costa Rican retail group Grupo Monge, for example, was born as a popular

---

Box 2   Grupo Monge

Founded in Costa Rica in 1970, Grupo Monge is a leading family-owned retailer of consumer electronics, household appliances and furniture in Central America, serving mainly low- and middle-income consumers in Nicaragua, Honduras, El Salvador and Guatemala, in addition to its home country, with 325 stores operating in the region. The company's activities include a wholesaling operation (under brands El Gallo Más Gallo, El Verdugo, Importadora Monge, Prado and Play) and a consumer finance arm that complements the retailing business by providing customers with financing for in-store purchases. Grupo Monge's innovative business model consists of applying the latest retailing processes to an underserved market segment traditionally serviced by informal, unorganized and often more expensive stores. Another distinct aspect of Grupo Monge is its strong corporate social responsibility programs, such as *A Centroamérica le tengo Fe* (I have faith in Central America) and *Apoyo Comunitario* (Community support). These two programs have granted 1,000 scholarships and helped over 10,000 families in the region by introducing information and communication technologies into schools. The group has helped Costa Rica achieve one of the highest concentrations of computers in classrooms in Latin America. In 2009, Grupo Monge launched a new furniture line made from wood and renewable materials to promote environmental best practices in the manufacturing process. Currently seven Grupo Monge's suppliers are implementing these practices, and their products are stamped with a green line seal. Grupo Monge's goal is to consolidate their brand throughout Latin America.[4]

supermarket chain El Gallo Más Gallo. Following the evolution of its customer base, it stepped into the furniture and domestic appliances market and developed middle- and high-end brands (box 2).

Latin America's recent retailing boom has benefited companies of every size. Multinational players such as Wal-Mart, Best Buy, Home Depot and Casino arrived during the last fifteen years, looking to emerging markets for a safe harbor during the economic crisis. In 2011, the French chain Casino saw its sales decrease by 4.3 per cent in Europe, while in Latin America they increased by 8.4 per cent. FEMSA, the largest independent Coca-Cola bottler in the world, entered the convenience-store market in 1977 with OXXO, the largest and most profitable chain in Latin America (box 3). In November 2012, FEMSA tapped into the drugstore segment by acquiring one Mexican drugstore chain and then another in May 2013, totaling more than 430 sale points (*CNN Expansión*, 2013). However, Wal-Mart, which insists on transplanting models successful in the US to emerging markets, has suffered (*BusinessWeek*, 2014). Wal-Mart, Brazil's fourth largest retailer, has seen its Brazilian store traffic decline in the last quarter of 2013 by 3.4 per cent. Wal-Mart's strategy of everyday lowest prices does not fit the buying patterns of the new Brazilian middle class, price sensitive and looking for the best bargains at different stores.

Financial Products: Mortgages and Consumer Finance

Rising consumer spending in Latin America can be explained by the expansion in the ranks of the middle classes, which brought increased availability of credit. According to the International Monetary Fund, real banking credit to the private sector grew 12.4 per cent a year in the region between 2004 and 2007, remained positive during the 2008–09 crisis and recovered strongly afterward to grow nearly to the pre-crisis level (Hansen and Sulla, 2013). In 2011, real credit growth was faster than in both

---

Box 3 OXXO

Established in 1977 in Monterrey, Mexico, OXXO was initially devised to be an outlet for beer and soft drink products by the beverage company FEMSA. It grew to become the largest chain of convenience stores in Latin America with over 10,700 small stores in Mexico and thirty-four in Bogotá, Colombia.[5] Still wholly owned by FEMSA, the unit has delivered double-digit sales growth in recent years through rapid expansion, reaching sales of $6.7 billion in 2012. OXXO's success lies in the development of a computerized operating system that tracks merchandising, warehouse operations, assortment planning and pricing. The company expects to operate 12,000 stores by 2015, thus taking advantage of changing lifestyle and consumer tastes.

Emerging Europe and Asia. Moreover, in most Latin American countries, household credit (that is, mortgages and consumer credit) outgrew corporate credit, meaning that the flowering middle class benefitted enormously from this phenomenon. Consumer credit has been growing in Latin America as nowhere else in the world, driven mainly by Argentina and Brazil. The latter is also the only Latin American country among the largest consumer credit markets, ranking seventh, and is globally third in growth rate after China and Turkey. Brazil outranks both countries in customer credit per capita (Crédit Agricole Consumer Finance, 2011).

Interestingly, the traditional financial sector was not the first to perceive and respond to the opportunity represented by increasing income levels. As explained in the previous section, it was the retailing sector that spearheaded a revolution that not only supported the increase in consumption the retailers were longing for, but also allowed retailing companies to enter the financial services sector.

Lower-end retailers traditionally offered informal credit by allowing regular consumers to finish paying in their next shopping trip or even pay the entire due amount on the customer's payday. These are common practices in convenience stores throughout the Latin American subcontinent. Nevertheless, as the expanding middle class aspires to non-essential items offered by large retail chains, where purchases were infrequent, such trust-based relationships must be replaced by formal credit. Brazilian retailers pioneered the offer of installment payment plans, with booklets with payment dates and amounts due (including interest rate and fees) payable in the stores.

Over time, installment plans evolved into store cards, still providing for those customers not eligible for credit cards. The Chilean Cencosud first offered the Jumbo Más credit card more than ten years ago, in 2003, to facilitate in-store purchase (see box 4). The definitive step happened when the group acquired Banco París to become the company's financial retail division in 2005. This division now offers credit cards and insurance in addition to the brand-label cards and consumer credit and has expanded by opening its own bank in Peru and establishing joint ventures in Brazil and Argentina (Cencosud, 2012).

The banking sector, in turn, reacted to these developments by entering the white-label credit card business – that is, the management of credit cards branded after retail companies. In June 2013, for example, Cencosud sold a major share of its Chilean and Argentine credit card business to the Brazilian Itaú Unibanco (*Infobae*, 2013), which thereby increased its presence in consumer financing (see box 5). Banks also started offering payroll loans, or loans with repayments deducted automatically from the debtor's paycheck before the money could be spent elsewhere. This type of credit has expanded to virtually every country in Latin America as an alternative for customers with little collateral to offer and non-existent (or even negative) credit records. With pre-approved credits being offered at the automated teller machine (ATM) based on payroll account activity information, it is not surprising that payroll loans increased 16.5 per cent in Brazil to $88 billion and 32 per cent in Mexico to $9 billion in the twelve months through September 2012 (*The Wall Street Journal*, 2013).

Box 4 Cencosud

Centros Comerciales Sudamericanos S.A. was founded in 1960 in Santiago, Chile, and is now one of the largest conglomerates in Latin America. The company went public in 2004, although the original owner, the Paulmann family, retained control of the company. It expanded into Argentina, Brazil, Peru and Colombia through acquisition of local chains or the local operations of multinational retailers, such as Carrefour in Colombia. By the end of 2013, Cencosud operated 900 supermarkets, department stores, home improvement stores and shopping centers. In 2003, the company entered the financial retail sector with the creation of the store cards for the Jumbo supermarket chain. The financial branch of the company has been growing ever since through joint ventures, including one with Itaú-Unibanco, and acquisitions such as the specialty retail consumer bank Banco París in Chile. In 2010, the group established Banco Cencosud in Peru. As of December 2013, the group had revenues of $19.0 billion and net profit of $562.6 million, and a total of 4.7 million credit cards and other bank accounts in Chile, Argentina, Brazil, Colombia and Peru (Itaú, 2012).

Box 5 Itaú Unibanco

Itaú Unibanco S.A., headquartered in São Paulo, Brazil, is the largest financial group in Latin America, resulting from the merger in 2008 of Banco Itaú, founded in 1945, and Unibanco, which began in 1924 as the financial branch of a Brazilian retail chain. Itaú-Unibanco managed total assets of $523.5 billion in 2013, a net income of $7.3 billion with revenues of $41.4 billion. Itaú's shares are traded in São Paulo, Buenos Aires and New York, where the bank has been part of the Dow Jones Sustainability Index for the past thirteen years. The bank provides financial services including credit, insurance policies, investing tools, credit cards, saving accounts, pension plans, cash management, international trade financing, business transactions, mortgage loans, project financing and asset management. The bank has almost 100,000 employees in Brazil and in eighteen other countries, such as Argentina, Switzerland and the US.

This new breed of credit seems much easier to a customer base still uneasy in the face of financial operations. And because both installment cards and payroll loans have lower default rates than credit cards, these options are appealing for all parties involved.

As we can see above and in consumer finance, the boundary between the retail (Cencosud) and financial sectors (Banco Itaú-Unibanco) in Latin America is blurring. Both compete after the consumer appetite of the middle class. Technology offers an opportunity for different players from different sectors to offer financial services. The battle has just started, and there is no clear winner yet.

Housing demand has also increased. Around 40 per cent of families in Latin America live in inadequate housing conditions, but less than one-quarter of all housing is financed through formal mechanisms. Legal reforms and government subsidies therefore contributed to a sustained increase in mortgage portfolios of financial institutions throughout the continent. Moreover, this segment has experienced sustained growth for more than a decade without, according to some experts, signs of real-estate bubbles or housing prices misalignment (Cubeddu et al., 2012a), though others have voiced concerns about possible real-estate bubbles in São Paulo and Rio and other major cities in Latin America.

Furthermore, mortgage credit in Latin America stands well below the levels observed in other emerging regions. In the six most financially open Latin American economies – Brazil, Chile, Colombia, Mexico, Peru and Uruguay – mortgages average 7 per cent of GDP, versus 20 per cent or more in emerging Asia and above 65 per cent in the US (Cubeddu et al. 2012b). It is therefore not surprising that corporate credit has grown faster in the construction sector than in any other industry in Latin America (Hansen and Sulla, 2013).

The increasing household indebtedness and the possible negative consequences of credit oversupply (such as inflationary pressure and deteriorating quality of the financial sector's portfolio), as well as recent reports of cases of abusive practices by both retailers and banks, might increase government regulation and public mistrust. Nevertheless, these should not hamper the evolution of financial services for the emerging middle class.

Automotive Sector

Latin America is the most urbanized region in the developing world. Nearly 80 per cent of its population, or 470 million people, lived in urban areas in 2010, and there are fifty-one cities with populations over 1 million; overall car ownership and car use in Latin America are therefore higher than would be expected based on population and GDP per capita levels (IDB, 2013). Since 2005, South America has boasted the strongest growth rates in the automotive original equipment manufacturers (OEM) sector worldwide. Combined sales for OEM operations for Brazil and Argentina grew an average of 20 per cent per year between 2005 and 2010, ahead of Asia with 18 per cent and leaving North America and Europe far behind, with 7 per cent and 2 per cent, respectively (Powers, 2012).

Buoyed by renewed confidence in local macroeconomic stability, the emergence of the middle class in Latin America played a relevant role in the decision of automotive OEMs to invest in the region. During the 2008 crisis, companies enlarged their footprint in Latin America by modernizing plants and increasing productive capacity. Some firms used the opportunity to enter the region, such as the Korean Hyundai, which started operations in Mexico and Brazil, and the Chinese Chery with an assembly line in Brazil and auto parts manufacturing in Venezuela and Uruguay. Manufacturers that insisted on supplying Latin American markets with antiquated business models – for example, hand-me-down equipment and past-generation vehicles – will quickly be left behind by these more dynamic entrants (Powers, 2012).

With regards to the automotive industry, the region can be divided into three groups of countries. Brazil is the lone representative of the first group, the leading producing nation that largely consumes the vehicles it manufactures. The second group consists of countries such as Argentina, Colombia, Mexico and Venezuela, which are also major manufacturers that export part of their output, but which require substantial vehicle imports to meet domestic demand. Automobile ownership per capita is slightly above the world average in Argentina, Mexico and Brazil. These three countries alone account for the largest number of vehicles and the strongest increase in sales in the last ten years. In the third and final group are countries such as Chile, Paraguay, Peru and Uruguay, which import all the vehicles sold domestically. Peru and Colombia are far below world averages in terms of car ownership (IDB, 2013). Also, the fleet age in Latin America is older than the world average, providing a final additional push to demand in the region (BBVA Research, 2010; ANFAVEA, 2013).

Although the number of local players in the automotive sector is relatively small compared to its Asian counterparts, they include the Brazilians Troller (off-road vehicles), Agrale (motorcycles and agricultural tractors), Marcopolo, Comil, Neobus and Busscar (buses) and Randon S.A. (trucks and loaders); in Mexico, Mastretta (automobiles) and Dina (trucks and buses).[6] Many of the local manufacturers have reached a significant market share in excess of what would be expected given their size and the fact that they cannot compete with the world leaders; many even manage to sustain reasonable exporting levels.

Companies in the automotive manufacturing industry benefit from improved social and economic conditions in direct and indirect ways. Consider bus manufacturer Marcopolo, for example, the only local player to become a multinational company, while retaining 45 per cent of the Brazilian market. A larger middle class implies more people commuting. This places additional stress on already strained urban mass-transit systems and an increase in the use of bus transportation to cover the deficiencies. Brazil's failure to upgrade its mass transportation system on time is thus giving a boost to Marcopolo (box 6) (Bloomberg, 2013). In January 2013, the Brazilian government reduced excise taxes on buses and trains to support the renewal and expansion of municipal urban transportation systems. In addition, municipalities used subsidized credit to buy more than 23,600 buses between 2008 and 2012 to shuttle students from rural areas to school through the *Caminho da Escola* (Way to School, which also supported the acquisition of motorboats and bicycles for the same objective [*Blog Ponto de Ônibus*, 2013]). Marcopolo sold 3,911 schoolbuses to the state under that program in 2012 and was authorized to manufacture up to 4,100 by October 2013. Added to tax cuts designed to stimulate domestic industry that benefitted the capital goods sector, urban buses became the driving segment of the industry in Brazil (Marcopolo, 2013).

Box 6   Marcopolo

Marcopolo S.A. was founded in 1949 in Brazil. The company went public in 1973 and today manufactures almost half of all bus and microbus bodies built in the country. It is the third-largest manufacturer of bus bodies in the world. Its portfolio includes bodies for both urban and highway-transportation buses and for motor coaches, vans and recreational vehicles. The company produces 32,000 buses per year under brand names including Volare, Fratello, Andare, Paradiso, Viaggio, Torino and Viale in seventeen plants scattered across Brazil and five other countries: Argentina, Colombia, Mexico, Portugal and South Africa. In addition, the company has joint ventures with companies such as Daimler and Tata Motors in China, Australia, Egypt, India and Mexico. Net revenues reached $1.4 billion in 2013, and the company employs over 22,000 people worldwide. Although exports represent roughly 40 per cent of the total bus bodies manufactured by Marcopolo, they accounted for almost 70 per cent of the revenues in 2011. Marcopolo's exports from Brazil grew 25.9 per cent in 2012 in relation to the previous year (Marcopolo, 2013).

The auto manufacturing industry relies on a vast network to ensure the timely supply of all necessary auto parts. It is only natural that the industry also receives a boost from the greater demand for automobiles, motorcycles, buses and trucks. Protectionist policies in Brazil and Argentina are giving local suppliers further competitive advantage in the region over suppliers located abroad. High import tariffs on passenger cars (35 per cent in Brazil, 21.5 per cent in Argentina) and auto parts (16.5 per cent in Brazil and 17.5 per cent in Argentina) stimulate local sourcing. So, too, do local-content requirements: in Brazil, a bill mandates that as much as 30 to 60 per cent of a vehicle's components must be purchased from local suppliers. Some 17 per cent of major modules produced in South America are assembled in supplier parks within minutes of the vehicle assembly site. Ford's operation in Camaçari, on Brazil's east coast – a region with no previous history of auto manufacturing – arranged for twenty-six suppliers to establish operations in and around its manufacturing site, promising them a larger share of vehicle work content as an incentive (Powers, 2012).

In short, the key to survival in Latin America is to adapt to and exploit the characteristics and demands of the local market. Automotive multinationals are the winners in the region. The most successful model in Latin America in recent years was the American Ford EcoSport, an urban car with an off-road look conceived especially for the Brazilian market and launched in 2003. Special features included flex engines that run on either petrol or ethanol and a compact chassis to facilitate navigation in narrow and crowded streets. It has been a best-selling product in Brazil, Argentina, Venezuela and Mexico ever since, having sold more than 700,000 units through 2011. In 2012, Ford announced that the second generation of the model, developed by Brazilian engineers, was to be exported to India, China and Thailand.

Consumer Goods and Services

People living at the subsistence level often spend 100 per cent of their income on basic items such as food, non-alcoholic beverages and housing. This group of consumers has little money left over to purchase items other than those that cover their basic needs. Such items are typically included in the category of consumer goods, and their demand is both irregular (following the ebbs and flows of revenue from informal employment) and highly price-sensitive. Nevertheless, a significant portion of low- and lower-middle–income households in Latin America have running water, electricity and such basic appliances as refrigerators, televisions and radios. In many countries, a considerable number of urban households in that income range also have washing machines and access to cars. Penetration of mobile phones has gone beyond 100 per cent in most countries in the region.

As those households move into the middle class, the share of their expenditure dedicated to cover basic needs falls – perhaps 75 to 50 per cent of disposable income. The remainder is the discretionary income to be used for non-pressing needs. The fact that households are likely to already possess domestic appliances often means the budget surplus will be used to upgrade the quality of the consumer goods purchased. This means not only companies in the food and non-alcoholic drinks segment such as BRF (box 7) are expected to expand, but also a whole range of product segments could benefit as consumers widen their purchase choices. And because upper-income consumers divert a significant part of their budget to high-end categories (especially services, such as travel) and allocate only up to 35 per cent of their income to consumer goods, the growth of the middle-income tier might boost the consumer goods segment to unprecedented levels (*Euromonitor International*, 2013).

Companies that cater to the lower end of the socioeconomic spectrum are the first to benefit from the expanded purchasing power of consumers with modest incomes. Before moving on to higher-end products, households with rising incomes increase the frequency of consumption of lower-end staples. If the firm manages to capture the consumer at that point, it might succeed in diverting the consumer's attention from more celebrated brands. Peruvian Ajegroup is an example (box 8). In 1991, Ajegroup began selling homemade cola drink door to door. With a price point 30 to 35 per cent below those of Western brands Coca-Cola and Pepsi-Cola, and aggressive investments in cost reduction in production and distribution, it was able to retain consumers in twenty countries

---

Box 7   BRF (formerly Brasil Foods)

Headquartered in Itajaí, BRF is a company in the food-processing industry and one of the leaders in the world. BRF is the result of the 2009 merger of two Brazilian groups, Perdigão and Sadia. BRF raises, produces and slaughters poultry, pork and beef, as well as processing and selling fresh meat, milk and dairy products, pasta, frozen vegetables and soybean derivatives. With about 129,000 employees, it operates sixty-one plants in Brazil, five in Argentina, two in Europe and will soon open another in the Middle East. BRF's products are sold in more than 110 countries. The company had $13.0 billion in revenues and net profit of $465.5 million in 2013. BRF is traded on the São Paulo and New York stock exchanges. The company's main competitors are JBS, Marfrig, Tyson Foods and Bunge.

> **Box 8 Ajegroup**
>
> Founded in Peru in 1988 as Grupo Añaños, Ajegroup manufactures soft drinks and started distributing and selling them in 1991. It has been ranked twelfth on the list of the most global companies in Latin America compiled by the business magazine *América Economía*. For a family business owner, or for an entrepreneur looking for business pathways in Latin America, Ajegroup's strategic planning is exemplary, as they took advantage of expansion opportunities in the region. Ajegroup is present in more than twenty countries across the world and, in 2011, had sales of $1.45 billion.

throughout Latin America and Southeast Asia. As its loyal customers move up the social ladder and increase the consumption of carbonated sodas and other soft drinks, Ajegroup's brands remain a favorite. Its flagship brand, Big Cola, currently shows up fourth among the most recognized soft drinks in the world – after Coke, Pepsi and Sprite. Ajegroup had to compete with two global giants, Coca-Cola and Pepsi-Cola. If we consider revenues for both companies, Mexico is the second-biggest country and Brazil the third. The region is a major playing ground in beverages.

Operating against the 'bottom-of-the-pyramid' brand loyalty that accounts for the success of Ajegroup and others is the increased discrimination of consumers with rising incomes. As disposable income and purchasing power increase, Latin American consumers become more discerning, discriminating and demanding in their tastes and expectations. Consumers can indulge themselves with purchases of higher-end products on occasion, aspiring to buy brands (especially leading brands) regardless of price because they embody quality and status. In addition, households under tight budgets are more likely to suffer financial losses due to poorly performing lower-end products. This probability leads consumers to pay more for quality rather than risk a product failure. Products whose appeal lies in their low prices therefore lose their advantage. Companies have to consider how to satisfy this desire for individuality in the way they market products in high-involvement categories, such as cars and personal care, and also in more common categories such as food and household products (Corpart, 2012).

Also relevant is the increasing participation of women in the workforce, rising from 32 per cent in 1990 to 53 per cent of working-age women in 2008 (ILO/UNDP, 2009). By the end of 2012, Latin America's workforce had over 100 million women. As women gain financial independence and increased decision-making autonomy over household

> **Box 9. Natura**
>
> Natura is a Brazilian cosmetics company with a compelling brand and vigorous growth in international and domestic markets. Natura is the leading manufacturer and merchandiser of beauty products in Brazil: household and personal care, solar filters, cosmetics, perfume and hair care products. The company sells its products through agents. Luiz Seabra founded Natura in 1969 and it became a public company listed on the São Paolo Stock Exchange in 2004. In 2013, Natura had revenues of $3 billion and net income of $365.5 million with 6,260 employees. Natura emphasizes its image as an environmentally friendly, sustainable company using organic products, working toward a sustainable planet and social support. The company also takes satisfaction in its research and development activity.

consumption, the trend is toward consumer goods that make daily life easier, such as automobiles, technology and communication devices, processed foods, prepared beverages, health care and childcare (Corpart, 2012). An example of a company that excelled in selling to this increasing segment is the Brazilian Natura (box 9). Based on close attention to women's needs (for instance, by promoting its products by portraying ordinary-looking women rather than supermodels) and a direct sales model through a network of 1.2 million 'consultant resellers', Natura expanded to Argentina, Chile, Colombia, Peru and Mexico.

Future Opportunities and Risks

Latin America has been experiencing sustained economic growth since the turn of the twenty-first century. This growth has been accompanied by an increase in purchasing power and a decrease in poverty levels in nearly every country in the region. This phenomenon has allowed a massive upward mobility of many Latin Americans to the middle class and has contributed to a surge in demand for goods and services, ranging from cars to health care, from financial services to mobile phones. Local companies, which are more attuned to local demand and local economic changes, have taken advantage of this increasing purchasing power.

The growing availability of information on what drives this class of consumers has inspired novel approaches to tap the potential of the flourishing consumer market across the region. Successful companies were able to cater to this new middle class by adjusting their strategies and innovating in product design and services. For example, the boost in consumer credit originated not from financial institutions, but the retail sector. Firms with winning products and services invested in quality to retain their edge. Grupo Monge in Costa Rica accompanied the rise of the customer base into middle and high classes by creating high-end stores while maintaining the original El Gallo Más Gallo brand. Foreign products no longer appeal to Latin American consumers without significant tailoring and marketing plans suited to local demands. The success of Ford EcoSport is due to the alignment of high engineering and adjusting to customers' needs in congested Latin cities.

As economic activity remains brisk, citizens also benefit from the new dynamism in the private sector. Formal employment rates are at the highest for the last decades as a result of stronger private economic activity (ECLAC/ILO, 2013). Bigger profits seize the attention of the media, and the general public presses firms to become more transparent and aware of their responsibilities as members of the community. Thus Natura Cosméticos has built a brand based on environment-friendly products and Banco Itaú-Unibanco invests $12,000 per elementary school student through the educational program *Raízes e Asas* (Roots and Wings).[7]

Initial public offerings further reinforce this tendency to transparency and accountability, in addition to contributing to the development of local financial markets. Also, private companies join the social clamor for a public sector free of corruption and capable of providing efficient services. In short, the private sector does not merely make money from the economic changes taking place in Latin America, but also plays an increasingly key role in crystallizing the subcontinent's social achievements.

Furthermore, as overall income expands, the economy moves up the productive chain. The fastest-growing companies in Latin America will be in industries no longer related to commodities such as minerals, oil or grains, but rather in those sectors that cater to final consumers, lifted by growing domestic and regional markets (Molinski, 2011). This means more value added to the products manufactured or assembled domestically. Higher aggregate value allows, in principle, higher tax revenue for local and national governments. Finally, higher-quality products require specialized production methods and machinery, thus increasing demand (and wages) for skilled labor.

Times are good for business and companies must be careful not to disconnect from reality. On the one hand, the ascent of the middle class is not irreversible. Most households currently included in the middle class are near the lower income threshold, still a missed paycheck away, as it were, from social and economic vulnerability. In such a situation, overconsumption financed by overindebtedness may strain household budgets even more.

Moreover, the middle class in Latin America is unlikely to slavishly follow the steps and consumption patterns of their counterparts in developed economies. Latin Americans expect product safety and corporate ethical standards as high as those practiced in the developed world, even if local legislation is, for the moment, lenient. Similarly, local players are expected to hold to social responsibility actions and standards as high as those present in the developed countries. Also, governments play a larger role in these economies by providing services usually supplied in high-income countries by private institutions and by regulating private activity in sensitive markets such as oil, telecommunications and energy. Business strategies must therefore account for the local context and keep pace with the region's unique development path.

The rise of the middle class in Latin America represents tremendous opportunities for both global and local players. The emergence of a middle-income class presents a rich opportunity for any entrepreneur who is willing to brainstorm outside the developed market or upper-class box. But companies operating in the region have to adjust their business models and deliver affordable products better suited to this new customer base. Once the additional boost provided by credit and labor market dynamics fades out, the maintenance of current growth rates will require more productivity gains. Local companies must resist the temptation of merely refurbishing products originally designed for either upper or lower ends of the income distribution.

As we close the chapter, a word of caution regarding the forecast for the region. GDP growth in Latin America averaged 4 per cent between 2003 and 2012, but went down to 2.6 per cent in 2013, and the forecast is similar for 2014. According to the OECD (2014), this sudden deceleration is due to a decline in commodity prices, because of slower growth in China. However, it is interesting to note that the decline in prices has been in minerals, but oil and gas prices are still high and agricultural products as well. Latin America is a big exporter of both oil and gas and agricultural products. The second cause of this decline is purported to be so-called tapering of quantitive easing of monetary policy in the US, with subsequent higher interest rates in the US. This, in turn, would cause an exodus of capital from emerging markets to 'safer' markets, such as the US. However, the quantitative easing has not stopped and the capital exodus from emerging markets has not materialized except for a few months (July–September 2013). For that reason, this chapter maintains its positive tone regarding Latin America.

Local firms that have emerged as global leaders in recent years are those able to survive in volatile markets. Instead of giving up amidst economic turmoil, multilatinas retooled, readjusted to the new environment and developed the ability to manage risk and seize new opportunities. They acted promptly when foreign multinationals either signaled they were unprepared to identify the incipient opportunities or preferred to withdraw (Casanova, 2009). By expanding into the natural markets of neighboring countries, the Latin American giants learned the nuts and bolts of managing international supply chains and multicurrency accounting systems, thus paving their way into the selected group of multinational corporations. As this chapter illustrates, the processes of multilatina success and middle-class consolidation are intertwined.

Notes

1. See Chapter 1 in this volume, by Dayton-Johnson, for background on the various definitions of the middle class, and Chapter 2, by Azevedo et al., for more information on the World Bank measure.
2. The informal economy refers to the economy that develops beyond the formal labor market, avoiding taxes and regulations. Most transactions are made in cash. Experts estimate that the informal economy could account for as much as 40 per cent of economic activity in Brazil. In the manufacturing sector in Brazil, about 48.6 per cent of women and 31.1 per cent of men work in the informal sector. One can find similar percentages all over Latin America (ILO, 2012).
3. The thirteen Latin American companies in the Global 500 of *Fortune* (July 2013) are: Petrobras, Banco do Brasil, Banco Bradesco, Vale, JBS, Itaúsa-Investimentos Itaú, Ultrapar Holdings and Brazilian Distribution (CBD) from Brazil, Pemex, América Móvil and CFE from Mexico, PDVSA from Venezuela and Ecopetrol from Colombia.
4. Corporate website, http://www.grupom.net/, date accessed 3 July 2013.
5. Corporate website, http://www.oxxo.com/comunidad/m-xico.htm, date accessed 30 August 2013.
6. Airdin, a subsidiary of the Mexican Dina, has a plant in Argentina, but it produces no automobiles or auto parts, only air compressors.
7. Examples from L. Casanova and A. Dumas (2012).

References

A. T. Kearney (2013) *Global Retail Development Index*.

América Economía (2011) 'Almacenes Exito comprará cadenas minoristas en Uruguay por $746M', *América Economía* (30 June), http://www.americaeconomia.com/negocios-industrias/fusiones-adquisiciones/almecenes-exito-comprara-cadenas-minoristas-en-uruguay-po, date accessed 5 September 2013.

ANFAVEA (2013) *Brazilian automotive industry yearbook* (São Paulo: Associação Nacional dos Fabricantes de Veículos Automotores).

BBVA Research (2010) *Latin America Automobile Market Outlook* (Madrid: BBVA Economic Analysis), December.

BBVA Research (2013) *EAGLEs: Emerging middle class in 'fast-track' mode* (Madrid: BBVA Economic Analysis), January.

Blog Ponto de Ônibus (2013) 'Caminho da Escola: educação, indústria, números e política', *Blog Ponto de Ônibus* (21 April) http://blogpontodeonibus.wordpress.com/2013/04/21/caminho-da-escola-educacao-industria-numeros-e-politica/, date accessed 18 August 2013.

Bloomberg (2013) 'Failed World Cup Projects Producing Rally for Marcopolo', *Bloomberg* (27 February), http://www.bloomberg.com/news/2013-02-27/failed-world-cup-projects-producing-rally-for-marcopolo.html, date accessed 18 August 2013.

Boza, M. (2012) 'Middle Class Market Boom: The Growing Middle Class in the Hemisphere Is Creating an Entirely New Base of Consumers', *Americas Quarterly*, vol. 6, no. 4, 66–72.

BusinessWeek (2014) 'Why Wal-Mart Hasn't Conquered Brazil', *BusinessWeek* (May 12–18), http://www.businessweek.com/articles/2014-05-08/why-walmart-hasnt-conquered-brazil, date accessed 1 June 2014.

Casanova, L. (2009) *Global Latinas: Emerging Multinationals from Latin America*, www.globallatinas.org (Basingstoke and New York: Palgrave Macmillan).

Casanova, L., F. Castellani, J. Dayton-Johnson, S. Dutta, N. Fonstad and C. Paunov (2011) *InnovaLatino: Fostering Innovation in Latin America*, www.innovalatino.org (Madrid: INSEAD/OECD, Ariel/Fundación Telefónica).

Casanova, L. and A. Dumas (2012) 'Should poverty alleviation be part of multinationals' corporate responsibility?', in *Global Compact International Yearbook 2012*, 62–66.

Cencosud (2012) *Annual Report 2012*, http://www.cencosud.com/?lang=en, date accessed 30 August 2013.

CNN Expansión (2013) 'FEMSA sube al cuarto lugar . . . en farmacias', *CNN Expansión* (22 May), http://www.cnnexpansion.com/negocios/2013/05/22/femsa-liderara-farmacias-ya-es-cuarto, date accessed 3 July 2013.

Corpart, G. (2012) 'The Latin American Consumer of 2020', *Americas Market Intelligence* (4 September), http://americasmi.com/en_US/expertise/articles-trends/page/the-latin-american-consumer-of-2020, date accessed 25 August 2013.

Crédit Agricole Consumer Finance (2011) *Consumer Credit worldside at end-2010*, (August), http://www.slideshare.net/caconsumerfinance/consumer-credit-worldwide, date accessed 30 August 2013.

Cubeddu, L., C. E. Tovar and E. Tsounta (2012a) 'Latin America: Vulnerabilities under construction?', *IMF Working Paper* (July).

Cubeddu, L. C., E. Tovar and E. Tsounta (2012b) 'Finance: Latin America's Mortgage Market', *Americas Quarterly*, no. 416, http://www.americasquarterly.org/latin-americas-mortgage-market, date accessed 30 August 2013.

ECLAC (2013) *Social panorama of Latin America 2012* (Santiago: United Nations Economic Commission for Latin America and the Caribbean).

ECLAC/ILO (2013) *The employment situation in Latin America and the Caribbean* (Santiago and Geneva: United Nations Economic Commission for Latin America and the Caribbean and International Labor Organization).

Economist, The (2007) 'Adiós to poverty, hola to consumption', *The Economist* (18 August), http://www.economist.com/node/9645142, date accessed 2 September 2013.

Euromonitor International (2013) *Regional Focus: Latin America's Low-Income Consumers – A Large but Challenging Market* (28 March).
Ferreira, F. H. G., J. Messina, J. Rigolini, L. F. López-Calva, M. A. Lugo and R. Vakis (2013) *Economic Mobility and the Rise of the Latin American Middle Class* (Washington, DC: World Bank).
Globo, O. (2011) 'Chilena Cencosud compra rede de supermercados Prezunic', *O Globo* (16 November), http://oglobo.globo.com/economia/chilena-cencosud-compra-rede-de-supermercados-prezunic-3250377, date accessed 1 September 2013.
Gudlavalleti, S., S. Gupta and A. Narayana (2013) 'Developing winning products for emerging economies', *McKinsey Quarterly* (May).
Hansen, N. H. and O. Sulla (2013) 'Credit Growth in Latin America: Financial developoment or credit boom?', *IMF Working Paper* (May) (Washington, DC: International Monetary Fund).
IDB (2013) *Mitigation Strategies and Accounting Methods for Greenhouse Gas Emissions from Transportation* (Washington, DC: Inter-American Development Bank).
iEco (2012) 'América Latina se convierte en la nueva tierra prometida de la industria del retail', *iEco* (11 March), http://www.ieco.clarin.com/economia/America-Latina-convierte-prometida-industria_0_661734064.html, date accessed 3 July 2013.
ILO/UNDP (2009) *Work and Family: Towards new forms of reconciliation with social co-responsibility* (Geneva and New York: International Labour Organization and United Nations Development Programme). http://www.ilo.org/wcmsp5/groups/public/@dgreports/@gender/documents/publication/wcms_111375.pdf, date accessed 15 June 2014.
ILO (2012) Statistical update on employment in the Informal Economy (Geneva: Department of Statistics, International Labour Organization), http://laborsta.ilo.org/applv8/data/INFORMAL_ECONOMY/2012-06-Statistical%20update%20-%20v2.pdf, date accessed 10 June 2014.
Infobae (2013) 'El Banco Itaú compró las tarjetas de crédito de Jumbo, Disco y Vea', *Infobae* (18 June), http://www.infobae.com/notas/716031-El-Banco-Itau-compro-las-tarjetas-de-credito-de-Jumbo-Disco-y-Vea.html, date accessed 3 July 2013.
Itaú (2012) *Annual Report 2012*, http://www.itau.com/, date accessed 20 August 2013.
Latin Business Chronicle (2013) 'Top 500 Latin American Companies Ranking', *Latin Business Chronicle*, http://www.latinbusinesschronicle.com, date accessed 12 June 2013.
López-Calva, L. F. (2012) 'Meet Latin America's Real Middle Class: What they believe, what they purchase, what they want', *Americas Quarterly*, vol. 6, no. 4, 53–57.
López-Calva L. F. and E. Ortiz-Juarez (2011) *A vulnerability approach to the definition of the middle class* (December), (Washington, DC: The World Bank).
Marcopolo (2012) *Management Report 2012*, http://www.marcopolo.com.br/website/2011/marcopolo_sa/en, date accessed 30 August 2013.
McKinsey & Company (2011) 'In Latin America, a little respect goes a long way in retail', *Consumer and Shopper Insights* (September).
Molinski, M. (2011) 'Capitalizing on Latin America's middle-class rise', *The Wall Street Journal* (28 November), http://www.marketwatch.com/story/capitalizing-on-latin-americas-middle-class-rise-2011-11-28, date accessed 30 August 2013.

M2Farma (2013) 'Fusões e aquisições renderam R$9,12 bilhões às grandes redes de farmácia', *M2Farma Blog* (26 May), http://m2farma.com/blog/fusoes-e-aquisicoes-renderam-r912-bilhoes-as-grandes-redes-de-farmacia/, date accessed 2 September 2013.

OECD [Organisation for Economic Co-operation and Development] (2014) *OECD Economic Outlook* (Paris: OECD Publishing).

Powers, C. (2012) *South American Auto Manufacturing: The Supplier Localization Movement*, Oliver Wyman, available at http://www.oliverwyman.com/media/South_American_Auto_Manufacturing_FINAL.pdf, date accessed 29 August 2013.

RaiaDrogasil (2013) *Institutional presentation*, http://www.raiadrogasil.com.br/raiadrogasil/web/download_arquivos.asp?id_arquivo=AF52D37F-E400-41AC-9511-C61ED988358C, date accessed 10 September 2013.

Rigolini, J. (2012) 'Latin America's Middle Class in Global Perspective', *Americas Quarterly*, vol. 6, no. 4, 59–65.

Valor Econômico (2013) 'Drogarias Pacheco e São Paulo lucraram R$16,5 milhões no 4º trimestre', *Valor Econômico* (18 July 2012), http://www.valor.com.br/empresas/2756600/drogarias-pacheco-e-sao-paulo-lucraram-r-165-milhoes-no-4, date accessed 5 September 2013.

Wall Street Journal, The (2013) 'Latin America's New Credit Frontier', *The Wall Street Journal* (6 January), http://online.wsj.com/article/SB10001424127887323689604578222130866020660.html, date accessed 20 August 2013.

8
Feeling Middle Class and Being Middle Class: What Do Subjective Perceptions Tell Us?

Eduardo Lora and Johanna Fajardo-González

Economic definitions of middle class often rely on arbitrary boundaries defined by measures of central tendency, quantiles of the distribution or absolute thresholds based on a measurable characteristic, such as income or consumption.[1] In practice, there is little agreement on what and how big the middle class is (the variety of approaches undertaken by the contributors to this volume bears out this assertion). Likewise, most economists often ignore that membership in a given class is also driven by *social* status, the relative individual situation in a social hierarchy affected by life opportunities, lifestyles and a diversity of attitudes.

Understanding how perceived social rankings are formed and why those rankings differ from objective rankings may shed light on key political issues, such as attitudes toward income redistribution via taxes and public spending. Preferences for redistribution respond to individuals' beliefs regarding their own position in a social ranking and on how they achieved that position (Alesina and La Ferrara, 2005; Gaviria, 2007; Senik, 2009). However, those preferences may change when individuals are confronted with information about their actual standing in the social ranking (Cruces, Pérez-Truglia and Tetaz, 2013). In a similar way, those who perceive that their social position has declined hold more positive attitudes toward redistribution (Guillaud, 2013), while those who perceive that they have experienced higher mobility are less supportive of redistributive policies (Gaviria, 2007). Perceived social ranking – and the gap between perceived and objective social ranking – may also influence people's aspirations and their decisions regarding what they buy and whether they work in the labor market, among other key economic outcomes.

The existing literature on subjective social rankings indicates that self-rankings of social position offer a distorted picture of actual income rankings and of income distribution. Self-rankings tend to concentrate around the lower-middle points of the scales. While self-rankings are strongly associated with individuals' incomes, they are also influenced by many other individual and contextual variables. Beliefs of the income distribution are similarly distorted by these biases, as people underestimate income differences with respect to those far away from them in the income scale of their societies (Ravallion and Loshkin, 2002; Nuñez, 2005; Cruces, Pérez Truglia and Tetaz, 2013).

This chapter has three main objectives. First, it provides a subjective classification of the populations of sixteen Latin American countries into low, middle and high classes, based on a self-perceived social ranking. Second, it analyzes whether such a subjective classification matches two standard income-based measures of social class. Since the mismatches between the objective and the subjective classifications are fairly large, the third objective is to explore what factors, in addition to income, are associated with the self-perceived social ranking of Latin American households and to what extent those factors help to explain why so many people classify themselves as middle class, when they are not middle class if judged on the basis of their income levels.

Defining the Subjective Middle Class in Latin America

We propose a subjective definition of middle class based on the self-valuation of relative social position. Our main data source is the 2007 World Gallup Poll, which provides the most extensive coverage of both objective and perceived conditions of quality of life, including economic and social conditions. The samples are representative of the population aged fifteen or over in each country. In this study, we use information on sixteen Latin American countries, the only ones for which the Gallup Poll provides data on both perceived social ranking and on family income. Perceived social ranking is measured as follows: 'Please look at this card. Imagine in one end are located the "Richest people" of [COUNTRY] and in the other end are located the "Poorest people" of [COUNTRY]. Taking into consideration your current personal situation could you please tell me in which cell you place yourself?'

On average, Latin Americans rate their social position at rung 4.2. Roughly two in three Latin Americans classify themselves in rungs three through five, and only about 6 per cent consider themselves to be placed in the four highest rungs (see the 'Total' column of table 8.1).

Rung five is the mode for the whole sample. Therefore most people believe they belong to the lower-middle fraction of the social ranking in their countries. Those in one objective income decile (of their own countries) do not necessarily place themselves in that decile when answering the ladder-subjective question (table 8.2).[2] The mode for self-placement is rung five for all the deciles, except the two lowest ones, where the mode is rung three. Although objectively richer people classify themselves on higher rungs, the distribution of responses is not close to the NW-SE forty-five-degree diagonal that would be obtained if the subjective and the objective classifications matched perfectly. Therefore, the simple option of defining the subjective middle class as some central range of the ladder question on social ranking, or any other ad-hoc threshold, would be inadequate for our purposes. Instead, we propose a definition of subjective social classes that is interrelated with the sizes of the objective classes using alternative definitions established in the literature on (objective) middle classes, as explained below.

We estimate the size of the objective middle classes with two alternative definitions of middle class commonly used in the literature. The first corresponds to those households whose daily income falls in the

Table 8.1 Income Distribution and Self-Assessment of Social Position (percentage of individuals).

Self-assesment of social position	Decile of the Income Distribution										
	1	2	3	4	5	6	7	8	9	10	Total
Poorest	7.8	5.5	+	+	+	+	+	+	*	*	+
1	12.2	8.8	7.8	5.4	5.7	5.0	+	+	+	+	5.5
2	17.6	13.9	11.2	11.2	9.9	8.7	6.3	5.3	+	+	8.7
3	18.5	21.0	19.0	18.1	17.5	19.0	13.2	14.1	13.8	8.4	16.3
4	17.5	19.3	20.9	21.9	21.2	21.3	22.9	21.3	18.9	14.0	19.9
5	17.2	20.8	24.1	24.7	25.1	26.2	29.7	31.2	30.2	30.7	26.0
6	+	5.8	7.1	8.6	9.9	9.6	12.9	12.4	15.7	18.8	10.1
7	+	+	+	+	5.1	+	6.3	7.5	9.4	13.3	5.0
8	+	+	+	+	+	+	+	+	+	6.4	+
9	*	*	*	*	*	*	*	*	*	+	*
Richest	*	*	*	*	*	*	*	*	*	*	*

*Proportion is less than 1%.
+Proportion between 1% and 5%.

Note: The data in each column add up to 100%. Bold numbers represent the maximum percentage by column.

Source: Authors' calculations using Gallup (2007).

absolute range between $2 at 2005 prices adjusted for purchasing power parity (the median value of the poverty line in seventy developing countries) and $13 (the poverty line in the US), as proposed by Ravallion (2010). The second corresponds to those households that fall in the range between 0.5 and 1.5 times the median income, introduced by Davis and Huston (1992) and applied to Latin America and the Caribbean in OECD (2010).

We group households in a subjective middle class (by country) having the same size (by number of observations in the sample) as in the objective middle-class definition chosen. The procedure is as follows. First, we generate uniformly distributed random values on a range +/-0.5 to translate the categorical question of social ranking into a continuous variable for all the individuals in our sample. Second, we rank the observations in the sample for each country from the lowest to the highest value of this continuous variable and classify the lowest as subjective poor until the subjective-poor group size equals the objective-poor group size in their respective country. We repeat the second step to classify the following individuals in the sample by country into subjective middle class and rich, using the objective middle-class size and the objective rich-group size as references. As a result, for each class within a given country, the corresponding objective and subjective measures have approximately the same relative size. The procedure allows for direct comparisons with the objective definitions of middle classes without imposing ad-hoc criteria to the subjective data.

The Size of the Mismatches

Table 8.2 Matching Coefficients for Two Objective Definitions of Middle Class.

Subjective	Objective			Total Subjective
	Poor	Middle-class	Rich	
(a) Definition based on the absolute threshold of 2 to 13 USD PPP a day				
Poor	5.9	9.9	1.0	16.8
Middle-class	10.1	45.5	10.0	65.7
Rich	0.9	10.2	6.4	17.5
Total Objective	16.9	65.7	17.5	100.0
(b) Definition based on 0.5 to 1.5 times the median of the income distribution				
Poor	13.0	11.0	5.1	29.1
Middle-class	11.9	18.8	11.1	41.8
Rich	4.6	12.0	12.6	29.2
Total Objective	29.5	41.8	28.7	100.0

Source: Authors' calculations based on Gallup (2007).

By construction, the relative sizes of the classes are the same in the objective and the subjective classifications:[3] using the absolute threshold, roughly 17, 66 and 18 per cent for the poor, middle and rich classes, respectively (table 8.2). However, those that are classified consistently (and therefore are placed on the NW-SE diagonal of the table) represent only 57.9 per cent of the total sample. Of the total sample, 45.5 per cent are consistently classified as middle class in the objective and the subjective scales. Their 'matching coefficient' is 69.3 per cent,[4] defined as the percentage of correct subjective and objective classifications of those belonging to the middle class by country. In a similar way, in panel b),

Table 8.3 Correlation and Matching Coefficients by Country (objective definition).

	Middle Class Size		Correlation (a)		Matching Coefficient (b)	
	Based on absolute threshold	Based on the Median	Based on absolute threshold	Based on the Median	Based on absolute threshold	Based on the Median
Country						
Argentina	57%	46%	0.196**	0.196**	62%	47%
Bolivia	64%	42%	0.186**	0.186**	67%	45%
Brazil	67%	45%	0.166**	0.166**	68%	49%
Chile	71%	45%	0.341**	0.341**	77%	52%
Costa Rica	60%	42%	0.280**	0.280**	65%	41%
Dominican Rep.	61%	34%	0.292**	0.292**	66%	33%
Ecuador	69%	44%	0.267**	0.267**	72%	46%
El Salvador	66%	43%	0.218**	0.218**	71%	47%
Guatemala	71%	42%	0.174**	0.174**	73%	48%
Honduras	73%	45%	0.087**	0.087**	72%	45%
Mexico	66%	40%	0.308**	0.308**	71%	45%
Nicaragua	65%	41%	0.268**	0.268**	70%	46%
Panama	70%	41%	0.147**	0.147**	70%	45%
Paraguay	65%	39%	0.257**	0.257**	70%	44%
Peru	64%	39%	0.247**	0.247**	67%	44%
Uruguay	59%	39%	0.160**	0.160**	60%	36%
Average	66%	42%	0.285***	0.245***	69%	45%

Notes:

a. Kendall's Tau Coefficient; significant at the ***99 per cent level, **95 per cent level, *90 per cent level.

b. Matching coefficient: Full middle class size to average middle class size ratio, by country.

The absolute threshold definition corresponds to $2–$13 PPP a day.

The median-based definition corresponds to 0.5 to 1.5 times the country's median income.

Source: Authors' calculations based on Gallup (2007).

which uses the median income to define classes, those on the diagonal represent only 44.3 per cent of the total sample, and around 19 per cent of the whole sample are consistently classified as middle class in the objective and the subjective scales, with a matching coefficient of 45 per cent.[5]

With the absolute income definition, on average two-thirds of the populations of the Latin American countries are middle class, while with the median income definition, about 42 per cent are (table 8.3). The average matching coefficients for the whole sample, as mentioned, are 69 per cent and 45 per cent, respectively. Matching coefficients across countries show little variation around these averages. Despite the mismatches, there is a positive and significant degree of correlation between each objective measure of social class and the subjective definition. For the whole sample, the high significance of the Kendall[6] correlation coefficients of the relationship between subjective and objective social classes suggests that ranking by income is indeed relevant in the subjective valuation that individuals make of their relative wealth condition. However, the fact that those coefficients are consistently below 0.3 indicates that there are other factors affecting this valuation, to which we now turn.

What Influences the Perceived Social Position of Latin Americans?

What factors other than income seem to influence how people see themselves along a relative social scale within their countries? Answering this question may provide a useful characterization of the subjective middle classes in Latin America. In order to identify what factors people take under consideration when placing themselves on a subjective social ranking, we posit that perceived social ranking depends on all forms of wealth, actual and perceived. Following the classification proposed by IDB (2008), those factors can be organized in three main categories: 1) capabilities, 2) relational goods, which include family conditions and other interpersonal conditions, and 3) material conditions of life, which comprise income, financial circumstances and physical assets.

The first category, *capabilities*, includes variables that are specific to the individual, such as gender, age, health status (which can be measured by the EQ-5D, a standardized instrument that inquires about the presence of health problems in five dimensions: mobility, self-care, usual activities, pain/discomfort and anxiety/depression[7]) and education level.

Capabilities are necessary conditions for personal fulfillment and social development (Sen, 1985).

The second category, *relational goods,* is the group of variables referring to the individual in relation to others. It includes family conditions, such as marital status and childbearing, and other interpersonal conditions, which reflect the extent and depth of relations of the individual, including whether she declares to have friends to rely on, whether or not religion is important in her personal life and whether she is employed and has a supervisor.

The *material conditions of life* are subdivided into three groups: 1) income, 2) financial circumstances and 3) physical assets. The household's income per capita is the most obvious manifestation of wealth. If all forms of wealth were adequately measured through the other variables considered in our model, and if all of them had perfect functioning markets, it would be unnecessary to include income separately in the regression model, as total income would correspond to the flow of returns from all the different forms of wealth. Since these conditions are not met, the inclusion of income is clearly warranted.

Financial circumstances comprise actual and perceived circumstances. To summarize the information on access and use of financial services, we have constructed an Access to Financial Services Index, calculated with principal components analysis (PCA). For its calculation, we include the following list of dichotomous variables: whether or not the individual has a savings account, a checking account, an ATM card, certificates of deposit, a credit card and savings for retirement. Perceptions of financial circumstances may affect how people see themselves along the social ladder. They are measured with the answers to the questions of whether or not the individual has shortages of income to cover food costs and housing costs and a composite variable that summarizes the absence of other financial concerns.[8]

Finally, *physical assets* include variables of ownership of non-financial assets such as house, television, computer, automobile, washing machine and freezer. We also include in this subgroup variables of access to running water and electricity as well as the location (urban or rural) of residence as proxies of the possession of, or access to, other assets. Apart from the individual-level variables, country dummies are included in order to control for differences in unobservable country-specific characteristics, such as asset prices and all forms of social capital not differentiated across individuals.

To estimate the correlates of subjective social ranking, we implement an ordered logistic regression analysis on the ladder question variable (see Lora and Fajardo, 2013, for technical details). Namely, controlling for all of the variables enumerated above, what factors lead people to evaluate their relative position more highly? The main conclusion of our findings is that people judge their social ranking taking into consideration *all forms of wealth*, not just their current income.

First, individuals' judgment of their social ranking is affected by their human capabilities. Women tend to be more conforming than men: that is, they are more likely to place themselves in the higher rungs of the ladder. Age shows the familiar U-shape found in happiness studies, which in this context implies that, controlling for income and all the other factors mentioned, self-classification in a social ranking ladder declines with age until about seventy-two years of age and then increases. Other aspects of human capabilities that influence perceived social ranking are health status and education, consistent with the hypothesis that human capital is part of wealth, on the basis of which perceptions of social ranking are formed.

The same goes for the different forms of relational capital, which are sources of interpersonal relations and support, such as family, friends and religion. Thus, having a spouse and having one or more children are associated with a higher subjective classification. Surprisingly, being divorced, as compared with being single, is also associated with higher subjective social ranking. It should be noted in this respect that our estimates point only to correlates of subjective social ranking, without implying causality (divorce may be more common among those with more wealth, but may not necessarily be a *source* of higher subjective social ranking). Having friends is also associated with higher perceived social ranking, since they may be a source of help and support. We also observe a similar association between religion and the subjective social ranking. Of all the relational goods for which the Gallup Poll provides information, only having a job (after controlling for income) and having a supervisor are *not* associated with higher subjective social ranking among Latin Americans.

Material conditions of life are, of course, central in how people judge their relative standing in society. Income is a strong determinant of subjective social ranking, as already mentioned. Our estimates imply that when income doubles, keeping everything else constant, the probability of being at the sixth rung of the perceived social ranking ladder increases by 1.18 percentage points.[9] But apart from income, many other aspects of the financial and material situation of individuals affect their self-evaluation of relative social ranking. Having access to financial services and ownership of a variety of physical assets certainly contributes to feeling richer. Perceived social ranking is strongly associated with feelings of economic vulnerability (as captured in the variables which measure sufficiency of income to cover food and housing costs, and 'not being concerned with financial matters'). Finally, perceived social ranking is higher in urban areas.

Our results are largely consistent with those of Ravallion and Loshkin (2002) for Russia, where perceived social ranking is influenced not just by income, but also marital status, family size and composition, education, health, employment status and ownership of several assets (car, freezer, washer, television and VCR).

What Makes People Think They Are Middle Class (When They Are Not)?

The final step in our study is aimed at understanding what makes people think they are middle class when they are (objectively) classified either as poor or rich on the basis of their income. The inconsistency between objective and subjective social class has its origins, according to sociologists, in the imperfect correlation among income, occupation, education and some other factors such as local economic conditions, employment status, gender, marital status, talent and luck that create class ambivalence (Hout, 2008).

We use multinomial regressions (see Lora and Fajardo, 2013, for technical details) where the dependent variable is a categorical variable which equals one if an individual being objectively poor classifies herself as middle class; two if an individual being objectively middle class classifies herself as middle class; and three if an individual being objectively rich classifies herself as middle class. We present results using our two definitions of middle class. The set of explanatory variables is the same as in the previous section.

Since all forms of wealth, and not just income, are taken into consideration by individuals when judging their relative position in society, many of those forms help to explain why some people objectively classified as poor or rich see themselves as middle class. Among the capabilities considered, having at least completed secondary education is a consistent factor that helps explain why some people that are poor on the basis of their income classify themselves as middle class (while not having such education makes some rich people see themselves as middle class). Not being in good health contributes to explain why some people that make more than 1.5 times the median income (and are therefore rich on this criterion) consider themselves middle class. Among relational goods, having one or more children also consistently contributes to explain the mismatches. The contribution of children to mismatches suggests that people do not see children as household wealth: while having children is associated with a higher rung on the subjective social ranking, *not* having children makes some objectively poor people see themselves as middle class (and *having* children makes some rich people see themselves as middle class). Being married and having friends are relational goods that also help explain the mismatches, although in a less consistent way.

Among the material conditions of life variables, the following consistently contribute to explain the mismatches in both directions: 'access to financial services', 'not concerned with financial matters', 'has an automobile' and 'has a washing machine'. The following help to explain why some poor see themselves as middle class: 'access to running water service', 'access to telephone service', 'has a television' and 'has a freezer'. Since virtually all the objectively rich have these assets, these variables do not contribute much to explain why some rich people perceive themselves as middle class. Finally, not having a computer contributes to why some objectively rich people (on the basis of their income) perceive themselves as middle class.

We also found that in addition to all the individual variables, objectively poor persons of some countries tend to classify themselves more often as middle class than those of other countries, and likewise objectively rich people. The small number of countries in our sample (sixteen) prevents us from doing a rigorous analysis of the factors associated with those differences. However, and for illustrative purposes only, we estimate pair-wise correlations (see Lora and Fajardo, 2013, for technical details) between the country dummy coefficients and indicators of the state of development at the country level, namely income per capita, life expectancy and the set of variables of quality of public institutions developed by Kaufmann et al. (2009). Our results suggest that in more developed countries, fewer poor people tend to erroneously classify themselves as middle class, and more rich people tend to define themselves as middle class. In other words, the more developed the country, the stronger the downward bias in the subjective classification. This implies that the *relative* standards of reference that individuals use to judge whether they are middle class are consistently higher in more developed countries (when the definition of objective middle class is based on *relative* income).

Conclusions

Sociologists point out that proper analysis of social classes must consider both objective and subjective factors. However, economic literature often ignores the subjective aspect and opts for social-class analysis based on objective variables such as income and consumption. In this chapter we consider both strands of theory and use the subjective perception of social ranking to compare its match with two income-based definitions of middle class in Latin America using the rich data set of the 2007 Gallup World Poll.

The absolute threshold of daily incomes between $2 and $13 and the interval of 0.5 to 1.5 times the median income are two objective criteria to define the middle class widely used in the economic literature. With the first of these two criteria, only sixty-nine out of each hundred people that are objectively (subjectively) middle class classify themselves (objectively) as such, and with the second criterion only forty-five out of each hundred do so. Sociologists argue that inconsistencies between objective and subjective social class are due to a class ambivalence created by the imperfect correlation among standard economic variables such as income, occupation, education and some other factors such as local economic conditions, employment status, gender, marital status, talent and luck.

One of the objectives of this chapter has been to identify the factors behind the discrepancies between objective and subjective social classes. We have found strong and very consistent evidence that people consider many variables other than income when determining their social ranking. More precisely, they consider *all forms of capital*, be it personal capabilities, relational goods or material conditions of life, in their self-assessment of their position in society. The same set of factors that are associated with the self-ranking of individuals along the social ladder has been used in this chapter to explore why people who, based on income alone, are objectively not middle class define themselves as such. We found that having (or not) at least complete secondary education helps explain why some people that are objectively poor classify themselves as middle class (and why some rich people see themselves as middle class). *Not* having children makes some objectively poor people see themselves as middle class (and *having* children make some rich people see themselves as middle class). Among the material conditions of life variables, access to financial services, no concerns with financial matters, owning an automobile and owning a washing machine make some poor people self-classify themselves as middle class (and lack of those things make some rich see themselves as middle class). Access to running water service, access to telephone service and having a television and freezer increase the odds that a poor person sees herself as middle class, while not having a computer raises the odds that someone who is rich sees herself as middle class. Finally, persons of more developed countries within Latin America tend to classify themselves as belonging to a lower class than their exact counterparts (on the basis of their capabilities, relationships and belongings) in less developed countries of the region, implying that the standards of comparison do increase with social and economic development.

Notes

1. This chapter is an abridged and modified version of Lora and Fajardo (2013), and it is included in this volume by kind permission of Brookings Institution Press. The authors are grateful to Guillermo Cruces for extremely valuable support and advice during the preparation of the original article.
2. Since household income is reported in income brackets in the survey, we follow the methodology used by Gasparini at al. (2009) to estimate the intra-bracket distribution by assigning random income values in the corresponding income bracket.
3. Apart from minor differences that are below 1 per cent for all countries. This is due to inability to classify some individuals by one of the two criteria as some of them have missing values in either the income variable or the subjective classification variable.
4. Equal to 45.53/65.68, from panel (a) of table 8.2.
5. Equal to 18.79/41.75.
6. Kendall's rank correlation provides a distribution-free test of independence and a measure of the strength of dependence between two variables and the similarity between two different orderings.
7. The European Quality of Life-5 Dimensions Index (EQ-5D) is an indicator calculated on the basis of answers to quasi-objective questions of basic individual health conditions. The original EQ-5D studies were conducted in the United Kingdom and then implemented in the United States. See Dolan (1997) and Shaw et al. (2005).
8. A household head is considered to have financial worries if he claims to have one or more of the following problems: a) not having the capacity to pay for children's education; b) fears of not having enough money for retirement; c) not being able to maintain his current standard of living; or d) not being able to afford the medical costs of a serious illness or accident. The composite variable of not having financial concerns was calculated using the principal components analysis methodology.
9. By way of comparison, using the same Gallup data set and the question 'On what step of the ladder do you feel currently, with the highest step (10) representing the best possible life for you and the lowest step (0) representing the worst for you?', the ceteris paribus effect of doubling income implies that the probability of being at the sixth ladder in the life-satisfaction zero-to-ten scale increases by 0.37 percentage points.

References

Alesina, A. and E. La Ferrara (2005) 'Preferences for Redistribution in the Land of Opportunities', *Journal of Public Economics*, vol. 89, no. 5–6, 897–931.

Birdsall, N. (2010) 'The (indispensable) middle class in developing countries', in R. Kanbur and M. Spence, eds., *Equity and Growth in a Globalizing World* (Washington, DC: The International Bank for Reconstruction and the World Bank).

Cruces, G., R. Pérez-Truglia and M. Tetaz (2013) 'Biased Perceptions of Income Distribution and Preferences for Redistribution: Evidence from a Survey Experiment', *Journal of Public Economics*, vol. 98, 100–112.

Davis, J. and J. H. Huston (1992) 'The Shrinking Middle-Income Class: A Multivariate Analysis', *Eastern Economic Journal*, vol. 18, no. 3, 277–285.

Dolan, P. (1997) 'Modeling Valuations for Health States', *Medical Care*, vol. 35, no. 11, 1095–1108.

Gallup (2007) Gallup World Poll, http://www.gallup.com/strategicconsulting/en-us/worldpoll.aspx, date accessed 1 July 2014.

Gasparini L., W. Sosa, M. Marchionni and S. Olivieri (2009) 'Objective and Subjective Deprivation', in C. Graham and E. Lora, eds., *Paradox and Perception* (Washington, DC: The Brookings Institution).

Gaviria, A. (2007) 'Social mobility and preferences for redistribution in Latin America', *Economía*, vol. 8, no. 1, 55–96.

Guillaud, E. (2013) 'Preferences for redistribution: an empirical analysis over 33 countries', *Journal of Economic Inequality*, vol. 11, no. 1, 57–78.

Hout, M. (2008) 'How Class Works: Objective and Subjective Aspects of Class since 1970s', in A. Lareau and D. Conley, eds., *Social Class: How Does It Work?* (New York: Russell Sage Foundation).

IDB (2008) *Beyond Facts: Understanding Quality of Life*, Development in the Americas Report (Washington, DC: Inter-American Development Bank).

Kaufmann, D., A. Kraay and M. Mastruzzi (2009) 'Governance Matters VIII: Aggregate and Individual Governance Indicators 1996–2008', Policy Research Working Paper No. 4978 (Washington, DC: The World Bank).

Lora, E. and J. Fajardo (2013) 'Latin American Middle Classes: The Distance between Perception and Reality', *Economía*, vol. 14, no. 1, 33–60 (Brookings Institution Press).

Nuñez, J. (2005) 'Living under a Veil of Ignorance', mimeo (Santiago: Universidad de Chile).

OECD [Organisation for Economic Co-operation and Development] (2010) *Latin American Economic Outlook 2011: How Middle-Class Is Latin America?* (Paris: OECD Publishing).

Ravallion, M. (2010) 'The developing world's bulging (but vulnerable) middle class', *World Development*, vol. 38, no. 4, 445–454.

Ravallion, M. and M. Lokshin (2002) 'Self-Rated Economic Welfare in Russia', *European Economic Review*, vol. 46, no. 8, 1453–1473.

Sen, A. (1985) *Commodities and Capabilities* (Oxford, UK: Oxford University Press).

Senik, C. (2009) 'Direct evidence on income comparisons and their welfare effects', *Journal of Economic Behavior and Organization*, vol. 72, 408–424.

Shaw, J. W., J. A. Johnson and S. J. Coons (2005) 'U.S. Valuation of the EQ-5D Health States: Development and Testing of the D1 Valuation Model', *Medical Care*, vol. 43, no. 3, 203–220.

9
Political Attitudes of the Middle Class: The Case of Fiscal Policy

Christian Daude, Hamlet Gutiérrez and Ángel Melguizo

Fiscal policy – the way taxes and expenditures are allocated across society – reflects the political equilibrium within a given society.[1] This equilibrium is determined by multiple factors, such as the preferences of citizens for redistribution (that is, taxes and public spending that disproportionately benefit the least well off) and other socioeconomic and political dimensions, the distribution of power within society, the degree of influence of interest groups on the policymaking process and the political institutions that condition this process, just to mention some of the most commonly analyzed political variables.[2]

Given that in most middle-income or developed economies the median taxpayer is very likely to be part of the middle class or identify himself with middle-class values, it is important to understand the preferences and political influence of this group in shaping fiscal policies. In particular, for the case of Latin America, it seems puzzling that taxes and transfers are not more progressive, given the still high degrees of market-income inequality and the steady move toward democracy since the 1980s. Simply put, a median voter with low income in a democratic system would be expected to vote for electoral candidates campaigning on the promise of high taxes for the rich and generous social spending for the disadvantaged. As discussed in more detail below, the explanations for this apparent puzzle often relate to political factors, social mobility considerations as well as weaknesses in the provision and quality of public services. The question of the role of Latin America's middle classes in determining the level and composition of taxation as well as the priorities for public expenditures has recently received some interest in the literature, which we review in this chapter. The research reviewed relates more generally to the potential as well as effective role of the middle class in this context. The middle class is often seen as a key element that

Good sources and framework for ~~paper~~ 3rd essay

holds together the society and determines the social contract, through values such as meritocracy, patience and ethics (Doepke and Zilibotti, 2005). In this sense, Easterly (2001) and Easterly et al. (2006) present evidence that a broad middle class drives economic growth by increasing social cohesion and reducing political instability and conflict as well as shaping sustainable public policies in several areas, such as investment in infrastructure, health and education. More recently, Loayza et al. (2012) provide panel data evidence that societies with a larger middle class – controlling for income inequality, GDP per capita and poverty headcount – present higher levels of public expenditures (as share of GDP) on health as well as education.

At the same time, these authors find that a larger middle class is also associated with a higher quality of democracy and less corruption, as well as less distortive policies in the areas of trade protection and financial development. Therefore, cross-country analysis suggests that moving toward a society where the middle classes play a significant role in the economic and political arena could bring economic and social reforms that facilitate an inclusive development path. When looking at opinion polls regarding taxation services in Latin America, there is an association between different measures of tax morale – the degree to which people think that tax evasion is wrong – and perceiving yourself to be in the middle of the income distribution.[3] However, when other socioeconomic factors are taken into account, the perception of the relative position in the income distribution is only weakly related to attitudes toward taxation and redistribution (Daude and Melguizo, 2010).

In line with these results, distinct middle-class political values do not clearly stand out. For example, in a recent study López-Calva et al. (2012) find in six Latin American countries that '. . . values gradually shift with income, and middle class values lay between the ones of poorer and richer classes'. While the literature – and empirical evidence from developed economies – identifies the middle class as a potential source for demanding more public services and redistribution, Cárdenas et al. (Chapter 3 in this volume) show that for the case of Peru, the middle class does not favor redistribution from the rich to the poor or higher levels of taxation. Even its support for democracy is lower than among the poor. By contrast, the Peruvian middle classes seem to support growth-oriented and rather liberal economic policies. This result might be due to distrust toward the state because of corruption and weakness in the delivery of public services. Although it remains uncertain if these results also hold for the rest of the region, given the low levels of trust in government and public institutions, it seems likely that in several countries of the region the middle classes might follow a similar pattern of values and behaviors.

This chapter seeks to better understand the apparently conflicting role middle classes play in Latin America regarding fiscal policy and redistribution. In particular, we emphasize the role of relative income positions, social mobility and perceived quality of services as important factors to understand the level of tax morale of Latin America's middle classes. The remainder of the chapter is structured as follows. In the next section, we review the theoretical literature on middle class, social mobility and fiscal redistribution, putting emphasis on the alternative explanations that undermine the relevance of the median-voter theory for the case of Latin America's societies. Next, we discuss the empirical evidence of the different factors that affect tax morale and the demand for redistribution in Latin America and the role of the middle class. A final section concludes with some policy implications and points to some of the possible future directions of research needed.

The Median-Voter Model and Beyond

From a theoretical point of view, the median-voter model suggests that if *ex ante* inequality (i.e., before taxes and government transfers and other public expenditure) is high, as it is in Latin America, democracy should lead governments to raise revenues and carry significant redistribution (Downs, 1957). Simply put, in such a situation, the median voter is likely to benefit from progressive income taxation (which will fall more heavily upon voters with higher incomes than his) and progressive transfers and spending (which will disproportionately favor him). In this case, the middle class plays a key role, if they perceive a clear link between taxes and public goods and services. They are located in the middle of the income distribution and would determine whether the electoral equilibrium shifts toward higher taxes and better public services, on the one hand, or smaller governments and low taxation, on the other (OECD, 2010). Therefore, the quantity, and even more often, the quality of basic public services such as health, education, social insurance or security may significantly increase electoral support for higher taxes.

However, even in theory, a significant middle class and democracy may be a necessary, but not a sufficient condition for a bigger government and more redistribution. As surveyed by Alesina and Giuliano (2009), Alt et al. (2010) or Robinson (2010), preferences for redistribution stem from numerous sources. These include the individual's history (mobility experiences and perceptions might affect political attitudes toward redistribution; see Piketty, 1995), the political system, the organization of the family, nation- and region-wide cultural and social values (Bénabou and Tirole, 2006; Roemer, 1998), or even race (Alesina and Glaeser, 2004). Moreover, the demand for redistribution can also result from a balance between the aspirations of the middle and poor classes and the economy-wide disincentives to labor supply they expect from a higher level of taxation, as the seminal paper by Meltzer and Richards (1981) argues. In particular, if poor and middle-income voters (potential beneficiaries from redistribution) take into account the effects of taxation on labor-leisure decisions of their fellow citizens when voting, this will limit the size of government and the degree of redistribution.

Social beliefs about the degree of fairness in social competition also matter, according to Alesina and Angeletos (2005a). If members of society believe that they live in a 'meritocracy' (where individual effort determines income and that all have a right and opportunity to enjoy the fruits of their effort), they will support low redistribution and low taxes. Consequently, in equilibrium effort would be high, and the role of luck, birth, connections or corruption limited.[4] Additionally, Corneo and Grüner (2000) highlight the role of social incentives. Even if the middle-class households may benefit from larger redistribution, the fear of losing relative social status vis-à-vis the poor may align them more closely with the political preferences of conservatives in society.

The 'prospect of upward mobility' (POUM) hypothesis adds a dynamic dimension, stating that not only the middle class, but even the poor may vote for lower levels of redistribution than the median-voter theorem would predict. This could happen if they think that in the future, they or their offspring could progress, becoming a net payer and not benefiting from higher tax rates and redistribution (Bénabou and Ok, 2001). Thus, societies with high mobility, or more precisely where people perceive there is high mobility, may opt for low levels of redistribution. Conversely, in societies where mobility is perceived to be low, the median-voter theorem will rule and the poorer would vote for more redistribution.[5] It is important to note, though, that for the POUM to hold, some premises must be in place: policies should be expected to persist, agents should not be very risk-averse and those poorer than the average should expect to become richer than the average (Bénabou and Ok, 2001). In practice, some or all of these factors may be temporary. As illustrated by the 'tunnel effect' of Hirschman (1973), poor and middle-class individuals may be willing to accept and support high (or even increasing) levels of inequality during the early stages of development (staying in the slow lane of the traffic jam in the tunnel, according to his evocative metaphor). But they will only do so as long as they keep their hope in progressing (that is, that their lane starts to advance faster as well). Government credibility, risk aversion and expectations therefore play a crucial role.

There are political explanations for why the poor and middle classes, even if they constitute a majority, are unable or unwilling to use their political rights to equalize wealth, incomes or even opportunities: not only because they expect to become rich, but also because of ideological domination, since the media is owned by the elite. Or the poor may face difficulties in coordinating political action when they have heterogeneous preferences over aspects of life not immediately related to the economy (Przeworski, 2007). In a somewhat related vein, Chong and Olivera (2008) show empirically that those countries with compulsory voting exhibit less income inequality. Therefore, since poorer countries also have relatively more unequal distributions of income, the authors support the promotion of such voting schemes in developing countries.

Even in situations where governments are elected with the support of the poor to equalize income, they may then try to do so but fail, given different starting points. Modern redistributive policies mainly aim at equalizing human capital by investing in health and education (in contrast to the focus on redistribution of land or industrial capital witnessed in the past). Such redistribution may not result in an equalization of outcomes as in the past, since the same educational system may produce different outcomes depending on the socioeconomic background of pupils (Przeworski, 2007). In other words, the equalization of opportunities may not be enough to reduce inequality. Furthermore, if people are aware of the weak capacity of publicly provided services to reduce inequality, they will attach low value to these services and hence be unwilling to fund them through taxes.

Finally, tax evasion may also play a role. As formalised in Traxler (2009), individuals' preferences over alternative tax rates are determined by their true pre-tax incomes, which may differ from the declared income. Besides, due to the definition of tax bases, the ranking of agents according to pre-tax income does not necessarily correspond to the ranking of taxed incomes. This implies that voters' preferences for taxation might not decline in a straightforward way as their true income rises. Based on this, he shows that some unconventional patterns of redistribution may arise, even from the middle class to the poor and the rich.

Empirical Evidence for Latin America

In contrast to the extensive theoretical literature reviewed in the previous section of this chapter, there are relatively few rigorous empirical studies of the role of socioeconomic and institutional factors in determining the level of taxation and the willingness to raise public revenues in Latin America, in particular taking into account the role of the middle class in this process.[6] Nevertheless, the issue has recently received more attention in academic and policy research as seen in reports by international organizations such as the OECD (2010) and the World Bank (Ferreira et al., 2013). In what follows, we discuss the empirical evidence regarding the role of middle classes, social mobility, the quality of public services and relevant socioeconomic factors.

As mentioned, there are several reasons why demand for redistribution might be lower than expected in highly unequal countries, or why the middle classes might not be able to translate these demands into

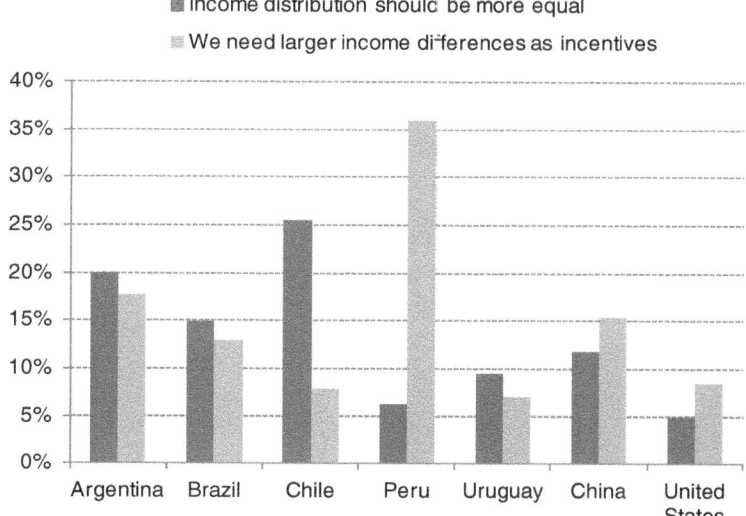

Figure 9.1 Demand for Redistribution by Self-Reported Middle-Class Respondents in Selected Latin American Countries, China and the US (%).

Note: The bars represent the percentage of total middle-class respondents that on a scale from one ('Income distribution should be more equal') to ten ('We need larger income differences as incentives') answered positively to either one or ten. Middle class includes the self-reported upper middle class and lower middle class.

Source: Authors' elaboration, based on *World Values Survey 2005*.

political change. There are significant differences in the demand for redistribution across countries within the region (fig. 9.1). While in some countries in Latin America the middle class leans more toward redistribution, in other cases the middle class tends to favor less redistribution. For example, in Chile more than 25 per cent of middle-class respondents say that they agree completely with the concept that income inequality should be reduced in the country (and just under 8 per cent think that income inequality should actually increase). In Peru, meanwhile, the situation is the opposite: middle-class respondents overwhelmingly think that income inequality in their country should be higher (almost 36 per cent of respondents) versus just 6 per cent who think the opposite. In other countries, such as Argentina, Brazil and Uruguay, middle-class respondents prefer slightly more redistribution.

The results for Peru are also in line with those of Cárdenas et al. (Chapter 3 in this volume), according to which the middle class in Peru supports mainly free-market policies and does not trust the government. As Peru still presents high levels of income inequality (with a Gini of 0.5 in 2011 according to ECLAC statistics) and low levels of social mobility (Daude, 2012), one hypothesis could be that government failures such as corruption and inefficient public expenditures have eroded the social contract in the country more than in other countries in the region. We discuss these issues in more detail below. For the sake of comparison, in the US or China, middle-class respondents tend to prefer more inequality in income. While there are of course multiple reasons behind these differences, it is interesting that in the US people tend to think that social mobility is high and hard work usually pays off (belief in meritocracy), while in China millions of people have objectively experienced absolute mobility out of poverty in the last two decades.

Fiscal Policy, Democracy and Social Mobility

Several institutional factors in Latin America may prevent democratic politics from having a significant effect on either the level of taxation or on its progressivity. As analyzed in Profeta and Scabrosetti (2008), the region still exhibits a low institutional capacity (especially in tax administration), a low quality of democracy (vulnerable to populisms, 'termites' which erode the tax bases and '*devoradores*' who capture social expenditure, as Elizondo and Santiso [2012] put it so suggestively for Mexico and Brazil, respectively) and inefficiencies in the budgetary and tax systems (in the sense that expenditure and tax benefits tend to benefit the high-income population; see Breceda et al., 2008; OECD, 2008; López-Calva and Lustig, 2010).[7] More formally, Profeta and Scabrosetti

(2010) test empirically this hypothesis for emerging Europe, Asia and Latin America, from 1995 to 2004. Standard indicators to characterize political aspects such as democracy and its quality are significantly associated with higher tax revenues (especially among European countries) and with higher direct and indirect taxes. However, both Asia and Latin America show significantly lower levels of tax revenues than European counterparts, even when controlling for differences in political institutions, indicating that other factors are at play.

Most empirical studies focus on explaining the low levels of tax morale in Latin America, analyzing perceptions and how they relate to socioeconomic and policy-related factors. Torgler (2005) highlights the significantly lower tax morale (by which he means the values and attitudes regarding tax compliance) in Latin America, using the Latinobarómetro 1998 survey and World Values Survey 1981–1997. According to the author, the main explanations for this low level of tax morale in Latin America are the perceived tax burden, low levels of honesty within society and government and corruption. Taxpayers perceive their relationship with the state not only as a relationship of coercion, but also as one of exchange. When they feel they are treated unfairly, they are less willing to pay taxes. This assessment tends to be confirmed by Gaviria (2007), based on the Latinobarómetro 1996 and 2000 survey rounds. Gaviria argues that the high demand for redistribution and the weak support for market outcomes in Latin America in the late 1990s and early 2000s stem from pessimistic views regarding social justice, equality of opportunities and social mobility in Latin American societies. Differences in expressed attitudes between rich and poor are substantial (in fact, larger than in other regions), and the poor are more likely to demand redistributive policies. Finally, although enforcement of the tax code and overall trust in the legal system tend to be correlated with higher levels of tax morale, some studies find that the fear of being caught evading taxes is not significant (Torgler, 2005).

There are some other studies that point to potential policy levers to raise more taxes based on the willingness and support from citizens, notably the quality of public services. Marcel (2009), based on the ECOsociAL 2007 survey, shows that only a minority of Latin Americans believes that the low- and middle-income population will progress (e.g., acquire a university education, own a house or establish their own business) with high probability. But at the same time, according to the same study, Latin American citizens have strong beliefs in the value of effort, in the benefits of education and in the shared responsibility of the state and the individual, backed by a willingness to pay more taxes to finance social insurance. Daude and Melguizo (2010), using the 2007 and 2008 rounds of the regional Latinobarómetro survey, confirm that perceptions regarding the quality of public services, and more generally the perception of how democracy works in the region, matter for survey respondents' expressed willingness to pay taxes. In particular, satisfaction with health care and education reinforce the belief that good citizens should pay taxes, and, in general terms, reduce the share of the population that thinks that taxes are too high. The conclusion seems to be that currently the middle classes might actually be an 'unsatisfied customer', in the sense that while they value democracy and in principle demand more public services and are willing to finance them, they are not satisfied with how democracy works in their countries.

Focusing on meritocracy and social mobility, recent results allow for some degree of optimism if reforms advance in the right direction. The majority of those who think that success depends on hard work rather than connections, and that a poor person in their country can become rich by working hard, also think that taxes are not too high (Daude and Melguizo, 2010). Furthermore, these authors find that the people who experienced a higher past mobility, and those who forecast a higher future upward mobility, tend to agree more frequently that good citizens should pay taxes and are less likely to think that current taxes are too high. As a consequence, these results suggest that risk aversion and the demand for social insurance against the risks of downward mobility or public goods that do not necessarily redistribute income may dominate the POUM effect introduced earlier in the chapter. Thus, people who expect to move up in the social ladder or have experienced such moves in the past could in principle support raised revenues for such policies. Finally, it is important to point out that many of these studies focus on the perceived relative economic status of people rather than their real position in the income distribution. A recent study by Cruces et al. (2013) finds that there are actually significant biases in these perceptions due to the group to which people compare themselves (see also Chapter 8 in this volume, by Lora and Fajardo). Furthermore, they find that once people find out about their real relative position, this extra information has a significant impact on their demand for redistribution, in particular for those who overestimated their position. Thus, perceptions and information about relative positions matter to understanding demand for redistribution.

The Quality of Public Services and Tax Morale

The relationship between the quality of services and tax morale could be a virtuous circle between good governance and tax collection. Good quality in public spending and tax morale can be linked through the literature of fiscal exchange theory of taxpayer compliance (Buchanan, 1976). This author argues that fiscal policy is political in nature, such that fiscal outcomes (levels and distribution) are the result of a bargaining process among different economic and political actors. At the same time, it is relevant to analyze simultaneously both taxes and expenditures as a process in which a contract-like negotiation takes place.[8] Moreover, Alm et al. (1993) argue that if taxpayers are somehow involved in the decision process of taxes and expenditures (e.g., through voting), they will feel more inclined to fulfill their tax obligations.[9]

This reciprocity can act as complement to coercion from government and 'peer pressure' or social attitudes to influence tax compliance (Ali et al., 2013; CAF, 2012; Fjeldstad and Semboja, 2001). While the nature of the coercive system will depend on the strengths of the institutional framework and the perception of individuals on the probability of being caught, we turn our attention now to elements of reciprocity as a key aspect in the relationship between middle classes and fiscal policy.

A central, if implicit, element to the notion of this virtuous cycle is that the quality of public goods and services is high. In assuring the latter, it follows that tax morale will also be high. If the mechanism between taxes and expenditure can be seen as a contract, then citizens regard public goods and services as a counterpart of taxes already paid. Thus high tax morale can act as powerful complement to the element of coercion in taxation. Then even in an environment where tax administration is weak (a weak coercive environment), high tax morale can boost collection. This notion is based on the idea that good management can reinforce the mechanism of reciprocity (CAF, 2012).

Therefore, the quality of the provision of public services is key to assure a minimum of support for public policies and their financing. A low perception of the quality of public services can affect the willingness of citizens to comply with their tax duties (Daude et al., 2013). The recent literature focusing on the determinants of tax morale has given importance to the role of quality in public spending, especially in developing economies. Daude and Melguizo (2010) and Torgler (2005) find a positive relationship between satisfaction with health care and education, on one side, and the belief that good citizens should pay taxes. More tellingly, there is the existence of a 'dissatisfied customer' relationship, especially for the middle class: as described above, while they recognize the necessity of paying taxes, citizens are not satisfied with the services provided by the government.

The quality in the provision of public goods and services plays an important role in the bargaining process of the social contract among several actors, which can relate to the theories of mobility and inequality described above. OECD (2008) puts the quality of public spending at the heart of possible multiple equilibria between taxes and expenditures. In a first equilibrium, a combination of low taxation and low (and poor quality) public spending is achieved, where fiscal legitimacy is therefore also low. In a second equilibrium, a combination of relatively high taxation and high-quality spending is produced,[10] which is accompanied by high public support. Under these circumstances, a minimum level of social insurance is provided, which enables a dynamic reduction of inequalities.

Finally, there is an important correlation between the willingness to pay taxes and the perception of the quality of governance. This perception can prove to be a powerful determinant, as is the case when there is actually low taxation but citizens feel they may be paying too much (CAF, 2012). The literature points to a high correlation between willingness to pay and the perception of government quality, so when people feel the government looks after their well-being, this might help reduce the natural resistance to paying taxes. There is a large interaction between the quality of services and trust in government, similar to the relationship with the former and tax morale, a concept also explained

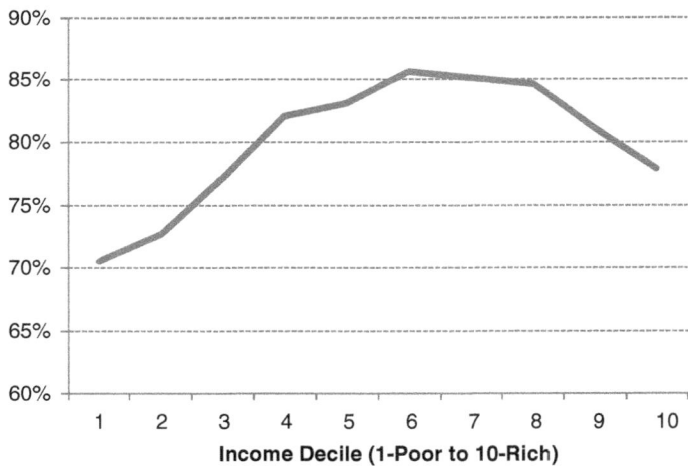

Figure 9.2 'Corruption among Government Officials Is Common or Very Common' in Latin America (% of respondents, by income decile, 2010).

Notes: Mean among respondents in Argentina, Bolivia, Brazil, Chile, Colombia, Costa Rica, Ecuador, El Salvador, Guatemala, Honduras, Mexico, Nicaragua, Panama, Peru, Paraguay, Uruguay and Venezuela.

Source: Authors' elaboration, based on LAPOP Barometer 2010.

by the fiscal exchange theory. The empirical literature, however, at times has struggled to lend support to this notion, where satisfaction with public services is the main factor behind the variation in results (Ali et al., 2013). Of course, as both variables tend to move together, it might be the case that public service quality and provision are much easier to spot than the institutional quality or corruption if it occurs at a high level. In this sense, the relatively critical appraisal of the Latin American middle classes regarding government failures, such as the perception of corruption, can be a strong hurdle for an effective fiscal exchange to take place (fig. 9.2).

Empirical literature for other regions of the developing world tends to focus on the determinants of tax morale based on socioeconomic patterns, as in the Latin American research. More importantly, several studies point toward public service delivery as an important factor that shapes the relationship between citizens and governments. In one of the early empirical works on tax morale determinants, Torgler (2004) finds high overall levels of tax morale in Asia, a characteristic the author attributes to cultural factors and national pride. However, he highlights that 'trust in government and the legal system and the satisfaction with national officials have a significantly positive effect on tax morale'. This result is corroborated by Daude et al. (2013), who also find a positive correlation between tax morale and satisfaction with public services in Asia.[11] In turn, D'Arcy (2011), using the Afrobarometer survey, targets the provision of public services in Africa, finding a positive relationship as well between tax morale and public access to health care. Ali et al. (2013) confirm these results using an updated version of the survey, which measures the question of tax morale more accurately.[12] Interestingly, while finding that, overall, those who are satisfied with public services are more likely to comply with their tax duties, the link for each country depends on the specific services being provided.

From a policy perspective, considerations about institutional aspects can shed light on potential policy actions. Thus, the quality of public services can positively influence trust in government. Using the Afrobarometer and Asiabarometer surveys, respectively, a positive and significant relationship is found between the quality of public services and trust in government (Daude et al., 2013). Torgler (2004) explores the links between satisfaction, trust in officials and tax morale, finding a reinforcing behavior between the variables. Elsewhere, the direct links between the former two have not been fully exploited, but the empirical literature of tax morale suggests that the relationship holds as well. Therefore, reforms aiming at greater efficiency on the use of resources (which in turn can affect the quality of public goods and services) can also help to increase tax morale and trust in governments.

Conclusions

In many respects, the challenges faced by Latin American societies in the areas of taxes and public spending are significant. This chapter discussed the literature and evidence on the relationship between the middle classes in Latin America and fiscal policy. In particular, we emphasize the relationship between social mobility, politics and the quality of public services. In most countries in the region, the current equilibrium is one of low effective taxation, resulting from a combination of narrow tax bases, low rates, low compliance and a limited effort regarding tax law enforcement. This is reflected in the amount of resources available to the public sector. The average tax intake of eighteen Latin American economies in 2012 was about 21 per cent of GDP, while for the OECD it was almost 34 per cent (OECD-ECLAC-CIAT, 2014). On the expenditure side, the provision of public services is insufficient in quality and quantity to solve pressing development problems, but also to satisfy the increasing demands from the emerging middle classes as people move out of poverty. This puts the state in a difficult position. On one side, it is pressed to supply more public goods and services and to do so in a more efficient way. On the other, citizens distrust the public sector because of lack of transparency and misuse of funds. The state still suffers from low levels of legitimacy in many countries in the region and the middle classes do not differ from the rest of society in their assessment of the state's legitimacy.

The potentially positive role of the middle classes in Latin America in creating a new and stronger social contract will probably depend on how governments react to new and evolving demands from this segment of society, but also how the elites and less-privileged sectors of society interact with them. In principle, the middle classes of Latin America could be a key player in transforming their societies and bringing modernization not only in the domain of social policies, but also in a broader sense. However, at present the Latin American middle classes are still critical of the effectiveness of the public sector to deliver on their aspirations and needs. As shown, they are particularly concerned about corruption and lack of transparency in the area of fiscal policies, more than the poor or the rich. Thus, the rise of the middle class is not a sufficient condition to achieve more political support for a progressive political agenda. Some critics may even argue the opposite; if this rise takes place in an environment where people think that they progress despite the inefficiencies of the public sector, this social group will be especially critical of the public sector's role. Therefore, the challenge is to transform these demands into a positive force that modernizes Latin American societies and makes them more inclusive. Furthermore, the middle class is also composed by more traditional sectors, beyond those who recently 'graduated' from poverty. If these sectors feel that they have been forgotten by the state, in favor of the new ranks that join the middle class from below, they will have a critical attitude toward fiscal policy, in particular transfers to the poor. In this sense, they could demand more expenditures or tax relief relative to the poor. This is not an inevitable or bad outcome, but it stresses the complexity of the emerging social issues due to the progress many societies in Latin America are starting to face. The stakes are high, but if managed properly, this process could be the starting point to move toward a better and more integrated system of social protection.

This latter issue relates to how middle classes shape social and fiscal policies in Latin American societies. In particular, social protection and social insurance systems in the region tend to be fragmented and are often an uncoordinated collection of small programs (see Chapter 6 in this volume, by Daude, de Laiglesia and Melguizo). Furthermore, since the 1990s, these policies have tended to be targeted toward the poor. In this sense, the expansion of the middle class changes the required set of policies, as the focus should shift from a system that mainly provides income support and some assets to the poor toward one that also allows for social insurance to reduce the vulnerability and foster resilience of those with incomes closer to the average. Again, these reforms are no free lunch and should be discussed jointly with a strategy of how to finance them, not only in terms of funding, but also regarding the incentives created by the way they are financed.

This chapter has highlighted several aspects that matter for effectively involving the middle classes in a renewed social contract in Latin America. The emphasis from country to country of course changes, as might also the sequencing of some of the elements of reform. However, some are common to the concerns of middle classes and citizens more generally across the region. For example, the quality of public expenditures, as well as the transparency in their administration, represents an area for improvement in most Latin American economies. It would be politically difficult to raise more revenue without also making efforts in this dimension. In a similar way, reforming the tax administration in terms of modernization, professionalization and transparency can also create a greater sense of fairness needed to enable other far-reaching reforms. A final aspect is that reforms might be initially possible only in areas where there is a common 'enemy' – a wide consensus across social classes to act – such as crime and public safety, basic education, universal social protection or the fight against hunger. Better policies in these areas might benefit not only the middle class, but also the rest of society, while the concerns of the middle class might be especially acute.

Finally, a better understanding of the evolving middle classes in Latin America is definitely needed. Despite referring to this social group loosely along this chapter, it is clear that today it is a rather heterogeneous group of people, with significant differences across countries and even cohorts within each country. Whether this grouping will transform into a class with more identity and political voice is not clear, but it is definitely a relevant field for research in the years to come.

Notes

1 The views expressed herein are the sole responsibility of the authors and do not necessarily reflect the opinions of their institutions.
2 See Profeta and Scabrosetti (2010) for a recent survey on the political economy of taxation and tax reform in developing countries.
3 The concept of tax morale is far from uniform. Other definitions found in the literature are 'the degree to which the population perceives that paying taxes is a civic duty and should not be avoided' (CAF, 2012), or more simply 'citizens' confidence in the tax system' (OECD, 2008).
4 These authors add a second and opposite equilibrium. If society believes that luck, birth, connections or corruption determine wealth, it will levy high taxes, and social beliefs will be self-fulfilling as well. In a parallel paper, Alesina and Angeletos (2005b) develop the latter argument: 'Big governments raise the possibilities of corruption; more corruption may in turn raise the support for redistributive policies to intend to correct the inequality and injustice generated by corruption'. We are not so convinced on the latter point. Alternatively, citizens may start avoiding paying taxes, ending up, again, with a small(er) government and low redistribution. Evidence by Friedman et al. (2000) supports our argument. They show that informality and tax evasion are higher in countries with high levels of corruption and conclude that only honest governments can sustain high levels of taxation.
5 Rodríguez (2004) proposes the following reassessment of the POUM effect: In societies where the rich can influence politics so that they pay little or no taxes, the median voter will prefer low levels of taxation to reduce the incentives of rent seekers.
6 For an analysis of the determinants of tax morale in different regions, and a survey of the empirical literature, see Daude et al. (2013) and the references therein.

7 López-Calva and Lustig (2010) document the recent significant and widespread reduction of income inequality in Latin America between 2000 and 2006. In particular, they study in depth the cases of Argentina, Brazil, Mexico and Peru, where inequality has been reduced due to the fall in the earnings gap between skilled and low-skilled workers and the impact of conditional cash transfer programs such as *Jefas y Jefes del Hogar* in Argentina, *Bolsa Escola/ Bolsa Família* in Brazil, *Progresa/Oportunidades* in Mexico and in-kind transfers in Peru. However, the same authors stress that the reduction in skill premiums is probably temporary and that a large share of government expenditure remains neutral or even regressive.
8 There has been a discussion on whether this theory would hold when there is abuse of power and the possibility of a majority exploiting a minority. Moreover, where democratic institutions are weak, questions arise as to whether this framework can properly account for this shortcoming. For more details see Frey (1976).
9 Theoretically, the fiscal exchange theory is fairly straightforward. However, empirical support to this theory is not definitive, especially when the issue of satisfaction with the provision of public goods and services is addressed (Ali et al., 2013).
10 Evidently, the relationship between taxes and (good) expenditures is not a monotone one, and greater efforts on the spending side must be made to assure that higher taxes will not end up financing wasteful spending.
11 The authors use the Asiabarometer survey, which does not address directly the concept of tax morale as has been previously described.
12 In previous versions of the Afrobarometer tax morale was proxied by the question 'the tax department always has the right to make people pay taxes', which puts the burden on enforcement and created a bias in the responses. The updated version treats the issue of tax morale more accurately, in our view, by asking if they thought it was wrong for people not to pay taxes on their income (possible answers are 'not wrong at all', 'wrong, but understandable' or 'wrong and punishable'), very much compatible with the 'acceptance of tax evasion', our preferred definition.

References

Alesina, A. and G. M. Angeletos (2005a) 'Fairness and Redistribution', *American Economic Review*, vol. 95, no. 4, 960–80.

Alesina, A. and G. M. Angeletos (2005b) 'Corruption, Inequality, and Fairness', *Journal of Monetary Economics*, vol. 52, no. 7, 1227–44.

Alesina, A. and P. Giuliano (2009) 'Preferences for Redistribution', NBER Working Paper 14825 (Cambridge, MA: National Bureau of Economic Research).

Ali, M., O.-H. Fjelstad and I. H. Sjursen (2013) 'Factors Affecting Tax Compliance Attitude in Africa: Evidence from Kenya, Tanzania, Uganda and South Africa', Paper prepared for the Centre for the Study of African Economies 2013 Conference, Oxford University.

Alm, J., B. Jackson and M. McKee (1993) 'Fiscal Exchange, Collective Decision Institutions, and Tax Compliance', *Journal of Economic Behavior and Organization*, vol. 22, no. 3, 285–303.

Alt, J., I. Preston and L. Sibieta (2010) 'The Political Economy of Tax Policy', in J. Mirrlees, ed., *Dimensions of Tax Design: The Mirlees Review* (Oxford: Oxford University Press), 1204–79.

Bénabou, R. and E. A. Ok (2001) 'Social Mobility and the Demand for Redistribution: The POUM Hypothesis', *Quarterly Journal of Economics*, vol. 116, no. 2, 447–87.

Bénabou, R. and J. Tirole (2006) 'Belief in a Just World and Redistributive Politics', *Quarterly Journal of Economics*, vol. 121, no. 2, 699–746.

Buchanan, J. (1976) 'Taxation in fiscal exchange', *Journal of Public Economics*, vol. 6, no. 1–2, 17–29.

CAF (2012) *Finanzas Públicas para el Desarrollo: Fortaleciendo la conexión entre ingresos y gastos* (Caracas: Corporación Andina de Fomento).

Chong, A. and M. Olivera (2008) 'Does Compulsory Voting Help Equalize Incomes?', *Economics & Politics*, vol. 20, no. 3, 391–415.

Cruces, G., R. Pérez Truglia and M. Tetaz (2013) 'Biased Perceptions of Income Distribution and Preferences for Redistribution: Evidence from a Survey Experiment', *Journal of Public Economics*, vol. 98 (February), 100–12.

D'Arcy, M. (2011) 'Why Do Citizens Assent to Pay Tax? Legitimacy, Taxation, and the African State', Afrobarometer Working Papers 126.

Daude, C. (2012) 'Education, Middle Classes and Social Mobility in Latin America', *Pensamiento Iberoamericano*, vol. 10, 29–48.

Daude, C., H. Gutiérrez and A. Melguizo (2013) 'What Drives Tax Morale? A Focus on Emerging Economies', *Hacienda Pública Española / Review of Public Economics*, no. 207 (April), 11–26.

Daude, C. and A. Melguizo (2010) 'Taxation and More Representation? On Fiscal Policy, Social Mobility and Democracy in Latin America', OECD Development Centre Working Paper 294, (Paris: OECD Publishing).

Doepke, M. and F. Zilibotti (2005) 'Social Class and the Spirit of Capitalism', *Journal of the European Economic Association*, vol. 3, no. 2–3, 516–24.

Downs, A. (1957) *An Economic Theory of Democracy* (New York: Harper).

Elizondo, C. and J. Santiso (2012) 'Killing Me Softly: Local Termites and Fiscal Violence in Latin America', in J. Santiso and J. Dayton-Johnson, eds., *The Oxford Handbook of Latin American Political Economy* (New York and Oxford: Oxford University Press), 457–502.

Easterly, W. (2001) 'The Middle Class Consensus and Economic Development', *Journal of Economic Growth*, vol. 6, no. 4, 317–35.

Easterly, W., J. Ritzen and M. Woolcock (2006) 'Social Cohesion, Institutions, and Growth', *Economics & Politics*, vol. 18, no. 2, 103–20.

Ferreira, F. H. G., J. Messina, J. Rigolini, L. F. López-Calva, M. A. Lugo and R. Vakis (2013) *Economic Mobility and the Rise of the Middle Latin American Middle Class* (Washington, DC: The World Bank).

Fjelstad, O.-H. and J. Semboja (2001) 'Why People Pay Taxes: The Case of the Development Levy in Tanzania', *World Development*, vol. 29, no. 12, 2059–74.

Frey, B. (1976) 'Taxation in Fiscal Exchange: A Comment', *Journal of Public Economics*, vol. 6, no. 1–2, 31–35.

Friedman, E., S. Johnson, D. Kaufmann and P. Zoido-Lobatón (2000) 'Dodging the Grabbing Hand: the Determinants of Unofficial Activity in 69 Countries', *Journal of Public Economics*, vol. 76, no. 3, 459–93.

Gaviria, A. (2007) 'Social Mobility and Preferences for Redistribution in Latin America', *Economia*, vol. 8, no. 1, 55–88.

Hirschman, A. (1973) 'The Changing Tolerance for Income Inequality in the Course of Economic Development', *Quarterly Journal of Economics*, vol. 87, no. 4, 544–66.
Loayza, N., J. Rigolini and G. Llorente (2012) 'Do Middle Classes Bring Institutional Reform?', Policy Research Working Paper 6015 (Washington, DC: The World Bank).
López-Calva, L. F. and N. Lustig, eds. (2010) *Declining Inequality in Latin America: A Decade of Progress?* (Washington, DC: Brookings Institution Press and United Nations Development Programme).
Marcel, M. (2009) *Movilidad, Desigualdad y Política Social en América Latina*, Documento de Trabajo CIEPLAN (Santiago: Corporación de Estudios para América Latina).
Meltzer, A. G. and S. F. Richards (1981) 'A Rational Theory of the Size of Government', *Journal of Political Economy*, vol. 89, no. 5, 914–27.
OECD [Organisation for Economic Co-operation and Development] (2008) *Latin American Economic Outlook 2009* (Paris: OECD Publishing).
OECD [Organisation for Economic Co-operation and Development] (2010) *Latin American Economic Outlook 2011: How Middle-Class Is Latin America?* (Paris: OECD Publishing).
OECD-ECLAC-CIAT (2014) *Revenue Statistics in Latin America* (Paris: OECD Publishing).
Profeta, P. and S. Scabrosetti (2008) 'Political Economy Issues of Taxation in Latin America,' in L. Bernardi, A. Barreix, A. Marenzi and P. Profeta, eds., *Tax Systems and Tax Reforms in Latin America* (Abingdon: Routledge), 63–76.
Profeta, P. and S. Scabrosetti (2010) *The Political Economy of Taxation: Lessons from Developing Countries* (Cheltenham: Edward Elgar).
Przeworski, A. (2007) 'Democracy, Equality, and Redistribution', mimeo (New York: New York University).
Rodríguez, F. (2004) 'Inequality, Redistribution, and Rent-Seeking', *Economics and Politics*, vol. 16, no. 3, 287–320.
Torgler, B. (2004) 'Tax morale in Asian countries', *Journal of Asian Economics*, vol. 15, no. 2, 237–66.
Torgler, B. (2005) 'Tax Morale in Latin America', *Public Choice*, vol. 122, no. 1/2, 133–57.
Traxler, C. (2009) 'Voting over Taxes: the Case of Tax Evasion', *Public Choice*, vol. 140, no. 1, 43–58.
Robinson, J. A. (2010) 'The Political Economy of Redistributive Policies', in L. F. López-Calva and N. Lustig, eds., (2010), 39–71.
Roemer, J. (1998) 'Why the Poor Do Not Expropriate the Rich: An Old Argument in New Garb', *Journal of Public Economics*, vol. 70, no. 3, 399–424.

Index

Afrobarometer survey, 197
age, and middle-class status, 108, 112, 179
Agrale, 161
Ajegroup, 164–5
América Móvil, 153
Argentina, 53, 56, 106
   economic crisis of 2001–2, 151
Asia,
   economic crisis of 1997, 151
   global middle class, 58–9, 151
Asiabarometer survey, 197
automobile sector, and middle-class demand, 160–3

Banco do Brasil, 153
Banerjee-Duflo measure of middle class ($2–$10/day), 8–10, 15, 16, 38, 39, 103, 106, 131
Batlle y Ordoñez, José, 5
Belindia (Brazilian income distribution), 17, 75, 95
Benedetti, Mario, 6
Bolivia, 53, 54, 57, 106
Bolsa Família, *see* Brazil
Bradesco, 153
brand loyalty, 165
Brazil, 56, 150, 153
   Bolsa Família, 19, 34, 83, 94
   Brasil Carinhoso, 82
   Camino da Escola, 162
   class C, 17, 78, 85, 92
   demonstrations, 2013–14, 1, 4–5, 22
   economic classes in, 78, 79
   fiscal policy in, 192
   forecast of middle-class growth, 78–83
   geography of middle-class growth, 80–1
   income distribution, 17, 71–4
   middle class in, 70–95
   National Social Security Institute, 83
   see also Belindia

BRF, 164
Busscar, 161

capabilities, 39, 178
CASEN (Encuesta de Caracterización Socioeconómica Nacional; National Socio-economic Characterization Survey, Chile), 132
CBD, 153
Cemex, 152
Cencosud, 155, 158, 159, 160
Chauí, Marilena, 23
Chile, 56, 133, 150
   Subsidio Previsional a los Trabajadores Jóvenes, 144
   Subsidio al Empleo Joven, 144
   see also CASEN
China, 151, 153, 167, 192
   global middle class in, 59
   and global poverty, 72
   trade with Latin America, 4
class C (Brazil), 17, 78, 85, 92
Codelco, 152
Colombia, 56, 106, 133, 150, 153
   Multidimensional Poverty Index, 117–8, 124–6
   National Planning Department, 21, 117
   Servicio Social Complementario de Beneficios Económicos Periódicos, 143
   see also GEIH
Comil, 161
Comisión Económica para América Latina y el Caribe, see ECLAC
commodity boom, 35, 151
consumer credit, 156, 157–60, 179
consumer goods, and middle-class demand, 163–6; *see also* specific firms
consumer durables and middle-class status, 182

Costa Rica, 53, 54, 150
conditional cash transfer programs, 19, 33, 34, 36, 130; see also Bolsa Família; Juntos; Progresa/Oportunidades
Continuing Provision Benefit (Brazil), 95
corruption, middle-class attitudes and perceptions, 187, 196

da Silva, Luiz Inácio Lula, 23
decoupling, 3–4
democracy, middle-class attitudes toward, 187
Dina, 161
Dominican Republic, 56
Drogarias DPSP, 155
Dumas, Alexandre, 86

ECLAC [United Nations Economic Commission for Latin America and the Caribbean], xiii, 3, 15–16, 141, 192
Economic Commission for Latin America and the Caribbean, see ECLAC
ECOsociAL survey, 193
Ecuador, 56
education level, and middle-class status, 93, 95, 108, 112
emerging markets, 151
employment, and middle-class status, 109
Encuesta de Caracterización Socioeconómica Nacional (Chile), see CASEN
Encuesta Nacional de Hogares (Peru), see ENAHO
Encuesta Nacional de Ingresos y Gastos de los Hogares (Mexico), see ENIGH
ENAHO (Encuesta Nacional de Hogares; National Household Survey, Peru), 132
ENIGH (Encuesta Nacional de Ingresos y Gastos de los Hogares; National Household Income and Expenditure Survey, Mexico), 132
entrepreneurship, middle class and, 51, 61, 71, 101–2

EQ-5D (European Quality of Life-5 Dimensions Index), 178
Esteban-Gradin-Ray measure of polarization, 76, 82
Europe, 2, 3, 5, 13, 58, 139, 155, 157–8, 161, 193

family structure, and middle-class status, 108, 182
Fernández, Lionel, xiii
50–150 measure of middle class (OECD), 10, 11, 15, 19, 104, 105, 107, 132, 176
and non-income dimensions of poverty, 120–2
financial services, 179
fiscal exchange theory, 197; see also social contract
fiscal policy, 186; see also public spending; taxation
Ford EcoSport, 163, 167
Friedman, Milton, 86
Friedman, Thomas, 90
functioning, 39

Gallup World Poll, 90, 104, 174, 183
GEIH (Gran Encuesta Integrada de Hogares; Large Integrated Household Survey, Colombia), 132
gender, and middle-class status, 108, 112, 165–6, 179
Gini index of inequality, 12, 33, 34, 56, 57, 72, 192
global middle class measure ($10–$100/day, Kharas), 9, 52–3, 104
Gran Encuesta Integrada de Hogares (Colombia), see GEIH
Grupo Monge, 20, 156, 167
Gurría, Angel, xiii
Guyana, 53, 57

health and middle-class status, 179
Hirschman, Albert O., 189
Honduras, 53, 54, 57
household surveys, 7, 123, 132
housing demand, 160
Hyundai, 161

IDB, 141, 178
ILO, 133, 134, 141, 151

Index 207

income inequality, 19
  decline in, 2000s, 19, 33, 35, 73
  and economic growth, 21–2
  and middle class, 37–43
  wage premium and, 19, 33, 35
independent workers, 137
India, 151, 153
  global middle class in, 59
  and global poverty, 72
informal sector, 134
  ILO definition, 134
informality, 132, 133, 136–8
  ILO definition, 133
  see also informal sector; middle class, labor-market characteristics of; occupational status; social protection
Inter-American Development Bank, *see* IDB
International Labour Organization, *see* ILO
International Monetary Fund, 22, 151, 157
Irigoyen, Hipólito, 5
Itaú-Unibanco, 153, 158, 159, 160, 167
  Raizes e Asas, 167

JBS Friboi, 153
Johnson, John, 5, 22, 23

Kenya, 134
Kharas measure of middle class, *see* global middle class
Kubitschek, Juscelino, 5

Lafontaine, 87
Large Integrated Household Survey (Colombia), *see* GEIH
Latin American Decade (Santos), 2–3
Latinobarómetro surveys, 193–4
Lima, real estate values in, 14–15
Living Standards Measurement Study (LSMS) Survey, Colombia, 123
Lost Decade (growth slowdown in Latin America), 1, 3

Marcopolo, 21, 161, 162
marketing strategies, targeting middle-class consumers, 153
marketing innovations, 154

Mastretta, 161
matching contributions (pension design), 142–4
median voter theory, 22, 186
  and middle-class politics, 188–90
Mercosur, 151, 163
meritocracy, 189, 192, 194
Mexico, 53, 54, 56, 133, 153
  fiscal policy in, 192
  Progresa/Oportunidades, 19, 34
  stabilizing development model, 5
  see also ENIGH
middle class, attitudes and values of, 102, 109; *see also* middle class and politics
middle class, economic measures of, 7
  absolute-income definitions of, 8–10, 38, 52–3, 74, 103, 131; *see also* Banerjee-Duflo measure; Ravallion measure; global middle class measure
  comparisons of, 16–17
  labor-market characteristics, 132, 133
  multidimensional, 117
  occupational status and, 15–16
  poverty line and, 12–15
  relative-income definitions of, 10–12, 38, 74, 103, 131; see also 50–149 measure;
  see also specific countries
middle class, forecast of growth, 53–8, 78–83
middle class, labor-market characteristics of, 133–8
middle class as motor for growth, 20–2, 85, 102
middle class and politics, 22–4, 97–8, 187; *see also* corruption; democracy; median voter theory; social contract
mortgage credit, 160
Multidimensional Poverty Index (Colombia), 117–8, 124–6
multilatinas, 151

NAFTA (North American Free Trade Agreement), 151
National Household Income and Expenditure Survey (Mexico), *see* ENIGH

National Household Survey (Peru), *see* ENAHO
National Socio-economic Characterization Survey (Chile), *see* CASEN
Natura, 20, 166
Neobus, 161

occupational status, 15–16, 109, 130, 179; *see also* informal sector; informality; middle class, labor-market characteristics of;
OECD (Organisation for Economic Co-operation and Development), xiii, xiv, 10, 13, 16, 91, 132, 167, 176, 191
Organisation for Economic Co-operation and Development, *see* OECD
OXXO, 157

Paraguay, 54
Partido dos Trabalhadores (Brazil), 23
Partido Revolucionario Institucional (Mexico), 5
PDVSA, 153
Pemex, 153
pensions, 23, 138
  matching contributions, 142–4
  policy options regarding, 140–5
  social pensions, 141–2
Peru, 133, 150
  political attitudes of middle class in, 59–65, 187
  Sistema de Pensiones Sociales, 143
  see also ENAHO
Petrobras, 153
Piñera, Sebastián, 5
PISA (Programme for International Student Assessment), 91
PME (Brazilian Monthly Employment Survey), 83
PNAD (Brazilian National Household Survey), 77, 78, 82
POF (Household Budget Survey, Brazil), 77, 78
polarization, measures of, 74–77; *see also* Esteban-Gradin-Ray measure of polarization

poverty,
  declines in, 36–7
  and economic measures of the middle class, 12–15
PPP, *see* purchasing power parity
Prebisch, Raúl, 3
Progresa/Oportunidades, *see* Mexico
prospect of upward mobility (POUM) hypothesis, 189, 194
Protestant Ethic and the Spirit of Capitalism, The (Weber), 102
public services, perceptions of, 97, 111, 194
  and tax morale, 194–8
public spending, 186, 188, 195
purchasing power parity, 7

Randon, 161
Ravallion measure of middle class ($2–$13/day), 8–10, 16, 18, 38, 39, 53, 103, 131, 176
redistribution, preferences for, 22, 52, 65, 68, 152, 173, 186, 191
relational goods, 178
retail firms and middle-class demand, 154–7
Rousseff, Dilma, 23
Russia, economic crisis of 1998, 151

Santos, Juan Manuel, 2, 18
self-employment, 135
Sen, Amartya, 39
Servicio Social Complementario de Beneficios Económicos Periódicos, *see* Colombia
Sistema de Pensiones Sociales, *see* Peru
Smith, Adam, 13
social contract and the middle class, 4, 22, 23, 25, 90, 95, 187, 192, 195, 198, 199
social mobility, 90, 102, 103, 150, 187, 194
social pensions, 141–2
social protection, 130, 134, 138, 199; *see also* pensions
social rankings, self-perceived, 24, 103, 173–4, 175, 176, 194
  distortions and errors in, 174

social status, 173
Solís, Luis Guillermo, 5
South Korea, 153
strategic innovations (firms), 154
subjective middle class, 24, 103, 176
Subsidio Previsional a los Trabajadores Jóvenes, *see* Chile
Subsidio al Empleo Joven, *see* Chile

Taiwan, 153
tariffs, 163, 187
tax morale, 187, 193
  and perceived quality of public services, 194–8
taxation, 134, 186, 188, 195
Tregua, La (Benedetti), 6, 15
Troller, 161
tunnel effect (Hirschman), 189

United Nations Economic Commission for Latin America and the Caribbean, *see* ECLAC

United States, 1–5, 20, 53–5, 66, 71–2, 74, 143, 152, 157, 160, 168, 191–2
Uruguay, 53, 54, 106

Vale, 152, 153
Veloso, Caetano, 95
Venezuela, 56, 153
vulnerability, 21, 23, 39, 41, 84, 120, 130, 132

Washington Consensus, 151
Wealth of Nations, The (Smith), 13
Weber, Max, 102
World Bank, xiii, 13–14, 18, 19, 151, 191
  measure of middle class ($10–$50/day), 9, 14, 16, 41, 43, 45, 104, 131, 150
World Gallup Poll, *see* Gallup World Poll
World is Flat, The (Friedman), 90
World Values Survey, 59–65, 191

Printed and bound by CPI Group (UK) Ltd, Croydon, CR0 4YY